# PRAISE FOI

MW00618671

"Powerful and complete. Hellström and Dank are speakers for our times. HR in Silicon Valley or SpaceX is nothing like company policies from any textbook, or any book, until now. Finally, Hellström and Dank guide us through nurturing an ever-evolving, lightning-quick business that can keep up with tech giants, global shifts and the chain of firsts required to get us to Mars and beyond, address climate change, be the next Google and establish equitable psychological safety in an exhilarating, uplifting, profitable place to work. Welcome to Agile HR, we're so glad to have you."
**Joe Justice, Agile business innovator**

"Introducing scientific thinking when evolving our next-gen organizations is a gain not only to HR but to everyone touched by them. This is more than a book, this is a mindset leap."
**Mattias Skarin, Enterprise Agile Coach, Crisp**

"Dank and Hellström have distilled years of Agile HR knowledge and experience into one practical book. This is the toolkit every HR professional of the 21st century needs. I wish I had had this book years ago."
**Tracey Waters, Director of People Experience**

"A great book by the pioneers of agile HR, Dank and Hellström! They were able to capture their passion in this book, and I am sure many readers will be eager to follow their guidance."
**Tom Haak, Director, HR Trend Institute**

"Agile HR takes you from the sticky status quo to the future of work. It's a full toolkit that's pleasantly practical, relatable and relevant. This is a must-read for anyone who is passionate about HR."
**Arne-Christian van der Tang, Chief Human Resources Officer, TomTom**

"To see this book in print brings me more joy than I can fully express. The Agile HR movement has been growing organically for some years now and the more HR professionals and organizations can get onboard and inspired by this way of working, the more successful businesses will become. This is the book anyone curious about the Agile philosophy needs to read. It's also for anyone that's already taken a leap of faith to leave behind old hierarchical and traditional business approaches for something more effective, by providing inspiration on how to create a culture where the Agile mindset is lived and breathed by all. Once you start on an Agile journey you never go back."
Nebel Crowhurst, People & Culture Director and early Agile HR adopter

"This book brings the best of Scrum into People Operations."
Jeff Sutherland, Founder and Chairman, Scrum, Inc

"This book may become the foundational text for Agile in HR. It provides solid advice all the way through, accurate on Agile and HR, and easy to approach without prior experience in Agile. And while becoming an expert takes time and practice, this book will ease the process a lot, by connecting the dots to a coherent whole."
Petri Heiramo, Certified Scrum Trainer, Agile Enterprise Coach

"Never has the HR profession had such an opportunity to transform our workplaces and this is an essential read for anyone who has been looking for a better, more human way than traditional, legacy approaches. Natal and Riina provide inspiration along with practical tools and techniques to give everyone the confidence to take the next step on their Agile HR adventure!"
Charlotte Goulding, Director of People at Infinity Works

"This book should be mandatory reading for all HR professionals. Written by true experts in Agile who know exactly how to explain key concepts and facts in a way that makes them easy to apply in a commercial environment, this book will elevate your HR practice and will turn you into a raving fan of Agile HR. This book is a true game changer!"
Karen Beaven, Director – PXI, The Creative HR Agency

# Agile HR

*Deliver value in a changing
world of work*

Natal Dank and Riina Hellström

KoganPage

First published in Great Britain and the United States in 2021 by Kogan Page Limited

2nd Floor, 45 Gee Street
London
EC1V 3RS
United Kingdom
www.koganpage.com

122 W 27th St, 10th Floor
New York, NY 10001
USA

4737/23 Ansari Road
Daryaganj
New Delhi 110002
India

Kogan Page books are printed on paper from sustainable forests.

**ISBNs**

Hardback    978 1 78966 586 4
Paperback   978 1 78966 585 7
Ebook       978 1 78966 587 1

**British Library Cataloguing-in-Publication Data**

A CIP record for this book is available from the British Library.

**Library of Congress Cataloging-in-Publication Data**

Names: Dank, Natal, author. | Hellström, Riina, author.
Title: Agile HR : deliver value in a changing world of work / Natal Dank and Riina Hellström.
Description: London ; New York, NY : Kogan Page, 2020. | Includes bibliographical references and index. | Summary: "In the new world of work, agility is a business imperative. From small tech start-ups or large traditional companies, organizations need to be fast, flexible and digitally empowered to succeed. However, too many companies are stuck with siloed, compliance-driven HR processes that work in opposition to the business rather than supporting it. This results in the view that HR is slow and out of touch. However, Agile HR shows that this doesn't need to be the case. It is a practical guide written specifically for people professionals on how the HR function can develop agile processes and practices that save time, boost performance and support overall business goals. Covering every aspect of the HR unction from people processes, ways of working and HR services to organization design, operating models and HR teams, Agile HR is an essential guide for all HR practitioners wanting to make their HR practices agile and drive business performance but don't know where to start. As well as guidance on how to deal with resistance, manage a backlog and deal with constraints, there is also invaluable guidance on how HR can prioritize effectively and assess which activities to pursue, which to develop, which to rework and which to abandon in order to achieve continuous business improvement. Supported by case studies from organizations who have seen the benefits of an agile approach to HR including Sky Betting & Gaming and MUJI, this is critical reading for all HR professionals in organizations of any size needing to adopt fast, flexible and evolving agile approaches to effectively compete in the new world of work"– Provided by publisher.
Identifiers: LCCN 2020040546 (print) | LCCN 2020040547 (ebook) | ISBN 9781789665857 (paperback) | ISBN 9781789665864 (hardcover) | ISBN 9781789665871 (epub)
Subjects: LCSH: Personnel management. | Organizational change.
Classification: LCC HF5549 .D26 2020 (print) | LCC HF5549 (ebook) | DDC 658.3–dc23
LC record available at https://lccn.loc.gov/2020040546
LC ebook record available at https://lccn.loc.gov/2020040547

Typeset by Integra Software Services, Pondicherry
Print production managed by Jellyfish
Printed and bound by CPI Group (UK) Ltd, Croydon CR0 4YY

*RIINA:*

*To Miksu, Axel and Oscar,*
*Tack för ert stöd, era kramar och er kärlek. Jag älskar er.*

*To Natal,*
*For better or for worse… we made it.*
*Thank you and you rock!*

*NATAL:*

*To Tim,*
*I'm nothing without you.*

*To Riina,*
*Yeah, we did it!*
*Big hugs*

# CONTENTS

# LIST OF FIGURES AND TABLES

# PREFACE: AGILE HR AND THE AUTHORS

*Natal*

A turning point in my HR career was working as the Global Head of Talent at a large international bank and realizing that the time-consuming and difficult internal process I oversaw appeared to have little perceived value within the business. Over a period of almost six months we would ask managers at every level of the organization to painstakingly put their people into one of 25 talent boxes and then use the data to produce detailed reports for senior executives to review. While this alone might seem unproductive, what made it worse was the data didn't even seem to determine how people were selected for talent programmes or promotions. Indeed, most managers, including the senior executives, were fearful of discussing the information with employees and preferred instead to keep the whole process secret.

I've always believed there is a direct link between business success and inspired employees, and if given the right opportunity everyone has the potential to make a difference. Never a fan of hierarchy or adhering to the command-and-control ladder, at this point I became convinced that the main role of HR was to build great places to work, where people could be successful in their job and find purpose in their career. To achieve this, I also knew HR needed to move beyond traditional processes and begin to understand the human experience of work.

In search of this vision I decided to step out into the consulting world and when asked to help a successful start-up evolve their performance and reward structure, I literally stumbled upon Agile. With posters on the wall declaring 'No show ponies here' and 'We believe in the power of experimentation', I could sense from the minute I walked in the door this assignment would be different.

The project context reflects where a lot of tech departments are currently, with teams working Agile but still using a traditional approach to HR, for example with performance management based on managerial feedback, individual ratings and bonuses. Of course, I did what most HR consultants do and reviewed the engagement survey data, interviewed key people and looked at the best-practice examples from the industry. I then presented my masterplan to the sponsor and was dumbfounded when they asked: 'How do you know this will work?'

As I muttered stock phrases like 'HR best practice', I quickly realized that in this business, people were expected to validate decisions through experimentation and evidence, rather than through opinion or what was done before. Why should HR be any different?

Luckily, I was in the right environment to begin my Agile learning and people happily volunteered to participate in small, safe experiment teams that tested different ways to discuss and share feedback, use peer-based performance tools and even try different rating scales. After several months of listening and observing, we had the data to start making changes. The first was the removal of quarterly bonuses, based on evidence that performance conversations were heavily focused on money and ratings, rather than on career development and feedback.

In the past, just contemplating such an organizational change would have led to a huge project involving months of approvals and committee meetings. Instead, I discovered that by working *with* people rather than *on* people it was possible to achieve cultural and behavioural change that everyone simply got on with, rather than spending months, even years, resisting.

It was now clear to me why this company was way ahead of its competitors. Ever since, I've been on a mission to equip the HR profession with Agile skills and prepare us for the future of work. My aim is to build awesome places to work where great people want to be, and by doing so enable business success. Through my role as a coach, consultant and facilitator I've partnered closely with HR teams and business leaders from around the world to help them embrace an Agile mindset and reinvent how they work. This mission has led to some amazing experiences and an opportunity to collaborate with a wide range of different brands and industries.

In 2016 I hosted the first Agile HR Meetup in London with the aim of building a community of like-minded practitioners, which has since grown into a regular event held in cities across the world, from Sydney to Paris, as well as online. That same year I met Riina while tweeting my passion for Agile HR, and we made the commitment to positively disrupt the profession we love together.

## Riina

During my fifth year as a student in chemical engineering, I began to realize I was no longer enthusiastic about a career in chemistry or pharma and needed to redirect my studies towards something that felt right. I came across studies in learning organizations and systems thinking and immediately knew this was what I wanted to work with. After graduating, I aspired to a career in HR, ambitious to develop learning organizations and increase adaptability and self-directedness in work life. Though corporate reality and the traditional HR and management hierarchies toned down some of my idealism, they never put out the passion.

I worked a lot with frontline staff and managers, and started to understand their everyday work, their needs and their pain points. Many of the HR solutions we were offering were not appreciated at all. Realizing how broken the HR processes were for the users, I wanted to redesign HR. However, challenging the HR processes and management structures wasn't always that appreciated, and some considered me a bit of a rebel. Luckily, guided by a couple of coaching-oriented leaders early in my career, I could experiment and innovate within my own HR domain. I designed self-organized, team-based onboarding programmes and started corporate communities and networks – before social media existed. Keen to bring much stronger customer focus and business relevance to HR and wanting to build company cultures where people can bring their full potential to work, I did feel like a misfit in the traditional, bureaucratic and hierarchical organization. Being an organizational innovator without seniority or a mandate was challenging.

That was until 2010 when I read *The Scrum Guide*. This was a life-changing moment as I realized I had been Agile my whole life. It felt like everything just clicked, a career 'love at first sight' moment. Scrum described the adaptive, organic, self-managed and customer-focused way of living that I had been advocating throughout my career. I predicted that the Agile way of working was going to spread from software development to other domains of work life, too, but did not expect it to take this long! Agile would challenge the dusty corporate structures I had been reimagining for a long time. This was the decisive moment I decided to quit my job and start my own company, offering Agile HR and Agile management consulting and training when there was none of that in the market.

A lot has happened since then. Today I advocate and influence for Agile HR and Agile organization development globally, consult, and redesign organizations' and HR teams' operations. I work as an Agile enterprise coach helping executives, leadership teams and change programmes adopt the Agile mindset and practices, co-create their Agile transformation steps, and deliver value through new forms of organizational and management design. I also work with advanced people analytics development, advocating for evidence-based people leadership.

Natal shares the same passion of redefining the whole profession of HR, reinventing work and creating an awesome employee experience. We found none of the IT-focused Agilists could translate Agile to the HR context, and wanted to bring Agile alive to our peers. Agile HR Community was founded to deliver professional level Agile training and development to HR, by HR professionals, and I'm happy to be facilitating this journey.

### Together

This is the handbook we wish we had had when we started to apply Agile HR within our own work. It brings to life all the learning we've gained from our personal experiences over the last decade, as well as the recommendations and insights from the leaders and teams we've collaborated with across the globe. We can't wait for you to put the handbook into practice and join our mission in transforming the HR profession for the future of work.

# AGILE HR AND THE 2020 PANDEMIC

As we finished writing this book the coronavirus pandemic hit. Covid-19 is the biggest disruption most people have experienced to their working lives and it will most likely alter the business world forever. The crisis itself is still far from over as we write, with many countries remaining in lockdown, international travel at a standstill and most business meetings possible only via video conferencing.

The pandemic also serves as a great illustration of why organizations around the world, no matter the industry or size, require business agility to stay alive. Within days whole organizations were forced to shift their entire workforce to remote working just to remain in business. Many were also forced to make significant capacity decisions, such as rapidly deploying people towards areas of the business now experiencing huge increases in demand, such as supermarkets or online retailers making hygiene products like hand sanitizer. Others faced the tough decision of completely shutting down, halting trade and furloughing workers. The fact these decisions were often underpinned by serious health and safety concerns made them even more challenging, with some organizations asking their employees to accept high personal risk just to keep essential services operating or to care for vulnerable parts of society.

Covid-19 forced businesses to work Agile. Suddenly, everyone had to quickly assess their strategic business needs, what was happening for their end customer, not to mention the safety and well-being of their people, and rapidly reprioritize and pivot direction. They were also forced to do this incrementally and to quickly get a temporary plan up and running, knowing they would need to reassess and change the plan within weeks, sometimes days.

This need to pivot meant that organizations already using Agile practices were way ahead of their competitors. We've been inspired by the many stories of HR teams using Agile to respond to the pandemic to keep their businesses operational and, most importantly, their people safe. Great examples include HR teams using Agile tools and collaboration methods to quickly refocus their work and get employee helplines and leader support mechanisms up and running within a matter of days. Often, this meant a need to embrace the concept of delivering an MVP (minimum viable product) to quickly get something functional and valuable out to employees, which could then be incrementally improved once operational.

We also saw that organizations which had already embraced flexible working practices and used digital tools to visualize work and support transparent decision making were able to simply keep going with everyone logging in from home. One Agile HR team even called every single worker in their organization to ensure people were safe and to assess which employees were most at risk and who required extra support to continue working from home. For this team it was also easy to onboard new employees virtually and welcome these people to the business while maintaining social distancing rules.

What's significant in all of these stories is how the Agile mindset and ways of working meant that these HR teams and organizations could trust each other to simply get on with the job despite the crisis happening around them. This meant it didn't matter if people could no longer physically see each other doing the work, because the Agile practices and tools they were using ensured information was shared, decisions were made transparently and work schedules were easily adjusted. Examples of this in action include agreeing times when people should be available online for video calls versus times in the working day when it is OK not to be online, because they are caring for a child or going for a walk. For most, video call bombing by kids or pets has become the norm, as have bad haircuts and a casual dress code. For many of these Agile organizations a crucial activity throughout the crisis was senior leaders holding regular briefings to openly talk about their own stress from lockdown and the changing circumstances, a display of vulnerability that made it OK for others to take time out or to ask for help.

The benefits of embracing an Agile mindset illustrated by Covid-19 exemplify how we hope this book will help HR professionals navigate the complexity of what is being labelled our new normal. As organizations reopen their doors under strange new social distance laws and limitations in how we trade and do business, HR teams around the world will need to use the tools and skills outlined in this book to respond. Charlotte Goulding, a leading Agile HR professional from Infinity Works, sums up the new Agile HR future perfectly:

> In and among the chaos, it feels like a great time for a person-centred HR approach to show its value, to engage and look after people, and find new and varied ways of working to suit different people and their circumstances.

If HR can successfully take on this challenge, we have the opportunity of emerging on the other side of this pandemic with a new and modern world of work.

# ACKNOWLEDGEMENTS

Through our Agile HR adventures, we've been fortunate enough to collaborate and learn from some of the most inspiring, not to mention supersmart, people.

This book pays homage to all the wonderful trailblazers who have joined our mission and become active members of the Agile HR Community. We are in awe of the things you do and the passion you display. Thank you for positively contributing to the future of the HR profession and being the momentum that keeps us going.

We also want to thank and show our deepest respect to our awesome Agile HR allies and collaborators from whom we've learnt so much. Your partnership has meant the world. Big shouts to Tracey Waters, Josh Bersin, Amanda Bellwood and Kate Rand, as well as the Agile HR Finland initial group, Baris Bal, Karen Beaven, Helen Blässar, Taina Blom-Bohner, Icar Castro, Nebel Crowhurst, Yusuf Okucu, Eoin Cannon, Luisa Colombo, Jennifer Dawson, Joanne Edwards, Mikko Eerola, Matias Fourment, Robert Frohman, Tudor Gandu, Tom Haak, Tina Harms, Jaakko Hartikainen, Petri Heiramo, Bee Heller, the Nuoret Henryt group, Lea Hejn, Alize Hofmeester, Sanna Hokkanen, Ari Jokilaakso, Joonas Kiminki, Esko Kokkonen, Eeva-Maria Kytönen, Cristina Leal, Jukka Lindström, Leila Ljungberg, Leonie Lübbers, Leena-Maija Otala, Virpi Mattila-Manninen, Anna Marriott, Arto Miekkavaara, Tamara Molinas, Marjaana Murtomaa, Wayne Mullen, Eija Niininen, James Perez, Emilie Piolroux, Joanna Rosiek, Diana Russo, Melissa Sabella, Avril Scott, Rina Sirén, Cassie Soady, Luke Sondelski, Pia-Maria Thorén, Petteri Tuomimaa, Salvador Vartuli, Vesa Vuorinen and Jane Weir, and a special thanks to Jeff Sutherland.

# PART ONE

# Defining Agile HR

# 01

# What Agile HR is

## Introduction

Agile HR takes everything we know about the Agile mindset, alongside the tools and techniques that bring it to life, and translates these concepts into the context of human resources and people operations. Agile places the customer at the heart of everything we do, and our work becomes defined by the value we deliver to the customer. This definition of value also becomes the main way we prioritize and focus our work on the most important thing to deliver at any one point in time.

In Agile HR we aim to deliver this value to our customer incrementally, slice by slice, validating as we go through a test-and-learn approach. To achieve this, we build feedback loops directly into how we work in order to constantly validate the value we're delivering to the customer and to guide our next increment. Through Agile HR we begin to think more like a scientist and use experimentation and prototyping to continuously test what works and what doesn't. The outcome is a data-driven and evidence-based method of working that allows us to demonstrate why and how an organizational change should be made or a new people process introduced.

While this incremental development cycle of 'plan, do, check and act' may seem obvious once you are familiar with Agile, the practice is often revolutionary for HR teams. HR no longer needs to follow the traditional best practice because that's the way it's always been done or because it worked at a previous organization. In our ever-changing and complex world, not only is best practice too static, it also leads HR to blueprint one-size-fits-all HR processes and systems that are then implemented through big-bang, company-wide change.

For example, it's not uncommon to hear of new performance management systems being introduced in one go as full end-to-end solutions across whole organizations. Despite good HR intentions, this top-down, often hierarchical approach to process design means these systems end up being perceived as tick-box exercises by the users because it feels like yet another add-on to their everyday work. The consequence is HR teams spending the next couple of years trying to get buy-in and acceptance, and they're often overheard saying things like 'it's all about the conversation, not the tool', in an attempt to get employees and managers to use a system that is not adding the intended value. What's worse, the implementation of these heavy, top-down processes has left a legacy of HR as a compliance function, rather than enablers of great performance and people's careers.

Viewed through this lens, Agile HR heralds a whole new method and approach in how we design our HR services – one that fundamentally reshapes the concept of change management. No longer do we manage people 'through change' and deal with 'change resistance' along the way. We now 'co-create change' directly with our people.

---

**WHAT THEY SAY**

HR need to be the facilitators of success, not the dictators of best practice.

Kate Rand, Group Employee Experience & Inclusion Director, Beyond

---

### Agile HR – a way to deliver value

In HR we talk a lot about the need to 'add value' for the business but often struggle to clearly quantify and define what this value is. We also discuss the need for a 'seat at the table' and to be accepted as another business function rather than a transactional service provider. However, we've often lacked the data to back up our viewpoint and demonstrate why time and money should be directed towards initiatives such as people development or cultural change, which can be perceived as a cost to business rather than an essential component of building a successful company.

Most HR leaders express a keen desire to modernize their operations and start to deliver value at speed across their organization. Indeed, they face problems very similar to those of other business leaders, who need to innovate and respond rapidly to our ever-changing and extremely complex business world. In HR we also face the challenge of clearly articulating and measuring how our services directly contribute to the business bottom line and help delight the end-customer, not just our internal customers.

Most HR strategies contain big complex topics, such as designing a personalized employee experience for a diverse workforce or developing future leaders for roles that don't even exist yet. While these complex goals are worthy aims, the value being delivered at any one point in time is often left undefined or linked directly to big-bang releases, such as a new employee benefits package or leadership development programme. A good challenge to set ourselves is: if HR needed to stop 50 per cent of our work tomorrow, can we easily pinpoint which initiatives we should keep and what to remove, based on their value and direct impact on the end-customer? Indeed, too many times, HR projects can be seen by other parts of the business as blockers to getting work done, because HR often asks people to do extra tasks on top of their paid job, such as filling in a form or ticking a box.

As a remedy, Agile helps HR break down these big complex problems into achievable slices of value. It helps us prioritize our work based on value, and clearly articulate what we're delivering to the organization and why we're doing it. The first question we need to ask when embracing Agile HR is how to help our people succeed in their work, and through this help create value to the end-customer.

Employer branding is another important area where HR needs to embrace the concept of value creation in order to be successful. Building a place of work where talented people want to be is very much like developing a great product that customers want to buy. For HR, the ability to create an end-to-end employee journey where people feel connected to the purpose and vision of the organization is an essential part of 'winning the talent war'. As we will see in Chapter 17, one Agile HR team has been so successful with the product development of their employer brand that they're now hailed as an award-winning company that attracts, and more importantly keeps, elite tech talent despite not being a high-paying business.

While the Agile mindset helps businesses innovate and deliver great customer products, it is first and foremost a mindset that develops high-performing teams and organizations. It does this by building feedback loops directly into the cycle of work and inviting teams to continuously assess how they work, what they're achieving and what improvements need to be made. By further supporting this cycle of inspection and adaptation, with real data from both the customer and internal metrics, it also becomes an evidence-based way of working. In this sense, HR leaders look towards Agile HR as a proven method to lift the performance of their own teams, as well as a way to start ruthlessly prioritizing time, effort and budget.

The other key point Agile makes is: why hire great people only to tell them what to do? Agile releases the power of each individual by inviting them to work in a collaborative team whose members self-organize and make their own decisions based on what will deliver the most value to the end-customer. One of the biggest benefits HR professionals discover once they embrace Agile is the creative energy that Agile teamwork brings to their everyday job.

### Agile HR – a human-centric approach

For a long time now, the HR profession has talked about the need to become more human-centric in how we work – an aim that is intimately connected with a growing focus on the employee experience and a desire to understand how our people think, feel and act at work.

One of the most powerful elements of Agile HR comes to the forefront when we consider who is HR's internal customer. Within the organization, employees are the customer, and this means Agile HR places people at the heart of everything we do. As a result, HR's work becomes truly human-centric, with the aim of building human-friendly solutions that are not only validated and tested but, crucially, adapted and valued by the users of the employee experience – our people.

By focusing on the customer, and constantly exploring how to enrich our customer's or user's experience of work, Agile HR helps us build great places of work where high-performing teams are driven through purpose and the impact they have on the end-customer.

Interconnected with this focus on the human in Agile HR is the need to build psychological safety and feedback loops across our teams and organization. The ability to run safe but small experiments, where it is OK to fail, is a core component of the Agile mindset. Only through experimentation can we learn through retrospection and gather the evidence needed to make decisions. It's crucial that people and teams feel comfortable in seeking out and sharing feedback about how they work and what delights the customer – a mindset that has the power to drive continuous improvement not just at the team level but throughout the whole organization.

As the champion of continuous improvement, an Agile HR professional becomes a facilitator of the Agile feedback loop, helping leaders and teams give and receive feedback, openly sharing their learning when something goes wrong and actively planning how they can improve in their next increment of work. HR also needs to do this within our own teams and at a personal level if we are to truly live the mindset and behaviours that underpin Agile. All of this helps to build a new type of HR capability that moves the profession beyond the image of a transactional service provider to that of a true business collaborator and Agile HR coach.

---

**WHAT THEY SAY**

The network-based organization and the Agile way of doing things are growing at an explosive rate. So, every large company we're talking with is saying we're going Agile or we are Agile. Consumers, buyers and customers can switch so quickly that if you're not continuously altering and iteratively developing your product or service, you lose the market. So you have to operate like this.

Josh Bersin, Global Industry Analyst (Hellström, 2020)

---

## Agile HR – a new operating model

Excitingly, Agile HR promises a whole new operating model for HR and the end of the traditional HR silo. In Agile, the handovers and deferred decisions that are common in traditional project management methods or product design are viewed as slowing us down. Instead, Agile advocates small, multi-skilled, self-organizing teams that can make quick decisions in response to evolving customer needs. This means overcoming our traditional HR silos, made up of single-point topic owners, such as recruitment versus talent, and HR generalists versus specialists, to work together and solve problems for the business in a holistic way.

Agile HR also represents a whole new method of partnering and collaborating with the business. Rather than designing in isolation, different business roles and skills are now invited into the Agile HR team to co-design the solution and, more importantly, validate the user experience of what is being delivered.

All this leads HR to developing T-shaped people and T-shaped teams – people and teams that have a breadth of experience and can work across a range of different business scenarios and projects, as well as deep dive into specific specialisms as needed. One challenge, however, is how we build an HR operating model that can successfully manage both business-as-usual (BAU) and the more creative solution design. We'll explore this topic in Chapter 10.

*Agile HR – an unlearning of old habits*

For HR, adopting the Agile mindset is as much about letting go and unlearning old habits as it is about learning new ones – an acknowledgement that it's time to move beyond our traditional, top-down legacy and modernize the HR operating model.

For example, when HR teams work in Agile ways, they quickly discover that receiving feedback early and before a solution has been perfected is a positive, because that's the only way to incrementally develop a great product. In the past, we might have shied away from more critical feedback until we were happy with the end result. Instead, Agile helps us timebox work and control the length of time in which we might fail to achieve an intended result. We can then safely use these situations as learning opportunities to discover what improvements to make next, rather than perceiving the result as a costly mistake.

For HR, Agile means we should no longer work on a product design, such as a leadership programme or peer feedback tool, with a view to making it shiny and perfect before it's released. Indeed, what Agile HR teams quickly learn is that the longer we take to release it, the longer we wait to validate if it truly delights the customer. What's even worse is that all the upfront work we did to make it shiny and perfect becomes wasted effort or sunk costs if it fails upon the first interaction with the customer.

The Agile HR concept of testing and experimentation doesn't have to be elaborate or a time-consuming exercise. It could be as easy as walking down the corridor to ask five people what they think of a piece of company communication before we hit Send. Or it can be more involved, such as a deep dive into the user experience to unearth their pain points, followed by testing prototypes to discover what solves their problems before committing to an overall design. The key is designing a prototype in the customer's hands or creating an experience to assess their real-life reactions and responses.

## Agile for HR and HR for Agile

To help HR professionals conceptualize Agile HR, it is useful to divide the topic into two distinct sections.

### Agile for HR

The first section, Agile for HR, looks at how HR can apply an Agile mindset and various working methods *within our own* teams and projects.

Just as much as an Agile mindset can transform the wider business, Agile for HR has the power to help our profession modernize, innovate and deliver value at speed. Agile for HR also benefits HR professionals and teams no matter what the context. It's not necessary to work within an Agile organization or groovy tech start-up to embrace Agile HR practices and realize these benefits. By simply applying a few of the basic Agile steps outlined in this book, a more human-centric, performance-focused and value-driven approach can be achieved within any HR team.

## HR for Agile

The second section, HR for Agile, looks at *our role in helping the organization* transform to meet the challenges of an increasingly complex business environment. HR for Agile looks at how to design modern workplaces by combining all our previous know-how in organizational development and cultural change with Agile ways of working. HR for Agile also focuses on the need to redesign existing HR and people practices to enrich the employee experience and enable business agility throughout the organization in which we work.

## Finding your own Agile HR flavour

Like Agile itself, no blueprint exists for how to do Agile HR and it's important to find our own flavour based on culture, industry, team size and business needs. It's also essential to build this new model of working incrementally through a test-and-learn cycle. Many of the case studies we'll explore in this book look at how an emerging practice was formed over time as the HR teams experimented with different Agile techniques and found their own operating model by keeping what worked well and eliminating what didn't.

The other key message is that HR will not be able to lead on organization transformation and develop wider business agility if they do not embrace an Agile mindset themselves. Without this, there exists a real danger of HR teams rushing into organization-wide solutions in topics like performance and reward for Agile teams, without truly validating both the problem they're trying to solve and the stages of cultural and behavioural change people need to go through to accept new ways of working.

How does HR ensure they embrace both the mindset and the methodology? By ensuring they adopt 'Agile for HR', as well as 'HR for Agile'. Only by doing, being and experiencing Agile within our own teams and projects can we begin to understand how, why and what HR needs to redesign to support enterprise-wide business agility.

## Building a great place to work

In summary, Agile HR is all about building a great place to work, where awesome people want to be. It aims to be a shared value across the organization between the business, the customer and its employees – a virtuous cycle that attracts amazing talent who are inspired by the opportunity to see the impact of their work on the customer and a business that benefits from highly motivated people constantly improving their performance and results. All of which leads to a delighted customer who craves to be part of the experience their product creates.

Agile HR therefore not only helps HR truly transform their own results, but it helps build high-performing teams and hugely successful businesses.

# References

Dank, N (2018) What's Agile HR Certification Like? Ask Kate Rand of Beyond, *Agile HR Community* [Blog], 18 July www.agilehrcommunity.com/agilehr-community-blog/whats-agile-hr-certification-like-ask-kate-rand (archived at https://perma.cc/UJU2-6H2S)

Hellström, R (2020) Interview with Josh Bersin, Global Industry Analyst, 20 January

# PART TWO

# The Agile mindset

# 02

# Why Agile?

## Introduction

Amazingly, this entire book was written virtually by the two authors, Riina and Natal, who live and work in different countries and time zones. Every page was lovingly compiled, reviewed and edited online using internet-based tools, and each editorial discussion and co-writing session was hosted through video or smartphone messaging. In fact, the whole publishing agreement, not to mention the corresponding development meetings, feedback conversations and even the signing of contracts, all took place without a single face-to-face meeting required. While both Riina and Natal still found it useful to print out each page for review, this whole experience demonstrates how technology and digitalization have fundamentally reshaped how people work, interact and live in today's world.

To deal with this profound technological change and an ever-rising level of complexity, organizations across the globe are being forced to rethink how they operate and compete within the modern marketplace. In this chapter, we'll explore the dynamics of this constantly evolving business landscape and begin to appreciate why organizations of every shape and size are beginning to embrace Agile as a potential way to find the answers to the many challenges they face. This discussion will help HR professionals begin to appreciate Agile, and all the new methods of working the mindset offers, as something much more than the latest fad or hot topic. Furthermore, we'll explore how Agile ways of working not only help the business respond to complexity but also offer HR the methods and tools needed to modernize their own practices and become better equipped for the future of work.

*Our digitalized world*

Today, Gordon Moore's prediction (known as Moore's Law) in 1965 that computing power would double every two years is proving to be very real – a new norm that is characterized by exponential technological change and perfectly illustrated through the rapid advancement in smartphones to the point that they now navigate our lives and buy our things (Kurzweil, 2005). From small local shops through to large international banks, organizations need to redesign how they operate to remain competitive. If we consider the small local shop, it now needs a Google listing and Tripadvisor rating to attract passing trade, while the large international bank competes against new fin-tech disruptors that can transfer funds instantly across the globe for a fraction of the price.

The first shift towards this new working paradigm started in the 1960s as our world began to transform through digital electronics and the rise of the computer. Often coined the third industrial revolution, this saw white-collar knowledge workers begin to replace blue-collar factory workers as the mode of production evolved. By the 1980s, handheld phones were on the rise and the computer was no longer just a business tool; it had become personal. Then came the internet in the 1990s and this massive increase in connectivity and digital possibility transformed our lives forever.

So profound is the impact of digitalization on our society that many argue we're now entering a fourth industrial revolution, where the digital, biological and physical are merging in such a way that the natural and artificial are becoming impossible to decipher (World Economic Forum, 2020). The subsequent impact on the workplace now has us talking about robots taking our jobs and the need to reskill entire generations of workers.

Often, we don't even notice how this new digitized life has changed our everyday behaviour until we experience a non-tech or clunky service from the past. As consumers, we now expect 24/7 availability and one-click purchasing via our phone or tablet, and our shopping to arrive on our doorstep within days, if not hours. Our choice feels endless, with hundreds of alternatives instantly accessible through the gadget in our pockets. Given this digitized choice, the customer is now king. By voting with our wallets, the end-customer can dictate the rise and fall of a business almost overnight, and organizations unable to quickly adapt to shifting consumer preferences or deliver a user-friendly service are left behind.

WHAT THEY SAY

According to a recent study by MIT Sloan Management School, only 17 per cent of leading companies will be leaders five years from now. These companies – including organizations like Apple and Alphabet – continually find new sources of competitive advantage by reinventing their businesses and adapting to evolving market conditions.

Jeff Sutherland, 2020

## The search for business agility

Within this new paradigm of work, organizations require business agility to stay in the game. Intimate knowledge of the end-customer is now crucial to making decisions on where to focus our time, money and thinking power. Business leaders constantly struggle with choices about whether to shift organizational capacity towards innovation and new product development versus the need to maintain older products and supporting infrastructure. Even the decision to launch a new product is risky, because if a business moves too early, the tipping point of customer need may not yet be realized and the product may fail to sell. To combat these ever-changing demands on the modern business, our operating models now require a new type of design and flexibility. Teams need to rapidly scale up or down in response to market forces, and new skills and capabilities must be quickly deployed to adapt to the ever-changing dynamics of customer choice.

In this fast-paced business environment it's also wrong to assume that our competitors are playing the long game. Guided by aggressive investment strategies, some of these new growth companies offer free services, subscription-based business models or sharing platforms with the aim of achieving exponential growth and first-mover status. By being willing to risk millions for market share, they play on the promise of future profitability by quickly compiling masses of transactions or followers and may even sell this vision on for millions before any actual profit is realized, as infamously demonstrated recently by WeWork (Dvorak and Fujikawa, 2019). Spurred on by likes, recommendations and new user adoption rates, these companies constantly track the pulse of the market with the aim of creating intuitive user experiences based on customer needs and preferences. The fact that our product or service is 'free' does not mean the customer won't leave in a heartbeat if something better comes along. Until the business reaches market domination and our product becomes interwoven with everyday life, as those of Amazon or Apple have done, this risk continues. Indeed, even the big players can have their loyalty shaken overnight through social media backlash, such as with Facebook and the Cambridge Analytica scandal (Wong, 2019).

Our new strategic focus on developing business agility is also in response to widespread market disruption. Through an innovative and what we've started to label as an Agile business model, companies like Tesla are transforming how we drive cars, and businesses like Netflix are revolutionizing how we watch television. These disruptors have transformed not only whole industries but also how people behave and interact within society. These companies are taking market share away from long-established corporations and challenging the decades-old business models that have been built on long-term relationships and assumed ways of working.

---

### WHAT THEY SAY

Depending on the day of the week, one of three companies is the world's most valuable company in the world. It is either Amazon, Microsoft or Apple. All of them are moving into different industries, disrupting and innovating the whole domain. Microsoft went through massive Agile transformation back in 2005. They were doing 18-month releases when Ken Schwaber and I went in to help them transform. It took them until 2012 to be able to release every sprint, and until 2017 to release every day. And in 2019 they became the most valuable company in the world. Where did this start? With a massively ambitious statement by Steve Ballmer of a need to 'become ten times as fast and go ask the engineers how this is possible'.

The big challenge is Amazon. Amazon has 3,300 Scrum teams delivering a new feature once a second to the public. A lot of companies may say 'we're not a computer company, we're not a software company', as if they haven't realized that much of their business is disruptable. For example, I've talked to many banks over the years, and they have felt quite secure because of the heavily regulated environment, 'not needing to worry'. Quite recently, some bank employees told me that Amazon is offering loans in their market and having so much data on their customers that they have an ability to calculate the risk of a loan in a few seconds. While deciding on loans can take the normal bank days, if not weeks, Amazon can do it in minutes. This insight was so massive for the bank that they realized they had no way to compete with that speed and needed to start planning an exit from the loan market.

Companies that think they are safe wake up one morning and find there is no market left.

Jeff Sutherland, 2020

*Achieving agility and stability simultaneously*

Within our VUCA (volatile, uncertain, complex and ambiguous) world, business agility has become the modern mantra of CEOs and entrepreneurs. However, it would be wrong to assume that this constitutes only an ability to adapt and change in the face of competition. Business agility also demands a type of stability within the operating model to ensure consistency and reliability (Aghina, De Smet and Weerda, 2015). While parts of the business will constantly change, there is also a need for a strong backbone of governance, accountability and stable infrastructure to support this flexibility, especially as a company begins to grow and scale. To be successful in the modern world, a business needs the right balance of stability and predictability on the one hand, and adaptability and responsiveness on the other.

As we'll come to learn when we explore the concept of Agile ways of working in the next few chapters, this stability looks vastly different from the traditional bureaucratic decision-making processes that often characterize older and more established corporations. Instead, this stable backbone comes from the discipline, transparency and true team collaboration that shape Agile operating models.

*Decision-making latency*

When dealing with this amount of complexity, most organizations face a prioritization and decision-making challenge. It is not uncommon for people to talk about steering committees and executive-level bottlenecks slowing businesses down in today's marketplace. Often a result of tightly controlled and centralized structures, this extra need to constantly synchronize, align and navigate internal politics just to make a decision can lead to missed opportunities and business inefficiency, not to mention a delayed time to market.

To overcome such hurdles and evolve these methods of working, it is now vital for HR and business leaders to understand the different types of operating models available and learn how and when to apply them. For example, to what degree can an organization enable team-based decision making that is much closer to the end-customer? Also, how can the rules, policies and roles be simplified to allow for speed to market and real-time decisions?

WHAT THEY SAY

A discussion overheard at a business offsite:

We have overcomplicated so many things in our company. For instance, the instructions given for a simple thing like paying for this management offsite are so complicated. I don't understand why our manager can't just pay for the full offsite with her credit card and then take care of the cost allocation later. Instead, 13 management team members must read these complicated instructions on how to pay for the offsite, pay individually, and then create 13 individual expense reports. All of which will be allocated to the same business unit cost code anyway. It's like we're making more work for ourselves on purpose!

## Solving complex problems

All these factors lead us to now view an organization as a complex, adaptive system (Johnston, Coughlin and Garvey Berger, 2014) instead of a controlled and rigidly defined piece of machinery. These are interconnected ecosystems similar to a coral reef or rainforest, where patterns emerge over time. In this complex environment, our traditional, top-down and hierarchical decision-making processes, which are based on a clear relationship between cause and effect, are failing (Snowden and Boone, 2007). To solve our modern-day problems, organizations need to harness innovation and creativity, through which solutions can emerge, rather than impose predetermined results such as scorecards and pre-set metrics. Safe experimentation, where it's OK to fail, becomes an essential business tool that allows us to make decisions based on empirical evidence and data.

The challenge, however, is an initial sense of losing control for many business leaders, and indeed for HR, who are used to working in a pyramid structure and applying assumptions on what can be managed and predicted within the workplace. For example, consider the common use of key performance indicators (KPIs) to guide results rather than using experimentation to gather evidence and validate a decision. In most situations this sense of control is illusory, given the constant state of flux that defines our business world. Only by embracing the need to adapt and linking this directly to how we run an organization can we successfully solve our modern-day challenges.

## Our Taylorist HR legacy

The organizational design of many businesses today, alongside the HR processes and systems that support these methods of working, still often reflects a traditional, command-and-control pyramid structure – an environment that has also produced a top-down, hierarchical approach to managing people, who are generally viewed as a costly resource, rather than the complex, emotive human beings that we are. Much of this legacy can be attributed to ideas first presented by Frederick Taylor who wrote a book called *The Principles of Scientific Management* (Taylor, 1911). This historical influence has also led to HR being characterized by process-heavy, compliance-driven, static systems, shaped to manage the lowest performer rather than enable everyone to perform at their best.

Taylor proposed a ground-breaking idea, for the time, of dividing up the process of manufacturing a good into a series of small, specific and scientifically tested tasks. By designing what we now know as the production line, Taylor not only revolutionized the organizational design of factories and businesses of the time but set in motion a new management theory about how to structure work and manage people.

The production line saw the birth of many workplace practices that we still see today, such as workforce planning, performance management and pay for performance. Workers were matched to specific tasks or specialist areas based on skill, and then trained and monitored to ensure standardization and workplace efficiency. To maximize productivity, Taylor advocated a new way to reward and incentivize these trained workers. Rather than punishing them for mistakes, Taylor argued the need to reward individual workers for higher results and pay them for each piece of work they produced. He also thought that if a worker's basic needs were met through a decent living wage, the motivation for stoppages and strikes would be removed. While many of these ideas may seem overly simplistic today, this style of management thinking went on to shape US industrialists like Henry Ford and Alfred Sloan, and laid the foundations for the mass-consumerist society of the 20th century.

### THE SEPARATION OF THINKING AND DOING IN THE WORKPLACE

The implications of Taylor's Principles of Scientific Management for the development of HR and the theory of management are profound. Of significance was the separation of the thinking of work, such as planning, budgeting and monitoring of tasks, from the doing of work, such as driving a forklift or packing a box.

A fundamental distrust of the worker permeates Taylor's theory of scientific management. Motivated by money, a worker is seen as naturally lazy and expected to slacken off if not closely monitored. Close personal supervision and micro-management were the natural consequences of this negative human view – a management style that still impacts the workplace today and is often seen as highly demotivating when on the receiving end: 'what the workmen want from employers beyond anything else is higher wages: what employers want from workmen most of all is low labor costs in manufacture' (Taylor, 1911).

Many people liken this view to a later concept, developed by psychologist Douglas McGregor in the 1960s, of the theory X worker, and how our beliefs about what motivates people at work shape our management style (McGregor, 1960). McGregor argued that if we believe people dislike their work and have little motivation for what they do, known as theory X, our management style will be more autocratic. Alternatively, if we believe people are challenged by their work and take pride in their results, known as theory Y, we're more likely to engage in a more participatory style of management and trust people to take ownership of what they do.

While motivational theory has developed since these ideas were put forward, theory X can still be seen in some management practices today. Indeed, while one part of Amazon is characterized by technological innovation and Agile work practices, the other side is made up of tightly monitored shift work, where people are tracked and timed as they pack delivery boxes (Chamberlain, 2018). While it is important to create efficient and lean processes for production-line work, we should never do so at the cost of the human view. Production-line work shouldn't be valued any less than other parts of the business, and the more we empower people to make their own decisions and continuously improve their own processes in this area, the more successful we can be.

Interestingly, it was back at the production line where we first saw a questioning of this separation of doing and thinking when 'just in time' manufacturing was created by Toyota in the 1980s. In the pursuit of 'lean' efficiency and the removal of 'waste' from the system, Toyota encouraged managers and workers to come together in the form of 'quality circles' or 'kaizen' to continuously improve and solve problems together. Crucially, it was recognized that the workers, who were closest to the end-customer, held many of the answers, as opposed to the managers. An Agile way of thinking was just about to begin (Rigby *et al*, 2016).

## Our HR legacy

While much has changed since Taylor's time and a greater appreciation of the human side of work has influenced management thinking, many of our existing HR processes and systems still feel clunky and out of touch with the modern needs of people and business. This bureaucratic legacy has also seen HR become the enforcer of bad management decisions which often originate with senior executives but get executed by HR because they involve a financial or legal impact on people. A good example is the need for HR to step in and start a formal process to manage a low performer owing to repeated lateness or missed targets, when often these situations can be linked back to a bad recruitment decision or a lack of trust between the manager and the employee.

HR's history of top-down implementation of processes and policies also means that despite our good intentions and the many great, people-focused professionals working in HR, we often end up being perceived as a compliance, rules-driven department rather than as representing the people side of business success. For example, asking all our employees to complete a career development plan as part of their annual performance discussion has the right intent, but when it's deemed mandatory and is linked to ticking a box for approval in a top-down performance management system, the support of people's career development gets lost in the enforcement of the process.

### Moving beyond HR best practice

As business seeks out agility to compete in the modern marketplace, the static frameworks of HR 'best practice', such as annual performance appraisals, managed career pathways and documented job descriptions, are failing to meet the needs of our rapidly changing operating models. As technology and digitalization transform the workplace, knowledge has become intangible and multi-sourced, while jobs have fragmented and whole careers have even disappeared as industries quickly evolve. Also, because digitalization creates a personalized and enriched end-customer experience within the marketplace, our employees now demand the same personalized experience at work.

Adding further complexity to these HR dilemmas is that our employees are multi-generational, diverse and want constant communication, individualized feedback and a good values-fit. In this new working paradigm, the traditional career ladder that people climb for job status and pay increases no longer reflects the realities of the workplace. Now, an individual contributor or high-performing team can impact the bottom line more than all the managers put together. With this evolution of the workplace come increasing demands for more dynamic and meaningful ways to reward and recognize people's contribution, and for frameworks that move beyond the traditional system of performance ratings and individual bonuses.

These modern and complex challenges call for HR to embrace a different, more progressive way of working – one that builds a shared value for the business, end-customer and employee. Our existing HR portfolio is out of date and unable to deal with these new workplace trends and organizational design needs. It's also time to realize that HR alone cannot solve these complex problems and that only by working *with* people, rather than *on* people, can we end our Taylorist legacy and find the answers together.

## Conclusion

Organizations across the globe now operate within a business environment characterized by rapid technological change, disruption, economic uncertainty and an ever-increasing level of complexity. To deal with this new norm, business is seeking a type of organizational agility to adapt and quickly respond to changing end-customer needs.

Business agility begins to reshape the operating model of organizations, which we'll explore in more detail throughout this book. For now, it's useful to note that organizations can be anywhere along this Agile journey, which ranges from being fully traditional and based on a pyramid structure, all the way through to fully Agile and based on a fluid network of teams (Figure 2.1).

In summary, here are the main changes taking place within organizations as they shift towards a more Agile way of working:

FIGURE 2.1    From hierarchy to network

**FROM A HIERARCHICAL, TOP-DOWN,
MANAGEMENT-LED ORGANIZATION**

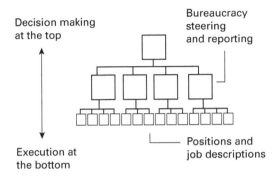

**TO A CUSTOMER-CENTRIC, ADAPTIVE,
NETWORKED ORGANIZATION**

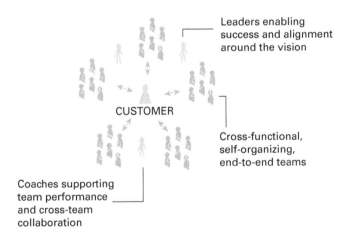

- **hierarchy to network** – reducing the dependency on hierarchical, management-heavy decision-making structures, and enabling business decisions organically through networked, self-organizing and team-based models;

- **functional roles to projects** – moving away from rigid resource plans, based on functional units and management reporting lines, towards project-based work, where the movement of people is more fluid, and based on end-customer needs and capability requirements;

- **customer value streams** – shifting from operating models based on product lines towards teams joined up along end-customer value streams with the aim of creating an end-to-end customer experience or journey;
- **transparency and knowledge sharing** – challenging the traditional culture of 'information equals power' and beginning to transparently share all available data across the wider business to enable real-time business decisions and team-based problem solving close to the end-customer;
- **doing one thing well** – shifting from detailed upfront planning, listing everything that will be worked on annually, towards developing a prioritized business portfolio that focuses effort on the most important end-customer need or business problem to ensure one job is done really well rather than spreading people's talents across multiple projects at the same time;
- **Agile business planning** – moving beyond the annual budgeting cycle, which doesn't allow the adaptation of how funds are allocated in response to changing circumstances, to a rolling and ongoing approach to budgeting and tracking company performance;
- **simplification and removing waste** – simplifying support functions and reassessing the value of internal processes so they enable rather than hinder the business – this is a key consideration for HR where a number of our projects are often imposed 'on the business' rather than being developed in conjunction with the business cycle.

---

### KEY POINTS FOR HR PROFESSIONALS

- Business now operates within a marketplace characterized by an ever-increasing level of complexity and profound technological change.
- A new type of organizational agility is required to quickly adapt and respond.
- As organizations seek out agility and fundamentally rethink how they operate, the static frameworks of HR 'best practice' and one-size-fits-all are rapidly becoming out of date.
- Most of our HR processes and systems still reflect a traditional, command-and-control pyramid structure, and need to evolve to meet the needs of organizational agility.
- Just like the business, it's time for HR to embrace a more progressive and Agile way of working so we can begin to co-create the solutions to the complex workplace problems we face.

---

# References

Aghina, W, De Smet, A and Weerda, K (2015) Agility: It Rhymes With Stability, *McKinsey Quarterly*, December www.mckinsey.com/business-functions/organization/our-insights/agility-it-rhymes-with-stability (archived at https://perma.cc/VQF9-SCGF)

Chamberlain, G (2018) Underpaid and Exhausted: The Human Cost of Your Kindle, *The Guardian* www.theguardian.com/technology/2018/jun/09/human-cost-kindle-amazon-china-foxconn-jeff-bezos (archived at https://perma.cc/EQ8H-JVRF)

Dvorak, P and Fujikawa, M (2019) SoftBank Founder Calls His Judgment 'Really Bad' After $4.7 Billion WeWork Hit, *Wall Street Journal* www.wsj.com/articles/softbank-books-loss-of-4-7-billion-on-wework-investment-11573024776 (archived at https://perma.cc/Z7E3-5RBQ)

Hellström, R (2020) Interview with Dr Jeff Sutherland, Co-creator of Scrum, 7 January

Johnston, K, Coughlin, C and Garvey Berger, J (2014) Leading in Complexity: What Makes Complexity Different and How Can Leaders Respond Effectively? *Cultivating Leadership* www.cultivatingleadership.co.nz/site/uploads/Leading-in-Complexity-CC-JGB-KJ-2014-4.pdf (archived at https://perma.cc/D5VE-BW2G)

Kurzweil, R (2005) Moore's Law: The Fifth Paradigm, *Wikipedia* https://en.wikipedia.org/wiki/Accelerating_change#/media/File:PPTMooresLawai.jpg (archived at https://perma.cc/M5QT-U7M2)

McGregor, D (1960) *The Human Side of Enterprise*, McGraw-Hill, New York

Rigby, D K, Sutherland, J and Takeuchi, H (2016) Embracing Agile, *Harvard Business Review*, May https://hbr.org/2016/05/embracing-agile (archived at https://perma.cc/QEB3-9Q2W)

Snowden D J and Boone, M E (2007) A Leader's Framework for Decision Making, *Harvard Business Review*, November https://hbr.org/2007/11/a-leaders-framework-for-decision-making (archived at https://perma.cc/9RKE-G6GQ)

Taylor, F W (1911) *The Principles of Scientific Management*, Harper & Brothers, London

Wong, J C (2019) The Cambridge Analytica Scandal Changed the World – But It Didn't Change Facebook, *The Guardian* www.theguardian.com/technology/2019/mar/17/the-cambridge-analytica-scandal-changed-the-world-but-it-didnt-change-facebook (archived at https://perma.cc/5FTF-MQAA)

World Economic Forum (2020) Fourth Industrial Revolution, *World Economic Forum* www.weforum.org/focus/fourth-industrial-revolution (archived at https://perma.cc/Z63U-GTXC)

# 03

# The Agile mindset

## Introduction

Agile means faster, doesn't it?

This is the most common misunderstanding of Agile. That all we need to do is work faster, while everything else remains the same. The reality couldn't be further from the truth. By embracing Agile we begin to work through a whole new set of beliefs and values that are fundamentally different from how we've traditionally worked in corporate settings. When we start to work Agile, the biggest and most lasting change is in our mindset.

In this chapter, we'll get comfortable with the core elements of Agile and how it differs from the 'waterfall' approach, a term used to describe more traditional ways of running a business project. It's important to highlight at this stage that we're not proposing that waterfall is wrong or bad, but rather that Agile is a very different mode of working that is best suited to the changing business world in which we now operate.

Where the problem starts, and why some view waterfall in a negative way, is that it's often been associated with the more bureaucratic and pyramid style of running a business – an operating model that we've come to see no longer fits with our modern working paradigm. However, the waterfall method as a way to run a project can still be relevant and sometimes even preferred, when we consider our HR context. In this chapter, we'll help identify these situations and explore how these differ from where and why we should embrace Agile.

By the end of this chapter, we'll begin to understand Agile on a deeper, mindset level, one that moves beyond the terms, tools and practices that we may have already come across. We'll do this because it's vital to clearly articulate what the Agile mindset is before we begin to translate it into our own HR context and start to apply the thinking to HR projects and working methods.

## The waterfall approach to projects

Waterfall project management is a body of knowledge built on upfront planning and long-term thinking. Before committing to a project, the plan needs to be defined, resources agreed and the budget fixed. This methodology is termed waterfall owing to the visualization of tasks and activities flowing down in a project Gantt chart (Figure 3.1).

Waterfall works on the premise that the more you plan every detail upfront, the better the project can be managed. In waterfall, all the specifications and deliverables are written and agreed *before any actual work begins.*

The Project Management Body of Knowledge (Project Management Institute, 2020) outlines the following five phases for a project:

1 **Initiate.** The business need for the project is established alongside the overall scope, budget and authorization. These project fundamentals generally require sign-off at each level of the company hierarchy to ensure visibility, stability and predictability.

2 **Plan.** A project management plan is set out by the project manager, containing detailed specifications on exactly what will happen, who will do it and how long it will take. This plan requires sign-off from stakeholders and sponsors to be official, and changes from this point need to be re-approved according to a predetermined change management

FIGURE 3.1  Gantt chart example

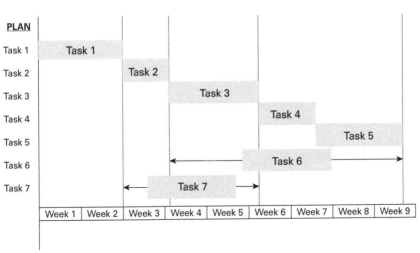

plan. Everything is agreed upfront, including project milestones, exact deliverables and their sequence, all types of resourcing from equipment to the people involved, contracts and vendors, and payment schedules, as well as activities like risk management, quality control, communication, training and expected documentation.

3  **Execute.** The project manager directs and manages the work, while the project team executes each step in the plan to get the job done. Generally, sign-off is required from the sponsors when the deliverables are produced.

4  **Control and monitor.** This phase happens alongside the above and is how the project manager ensures the work being carried out matches the plan, with any deviation tracked and reported. In waterfall, the schedule and budget are closely monitored and because everything is planned upfront, a change in requirements will have potential knock-on effects on all the other planned activities and costs. This means that any change is considered a risk that must be tightly controlled, re-approved and limited.

5  **Close.** Waterfall projects tend to have a separate implementation and closing stage. The implementation usually involves a large roll-out phase and the value of the project is only realized once all deliveries are fully implemented.

## Waterfall and predictable environments

The waterfall approach (Figure 3.2) works well in a stable and predictable environment. The detailed plans and specified processes also give a sense of control to those involved, who trust in the plan given the amount of upfront thinking and effort undertaken.

Standard process design also works well in predictable environments. If the conditions are stable, we can map out a standard process for how to execute different tasks or services. This approach is of particular value if we're delivering the same end result several times and want to regulate it.

In situations where dependencies are low, timeframes known and stakeholders minimal, waterfall is still a valid and preferred method. Essentially, waterfall is suited to projects where the impact of change can be easily managed, and the relationships between cause and effect are clear to all involved. Indeed, this way of working can help HR streamline processes and produce efficient, even automated, services. In these situations, following HR best practice still makes a lot of sense.

FIGURE 3.2    The waterfall approach

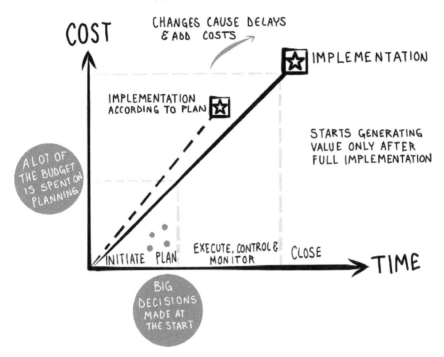

Here are some HR examples where the waterfall approach is beneficial:

- A payroll team needs to roll out a statutory raise in salary, only a basic level of approval is required, and the project can be easily planned and scheduled according to set deadlines.

- Organizing the logistics of a company-wide event that has already happened several times and the same detailed plan outlining venue, vendors and budget can be easily implemented. While every event is unique, once a set process has been established, and if the dependencies are minimal, a standard plan can be executed each time. It's good to note, however, that as soon as you want to innovate or improve the event, an Agile approach is preferred.

- A short and simple recruitment process for the replacement of a like-for-like role within a specified profession and when the required amount of experience and credentials is clear. For example, the recruitment of nurses for a specified area or a call centre operator. Again, it's good to note that as soon as the job profile or fit becomes more complex or we need to innovate the process, an Agile approach is needed.

- In the case of sexual harassment or violence towards an employee, it's essential to take immediate action to ensure people are safe. In these examples, HR follows a set, top-down waterfall process based on legal requirements and workplace safety. However, once the immediate issue has been resolved, an Agile approach would be best suited when exploring why the situation occurred in the first place and how to change any underlying cultural drivers that allowed it to happen.

### *When waterfall becomes a blocker*

The essence of waterfall is to stick to the plan. The key question to ask when considering this methodology is, if we plan the whole project now, how long can we trust the plan to stay unaffected by change? The biggest risk to waterfall projects is changes identified too late. A late change can have a massive impact on scope, schedule and cost. It can also lead to a large sunk cost, where a project team spends a lot of time and money on a delivery that isn't needed after all owing to a late change.

Therein lies the problem. Given the increasingly complex and changing business environment we now operate in, waterfall is less and less valid for larger-scale projects or when designing products. However, much of the corporate world is still overcommitted to the waterfall approach, with many traditional companies still reflecting these ways of working. In these models, the board of directors are personally liable for ensuring the long-term success of the business and set out a one- to five-year strategy to realize this vision. Everyone, from the C-suite down to first-level employees, is then directed towards this vision through cascaded goals and KPIs. In many companies, everything needs to be planned, budgeted and forecasted upfront, supported by quarterly or annual reporting. Often within these environments, waterfall-style planning offers a sense of certainty and control, much of which is quickly eroded once unforeseen market changes begin to bite.

If we then consider large HR initiatives, most still follow a traditional waterfall approach. The result is often called a 'big-bang implementation', where an end-to-end HR solution is designed upfront and then rolled out across the whole organization. These solutions usually demand a one-size-fits-all design, where all employees, no matter who they are or what they do, get the same standardized service or experience. Indeed, much of the language of traditional HR includes words like 'cascade', 'implementation' or 'roll-out', with the aim of hundreds, sometimes thousands, of employees adopting a new product or process at the same time. Also, once these predetermined HR solutions have been rolled out, the hope is to freeze and stabilize the process, with the assumption that all the right requirements have been identified upfront and only minor changes will need to be added once implemented and in use.

## Our complex and unstable HR environment

The modern reality of HR projects is multiple and highly opinionated stakeholders, organizational complexity and a need to change how people behave and interact within the workplace. Many HR professionals talk about how they're unable to trust their project plans to hold for long. Indeed, most of HR's work is impacted by change. Here are a few familiar examples:

- **Changing customer needs.** HR projects include several different stakeholders or users who are often unclear about their needs and requirements at the start. Often people only figure out what they really want once they use or experience the HR solution. It's common to hear of HR projects dealing with new, unplanned requirements after the final version is agreed, or discovering that major changes are needed once implementation begins.

- **Complex dependencies.** HR is often dependent on input from other teams or departments, whose changing priorities impact HR's delivery. Sometimes these dependencies go beyond the traditional boundaries of an organization and include entities like workers' councils, suppliers and freelancers. Such dependencies often mean that HR are unable to stick to their scheduled plan because they have to chase answers or involve others.

- **External disruptions.** There might be economic, political or competitor-related uncertainties hindering the business from deciding on long-term commitments, such as an investment in people development or recruitment. Union negotiations, changes in the talent market or a disruptive new competitor might also influence HR projects and greatly alter the scope.

LESSON

We tend to ask people in our Agile HR training workshops about their current approach to planning a project:

'When do you make all the big decisions in your projects?'

'In the beginning, when we're planning.'

'When do you know the least about the project and what to expect?'

'In the beginning, when we're planning.'

'Touché.'

The traditional waterfall approach is becoming less relevant for HR and can no longer be the only way to run a project or design a solution. It's time for HR to acknowledge that we face complex business problems and a rapidly changing workplace. We also need to innovate our speed of delivery and better demonstrate how we add value to the organization. Just like the wider business, it's time for HR to embrace the Agile mindset and evolve our operating model.

## Agile mindset

Agile is first and foremost a mindset. Agile starts from understanding that everything we do is focused on, and prioritized by, the value we deliver to the customer. Only by constantly validating the customer value can we create products and services that people want to adopt, use, recommend and pay for.

An Agilist accepts that everything cannot be planned in detail upfront and expects change to naturally shape their work. To develop products and services that maximize end-customer value, a lot of feedback and validation is required to ensure we're delivering exactly what the user needs. The only way to achieve this outcome is to work emergently, and embrace an incremental development cycle of plan, do, check and act.

To work Agile is to constantly seek out ways to improve and achieve our goal of delivering end-customer value at a faster rate. This means things like handovers, deferred decisions and stakeholder approvals slow us down. Instead, Agile advocates small, multi-skilled teams able to make their own decisions and prioritize their work according to the evolving plan. To help make this happen, all information available needs to be transparent and openly shared, and all the skills required to get the job done should be in the team.

Validating the customer value as we work through feedback from the end-customer also enables us to adapt and pivot along the way. To do this, it's important to release something of value early and regularly to constantly gather feedback and reassess the plan, rather than wait until the end of the whole project, like in waterfall. To achieve this, Agile looks at how to deliver the value step by step, or incrementally, often in smaller chunks to begin with, the aim being to build up the solution over time. Given this way of working, if we're then forced to stop the project halfway along, in waterfall nothing has been delivered, despite lots of work, while with Agile, small and regular slices of value have already been realized.

This is the insight that software developers had over 20 years ago. For all the same reasons, the waterfall approach was not delivering the right results and the changing business context meant that any detailed upfront planning was too rigid or static. The origins of Agile are therefore a direct response to these challenges (Figure 3.3).

FIGURE 3.3   The Agile approach

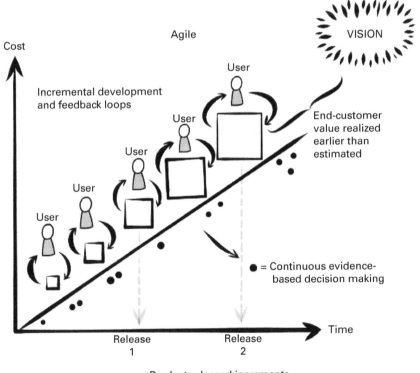

## The origins of Agile

It's important for an HR professional to know the origins of Agile, and where and why it started. Agile is nothing new. The software development community has been successfully evolving, testing and validating Agile ways of working for over 20 years. Today, within tech, Agile is already mainstream, and it's only during the past 5 to 10 years that other industries and functions have been catching up, aiming to replicate their successes.

It all started in software development, in the late 1990s, with an estimation of 31 per cent of IT projects failing (Standish Group, 1994). With the birth of the internet, technology was evolving so rapidly and the demand for new features and products was so intense that the waterfall approach just couldn't keep up. IT products were no longer staying relevant throughout their long development roadmaps and the investment budgets were too static. Another approach was needed, and a collection of forward-thinking tech leaders started to experiment with lighter, more adaptive methods for developing software. Some of these methods included Extreme Programming, Adaptive Software Development and Scrum (Highsmith, 2001). These leaders then got together to explore common ground and the word Agile was coined.

## The Agile Manifesto

Seventeen bright-minded thought leaders in software development, most of whom had been developing their own methodologies, were invited to gather in Utah in 2001. The group found they were committed to a certain mindset, alongside a collection of common values and principles that underpinned the various software development methods the different leaders were experimenting with in order to be more responsive and adaptive. As a result, the group compiled the *Agile Manifesto* (Agile Manifesto Organization, 2001) and the movement we know today began. The signers of the Agile Manifesto all remain well known in the Agile scene and continue to practise, publish and teach their various frameworks across the world.

The Agile Manifesto articulates the mindset, and even though it was written for software development, the words resonate strongly with HR and other non-tech areas of the business. Every Agilist should know the Agile Manifesto and reflect on its meaning.

THE AGILE MANIFESTO

We are uncovering better ways of developing software by doing it and helping others do it. Through this work we have come to value:

- individuals and interactions **over** processes and tools;
- working software **over** comprehensive documentation;
- customer collaboration **over** contract negotiation;
- responding to change **over** following a plan.

That is, while there is value in the items on the right, we value the items on the left more.

Agile Manifesto, 2001

## HR AND THE AGILE MANIFESTO

While some of these words might sound techie, HR can learn a lot from the Agile Manifesto. Much of our work can become overly focused on the processes and tools, rather than on the value our HR products and services deliver to the business and its people. There is also a tendency within HR to write policy or comprehensive documentation first, when the true need is to fix real-time problems and write the supporting documents only once the solution has been proven to work.

HR TOP TIP

Let's explore how the Agile Manifesto relates to our own HR domain.

'Individuals and interactions over processes and tools'

*HR example: Allowing teams to decide on their own learning budget*

Some companies allow their people to decide how to use their own learning budget instead of following a centrally managed learning and development process. This self-directed and just-in-time approach to learning often leads to a more creative use of the budget, as well as an increased utilization of free learning resources within the organization, such as mentoring, on-the-job learning and the formation of learning-based networks.

'Working software (product) over comprehensive documentation'

*HR example: GM's dress code*

General Motors' dress code is now described in two words, 'Dress appropriately' (Fessler, 2018), and is a great example of how we can evolve HR policy to reflect a positive human view and treat our employees as responsible adults.

'Customer collaboration over contract negotiation'

*HR example: Co-creating user-centric HR solutions*

Certain Agile HR teams invite other people from the business to actively participate in the design and development of specific HR products and services. The approach ensures the outcome not only reflects the input of ideas from the business, but the outcome is directly validated by the users of the subsequent solution.

'Responding to change over following a plan'

*HR example: Complex HR initiatives require adaptive planning*

Many people initiatives, such as culture change or post-merger integration projects, are hugely complex and contain a lot of uncertainty. These types of initiatives require an Agile mindset of adaptability and responsiveness to be successful, rather than being based on rigid, predetermined plans.

## Being Agile versus doing Agile

An Agile mindset is best developed by trying out different ways of working and building on direct experiences. To truly shift on a behavioural and mindset level, Agile practices need to be experienced first-hand. When people start learning about Agile, they begin to recalibrate their thinking patterns around a new set of beliefs and values. This process takes time and implies that the act of being Agile is much more than the visible activities of doing Agile, such as using a Scrum board or attending daily stand-ups.

The Agile onion, shown in Figure 3.4, is a great visual to help explain this concept. If the belief system is in place, Agile ways of working will flourish no matter what tools and techniques are utilized within an organization. The danger is when Agile practices are introduced without a corresponding shift in management thinking and organizational structure. Over time, traditional, top-down bureaucracy will simply frustrate and slow down

FIGURE 3.4   The Agile onion

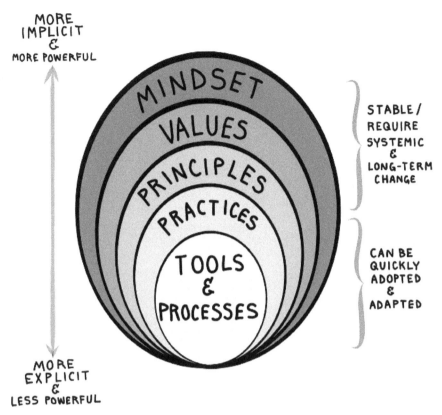

Reproduced with permission from Simon Powers, December 2019 (Powers, 2019)

Agile teams to the point where it may feel like Agile has failed. For an Agile mindset to take hold, a conscious change needs to take place in how people behave and interact. We'll explore these topics further in the upcoming chapters when we dive into HR's role in Agile organizational transformation and also how we use Agile practices within our own HR teams.

## Agile principles

The Agile mindset builds on the values outlined in the Agile Manifesto, as well as 12 guiding principles (Agile Manifesto Organization, 2020). We've compiled a list of core elements in this table to help HR understand the Agile mindset and begin to translate these values into our own HR context.

TABLE 3.1  Agile principles

**Customer centricity**

The aim is to delight the end-customer and user of the product or service. To do this we always start from the perspective of the customer and never assume we know what's right until we test.

- **Making it practical:** Agile teams use a strong product vision to guide their work, which clearly articulates the value the product or service will deliver to the end-customer.

- **Agile HR example:** For each HR initiative, outline the business value, employee value and end-customer value that we want to deliver. For example, can we assess how the onboarding process will deliver value to the end-customer for the business as well as to our employees?

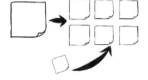

**Adaptive planning**

Agile teams embrace short cycles of 'plan, do, check, act' and welcome important changes even at the later stages of development. We are disciplined in how we prioritize and adapt our plans based on evidence and feedback.

- **Making it practical:** Agile teams understand that change will impact their work and that there is no use detailing everything upfront. Instead, they plan the most important things first and regularly review and update their plans based on data and feedback.

- **Agile HR example:** Avoid blueprinting the whole HR solution upfront and lose the ability to adapt and change the plan once we begin to test and validate what works.

*(continued)*

TABLE 3.1 (Continued)

**Incremental value delivery**

Through collaboration with the end-customer we discover how to deliver slices or increments of value. The goal is to develop the solution step by step, by delivering value early and often.

- **Making it practical:** An Agile team develops a 'good enough' product (known as a minimal viable product or MVP) and releases that to the end-customer, knowing they can continue to develop and improve the product based on feedback. A good illustration is mobile apps releasing updates every few weeks.

- **Agile HR example:** Break down big complex problems into smaller pieces of work and aim to deliver slices of value to our employees. For example, breaking down an organizational change project into smaller and more tangible deliverables, such as 'peer-feedback is frequently done by 60% of the employees in Unit X'.

**Continuous improvement**

Through the inspect-and-adapt cycle we aim to continuously improve how we work and what we deliver. We seek feedback from users and stakeholders to improve our solutions and test our hypothesis. At regular intervals we seek to improve our own performance and adjust behaviour accordingly.

- **Making it practical:** In the event of a failure, an Agile team uses the learning to understand what to do next.

- **Agile HR example:** An HR team invites other functions, like internal communications and compliance, to join them in a retrospective and assess how they can improve collaboration.

(continued)

TABLE 3.1  (Continued)

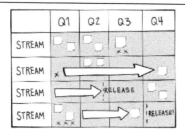

### Transparency

We embrace transparency in all our work to enable quick decision making and self-organization. By sharing information, we can quickly resolve dependencies and allow multiple teams and stakeholders to coordinate across the organization.

- **Making it practical:** Agile teams use visualization tools, like Scrum or Kanban boards (both digital and physical), to make their work transparent and to ruthlessly prioritize.
- **Agile HR example:** Set up an HR Kanban board in the main hallway to transparently share the work and progress on a large organizational development project with employees.

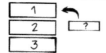

### Prioritization

We focus on the most valuable work and prioritize in a disciplined way. To avoid unnecessary tasks, we assess each requirement and only work on the things that deliver the most value.

- **Making it practical:** Agile teams understand that the end-customer will only use approximately 25% of the features initially planned (Sutherland, 2019). Instead of aiming to finish all the requested requirements, Agile teams constantly reprioritize their work based on value and use end-customer feedback to validate the most important features.
- **Agile HR example:** Rather than striving to make the product perfect, an HR team delivers the most important features first and then prioritizes what to focus on next, based on employee feedback.

*(continued)*

TABLE 3.1 (Continued)

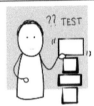

**Evidence based**

We gather evidence before making decisions and use prototyping and testing to understand the problem before committing to the project. Teams track success and continuously assess how they work to ensure the solution delivers value.

- **Making it practical:** An Agile team creates four different versions of a website and tests each version with a range of customers to gather data and assess which one works best.
- **Agile HR example:** An HR team does a mock-up of an example product using cardboard cut-outs and observes the reactions of employees to assess usefulness and impact.

**Sustainable velocity**

We limit the work in progress according to our true capacity and seek to discover a sustainable workflow. We know multitasking ruins performance and live by the mantra 'stop starting, start finishing'.

- **Making it practical:** Agile teams self-organize and pull work from a backlog, and no one pushes work on them from above.
- **Agile HR example:** An HR team limits the number of projects they are working on to ensure that they finish and achieve the desired results before moving on to a new initiative.

*(continued)*

TABLE 3.1  (Continued)

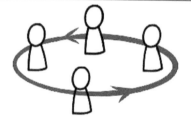

### Self-organizing teams

To solve complex business problems we need cross-functional teams that can self-organize and innovate together. Why hire great talent if we then just tell them what to do?

- **Making it practical:** An Agile team is given a set budget and allowed to test and experiment with alternative solutions within certain boundaries, without the need to ask for permission first.

- **Agile HR example:** An HR team redesigns their whole approach to learning and development and allocates a certain percentage of the overall budget to support self-directed learning. This allows individuals to make their own development investment decisions up to a certain budget limit, without the need for prior approval or sign-off.

### People and interaction

The best solutions are built through face-to-face collaboration. High-performing teams require time and space to build trust and collaborate effectively.

- **Making it practical:** A virtual Agile team makes sure they will meet face to face first for a decent kick-off and to get to know each other before they begin working on a project.

- **Agile HR example:** HR business partners and people from the centre of expertise get together for a monthly prioritization session and assess upcoming projects.

*(continued)*

**TABLE 3.1** (Continued)

| | |
|---|---|
|  | **Trust**<br><br>We trust our people and believe teams can solve problems given the right support. We aim to build psychological safety across the organization so that people feel comfortable to speak up and learn together.<br><br>• **Making it practical**: An Agile organization transparently shares the financial details of projects to allow teams to make their own spending decisions.<br><br>• **Agile HR example**: An HR team streamlines policy and trusts people to make adult decisions on things like travel and expenses. |

## Conclusion

While Agile is neither new nor a silver bullet that fixes every problem, the Agile mindset can help us find answers in an increasingly complex and volatile business world. Agile frameworks and practices have been fine-tuned over several decades, and we have evidence that they work. The essential thing is to identify where and when Agile is best suited to the context in which HR operates, and where waterfall may still be relevant.

Agile should seem self-evident and relatively simple as a concept. With a committed team it's possible to get started within a couple of months and begin to learn how to embrace the mindset within our everyday work. Bringing Agile alive at scale is much harder because in many organizations the structures, policies, systems and processes have been modelled according to a traditional, waterfall way of perceiving the world. We'll explore HR's role in Agile transformation when we discuss HR for Agile in later chapters, alongside the different organizational designs required for business agility to thrive.

KEY POINTS FOR HR PROFESSIONALS

- Agile ways of working differ from the traditional waterfall approach, and help teams manage projects more effectively in a complex and ever-changing business environment.

- Agile is first and foremost a mindset.

- Agile teams aim to deliver value to the end-customer incrementally, and constantly test and validate their work using end-customer feedback.

- Embracing an incremental approach to how we design and deliver HR products and services is a huge mindset shift for our profession, but one that can help HR teams add immense value to the business.

- Anyone can start using Agile tools and techniques, but to develop true business agility we need to build a new culture and mindset across the organization.

# References

Agile Manifesto Organization (2001) Manifesto for Agile Software Development, *Agile Manifesto Organization* https://agilemanifesto.org (archived at https://perma.cc/BSS4-ZN9Y)

Agile Manifesto Organization (2020) Principles Behind the Agile Manifesto, *Agile Manifesto Organization* http://agilemanifesto.org/principles.html (archived at https://perma.cc/S9GX-8K5C)

Fessler, L (2018) GM's Dress Code Is Only Two Words, *Quartz* https://qz.com/work/1242801/gms-dress-code-is-only-two-words (archived at https://perma.cc/W2LU-ZHFD)

Highsmith, J (2001) History: The Agile Manifesto, *Agile Manifesto Organization* https://agilemanifesto.org/history.html (archived at https://perma.cc/BSS4-ZN9Y)

Powers, S (2019) The Agile Onion, *Adventures with Agile* www.adventureswithagile.com/2016/08/10/what-is-agile (archived at https://perma.cc/87ZJ-SYZH)

Project Management Institute (2020) PMBOK® Guide and Standards, *Project Management Institute* www.pmi.org/pmbok-guide-standards (archived at https://perma.cc/6NGS-WAZP)

Standish Group (1994) The CHAOS Report (1994), *The Standish Group* www.standishgroup.com/sample_research_files/chaos_report_1994.pdf (archived at https://perma.cc/U262-UVC2)

Sutherland, J (2019) Scrum at Scale Licensed Trainer Training, Boston, MA, participation January 2019 by Riina Hellström

# 04

# Design thinking for Agile teams

## Introduction

Think about a service or product that gets us so excited that we find ourselves recommending it to others. What makes it special? How did the creators know to include such irresistible features? What were the key ingredients that made us become a loyal customer?

In this chapter we'll introduce how Agile teams and organizations use design thinking to solve problems for their customers and discover the products and services that delight us. Design thinking is an innovative design process that is an essential component of Agile, and as we'll explore later in this book, it can help Agile HR teams co-create a great employee experience. In this chapter we'll help you become comfortable with the core steps of design thinking within a business context, and then apply these same steps directly to an HR scenario in Chapter 9.

Design thinking is a collection of methodologies and tools that can be used at any stage in the product development and delivery cycle. First, it helps us fully understand and empathize with the end-customer or employee experience, as well as validate the business value and feasibility of our product ideas and solutions. Second, during the product development stage, design thinking ensures that we continuously test and validate all new features and product updates with real end-customers. The outcome is an incremental development process that aims to create loved products, great service experiences and unforgettable moments.

## Design thinking

It's useful to always keep in mind the Agile mantra, 'no product will survive its first contact with a real user'. We've all heard of costly product failures and companies misreading the market. As discussed in the previous chapters, to stay competitive, businesses now need to constantly track and predict the changing preferences of their end-customers and stay up to date with the next big trend, version or platform. There will always be the next gadget that everyone needs, the new restaurant that everyone must eat at and the new book that we all must read.

Success becomes much less about the *what*, and much more about *how* to stay relevant and *when to move*. As expressed by Peter Drucker (2017), 'there is nothing so useless as doing efficiently that which should not be done at all'. Furthermore, in a marketplace overwhelmed with consumer choice, it's vital to constantly seek out ways to differentiate our products and services, and to support this with a healthy pipeline of innovation and development.

While every business can enjoy a bit of luck, a much safer approach is to follow a method of validation that is based on the scientific principles of testing assumptions, evaluating hypotheses and prototyping solutions. This process forms the basis of design thinking and helps us make evidence-based decisions on what products to develop and invest in.

As explained by Tim Brown, CEO of IDEO and pioneer in the field, 'design thinking is a human-centered form of innovation' that aims to combine the needs of people with the possibilities of technology and the conditions necessary for business success (Brown, 2019). Adapted from the fields of ethnography and sociology, design thinking explores how humans function and the beliefs, values and customs that shape our experiences or how we engage with a product (Liedtka, 2018).

Through design thinking we aim to truly empathize with a user's real-world experience and explore the problems and pain points that our products and services can help solve for them. We need to research as much as possible about the user and then experiment and prototype to discover what the end-customer truly needs, wants and will pay for. Common questions that design thinking aims to answer are (Figure 4.1):

- Customer problems and needs
  - Do people want or need our product?
  - Why?
  - Why not?
- Feasibility
  - Is the product feasible and can it be developed in a profitable way?
  - What are the metrics and KPIs involved if we launch this kind of product?
  - How do we know it's creating the impact we want?

FIGURE 4.1  Design thinking questions

- Value of the product or 'sellability'
  - Will people pay for this product?
  - Why?
  - Why not?
  - How much will they pay?
  - Can they buy it elsewhere?
  - Why would they buy it from us?
  - What value does the user gain by buying the product?
  - Who else benefits from our product?
  - What's in it for them?
- Usability
  - Do people want to spend time using our product?
  - Why?

- o Why not?
- o How long will they use it for?
- Experience and user journeys
  - o How, when and where would people use the product?
  - o Do they have the ability and skills to use it?
  - o What is important for them when using it?
  - o What kind of experience is our product creating for them?
  - o What are the moments that matter?
  - o What do they like or dislike about the product?
  - o In which stages of the customer journey do people drop out?
  - o In which stages of the customer journey do we delight people?
- User groups ('personas')
  - o Who are the users?
  - o Can we profile them and find differences or similarities in their needs?
- Wanted features
  - o Which features do customers value or need most?

### Design thinking and Agile

We like to visualize the different stages of design thinking and how they link into Agile ways of working through Figure 4.2. Our loops combining design thinking and Agile have been inspired by Agile teams we've worked

FIGURE 4.2   Design thinking and Agile development

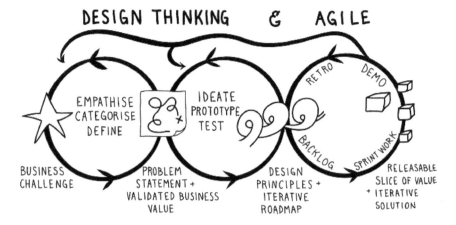

with both within business and HR, as well as the great resources provided by the Interaction Design Foundation, Stanford d.school and the British Design Council, which we encourage you to access after reading this book. While design thinking and Agile ways of working generally follow a sequence, it's important to appreciate that it's not a linear process and all the different steps feed back into each other, creating loops of discovery and validation. Depending upon what we discover at any one point, we might find it best to return to a previous step to perhaps reframe the problem and do more investigation or even jump ahead based on business needs. It's a dynamic cycle that encourages us to engage in both divergent and convergent thinking. Innovation and great product design take place when we stop ourselves from jumping immediately into the solution upon hearing the problem. This is particularly relevant for HR, where this thinking can lead us to redesign existing processes or systems, rather than moving beyond traditional HR best practice and discovering solutions that fit our specific organizational context and internal customer.

Let's now move through each of the main steps suggested in the first two design thinking loops within Figure 4.2:

1 **Business challenge:** why do it in the first place?

2 **Empathize:** deep dive into the employee experience.

3 **Categorize:** discover the moments that matter.

4 **Define:** what is the problem we need to solve?

5 **Ideate:** brainstorm and challenge assumptions.

6 **Prototype:** bring prioritized solutions to life to test with real users.

7 **Test:** does it delight the customer and what slice of value will we deliver first?

## 1. BUSINESS CHALLENGE

This step is about building our initial business case and why we should spend time on the design thinking process in the first place. While there is a lot of overlap with the next stages, here we look for evidence that a business challenge is worth pursuing and gain stakeholder buy-in for committing time and effort to investigating the problem further. In this first step, we might do an initial exploration of existing business metrics, market research and end-customer trends and data. Ultimately, we use this step to outline why we should commit time and people to the design thinking process; depending on the organizational set-up, this may require a short pitch or discussion with a potential sponsor or senior leader. Remember, we're not proposing the solution yet but the need to investigate a business problem or challenge. We also suggest referring to the template in Chapter 9 for a practical example on how to use this step within HR.

*Example*   Let's consider the example of a service development team working for a branded café, which is located at major international airports.
Their business challenge might be to encourage travellers to spend more
money at their cafés and increase revenue.

### 2. EMPATHIZE

This step helps us develop empathy with the end-customer's experience and
begin to reframe our business challenge in a human-centric way (Figure 4.3).
To do this we need to observe and explore how our users interact and
behave, as well as map out their everyday experience. In this discovery phase
we also intensely research the business problem to form multiple viewpoints
and challenge pre-set ideas and thinking patterns relating to the topic. We
want to build up a detailed narrative of the end-customer's needs, problems,
wants, dislikes, emotions, behaviours and touchpoints.

FIGURE 4.3   Empathizing with users' needs

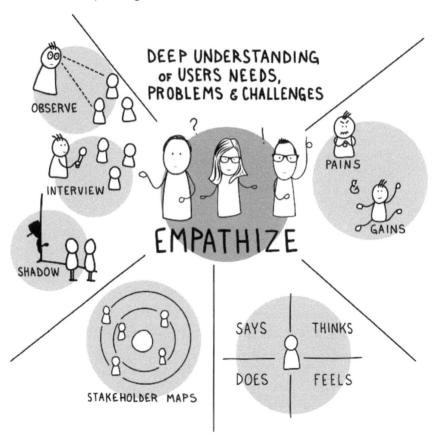

Table 4.1 lists some of our favourite empathizing tools, alongside tips on how to use each within the business and HR.

TABLE 4.1  Tools for the Empathize step

| Method | Tips |
| --- | --- |
| Human-centred user interviews | Ask why, encourage stories, explore feelings, look for non-verbal clues, don't suggest answers, be neutral and capture information by working in pairs or using voice/video recording.<br>*HR example: Explore what career development means for different people in the workplace.* |
| Five whys | Explore cause and effect relationships and go deeper into the root cause of problems by repeating why five times when you ask an investigative question. Also handy when brainstorming why a possible solution might work.<br>*HR example: Discover people's core motivational drivers when it comes to performance management.* |
| Camera study | Capture life and specific tasks through the user's eyes by asking them to take photos of their everyday experience, followed by an empathetic interview on the results.<br>*HR example: Observe people's working habits as part of a well-being project.* |
| Engage with extreme user views | Move beyond the common user and interview 'extreme users' to explore how needs might be amplified or workarounds created. Extreme users are real or fictional characters that don't fit the 'norm' regarding their views, behaviours, needs or expectations.<br>*HR example: Seek out extreme views when designing a new reward framework, explore HR practices through the lens of minorities (ie disabled, sexual minorities), take the view of a mentally unwell person or an extreme personality such as a person always looking for excitement.* |
| Saturate and group | Fill a wall with interesting findings, photos and experiences and seek out patterns and user needs.<br>*HR example: Collate all the information collected on career development to understand people's core needs.* |
| Empathy map | This can be used in lots of different ways, and we often link this to the use of personas and journey mapping (see below). An empathy map captures what a user says, does, thinks and feels, followed by needs and insights.<br>*HR example: Assess the onboarding experience for different people.* |

*(continued)*

TABLE 4.1  (Continued)

| Method | Tips |
|---|---|
| Journey or experience map | Helps to think more systematically about how the user moves through a product experience or service. See Figure 4.4 for an illustration.<br>*HR example: Map out the onboarding journey for new starters as part of a redesign project.* |
| Personas | Create fictional characters that represent a reliable and realistic version of our key user segments and base the information on qualitative and quantitative data.<br>*HR example: Build a collection of personas to represent the main employee types for an organization.* |
| Mystery shopper | Person poses as a real shopper and assesses the in-store or online experience for a product or service.<br>*HR example: Test the candidate portal used for the recruitment process by posing as a mystery applicant.* |

*Example*   Returning to our service development team studying user behaviour at airports, the team might interview specific target groups or observe travellers with the aim of recording the full end-to-end café experience at the airport. They create the personas of 'Barbara the Businesswoman', who travels weekly for work, and 'Mohomed the Dad', who has three kids under the age of seven and travels in holiday seasons. The team then study the same airport experience through the eyes of these different personas to explore alternative perspectives and insights in the service journey (Figure 4.4).

3. CATEGORIZE

Often completed in conjunction with the empathize step, we now need to analyse all the data sourced from user studies, business metrics, market trends and end-customer preferences. Through this analysis we seek patterns, test assumptions and disprove theories.

We also look for moments that matter for the user, key snippets of time that create a lasting impact on the end-customer. These moments can help us determine where we should ideate solutions first or help prioritize our future project backlog once we move into the Agile ways of working loop.

*Example*   The service development team map out all the information collected and study the different service journeys to find moments that matter

FIGURE 4.4   Journey mapping

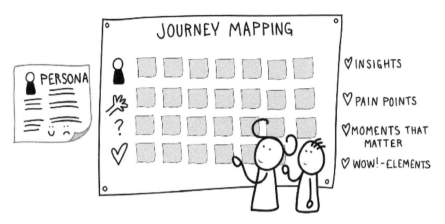

for their personas. The team might find that Barbara the Businesswoman stops to buy a coffee at the café but then leaves quickly when she is unable to find an electrical socket to charge her smartphone. Mohomed the Dad reviews the menu but leaves without buying anything when he can't find refreshments for his kids.

### 4. DEFINE

We now need to reframe our initial business challenge into an actionable problem statement. Also known as a point of view, the problem statement provides a clear summary of the business challenge through the viewpoint of the user. The aim is to build a hypothesis of what the actual problem is and what the impact of solving the problem would be for the end-customer and business, including metrics and KPIs.

It's also definitely worth creating design principles at this stage to help guide the future development of a product, which remains independent of any specific solution, for example that all designs need to be 'fit for purpose' and 'human-centric'. These design principles may even go into the Definition of Done for the subsequent project backlog (see Chapter 5 for more information).

Useful tools for this step are listed in Table 4.2.

*Example*   Returning again to the service development team at the airport, they may have assessed the potential sales lost when Barbara the Businesswoman and Mohomed the Dad didn't buy from their café, and calculate that they could increase revenue by 5–15 per cent if they had. This

TABLE 4.2  Tools for the Define step

| Method | Tips |
| --- | --- |
| Point-of-view statement | [USER] needs to [USER'S NEED] because [SURPRISING INSIGHT]. *HR example: A statement developed as part of a career development project is: 'Saskia, an employee over 50 years, needs to be a mentor because it gives her a sense of recognition for her skills.'* |
| Point-of-view analogy | Use an analogy, like a metaphor or simile, to distil insights and user needs into a catchy phrase. *HR example: As part of a performance management project, the phrase 'use feedback as a gift'.* |
| Checklist | Ask 'What's the point, who says, what's new and who cares?' *HR example: An onboarding project example is: 'Great onboarding is vital for business success; people say it determines whether they stay with the company in their first year; we can realize greater productivity by ensuring new starters contribute immediately; and it gives us a leading edge in the market.'* |
| How might we | Can be placed in front of statements to focus the ideas towards specific solutions, for example 'How might we delight the user when they first arrive at the airport?' *HR example: A talent acquisition project formulates 'How might we attract more senior female technical experts to join the business?'* |

leads the team to create a problem statement such as 'How might we entice Barbara the Businesswoman and Mohomed the Dad to choose our café instead of our competitors' at the airport with the aim of increasing sales by 10 per cent?'

## 5. IDEATE

Ideation is all about brainstorming, coupled with techniques to assess and rank our ideas according to business value and factors like effort, risk and budget. When brainstorming, it's healthy to encourage big ideas and to defer judgement and opinions to later. Be visual, use discussion techniques such as silent brainstorming or one conversation at a time, and encourage people to build on the ideas of others to see where they go.

We recommend learning different ideation techniques to avoid people jumping to quick conclusions, being influenced by group think or opting for logical ideas that already fit their current system or culture. We want ideas that open the hearts of the end-customer, and it's often useful to use different ideation methods in parallel to flesh out the bold and valuable solutions. Remember, our first ideas are generally not the best ones, and we often start with the most obvious answers that feel comfortable and immediately possible. Facilitating good ideation sessions is a fantastic skill for all HR professionals to develop further. Ideation is also a great team energizer, where people build on each other's hacks and unconventional thinking, and is extremely useful for HR teams just as much as the wider business.

Great methods are shown in Table 4.3.

TABLE 4.3 Methods for the Ideate step

| Method | Tips |
| --- | --- |
| 100 ideas | Group brainstorms 100 ideas in an hour on sticky notes.<br>*HR example: 100 ideas on how to build psychological safety in a business.* |
| Silent brainstorming | Individuals record own ideas (silently, often on a Post-it) first and then share and discuss as a group.<br>*HR example: Used as part of a recruitment process redesign project.* |
| Steal with pride | Look for solutions outside the immediate domain, for example study how another industry solves the same problem.<br>*HR example: Use HubSpot's culture code (HubSpot, 2020; see Chapter 9 for more information) as inspiration for designing an employee handbook at a manufacturing company.* |
| Benchmarking | Gain inspiration by assessing ideas from competitors or other companies, keeping in mind that we should never just copy and paste.<br>*HR example: Research what other companies are doing in performance management.* |
| Crowdsourcing | Open-source ideas from a crowd of people or online.<br>*HR example: Ask employees to submit ideas on how the business can be more sustainable and environmentally friendly.* |
| No constraints | Open the possibilities by saying that people have a magic wand or a billion dollars.<br>*HR example: Use this method to break down traditional thinking on communicating HR policies.* |
| Introduce constraints | Consider the impact of constraints such as budget or compliance, and encourage people to seek innovative ways to solve the problem and overcome the constraint.<br>*HR example: Introduce as a challenge to think out of the box on how to build a great learning and development framework with no money.* |

TABLE 4.4  Prioritization methods

| Method | Tips |
|---|---|
| Dot voting | Each person has a certain number of votes to place against their preferred idea. Can all go on one idea or be spread across several. *HR example: Use to pinpoint the most important moments that matter for an employee experience.* |
| Sorting | Sort ideas based on categories like rational choice versus long shot or types of prototypes such as digital versus experience. *HR example: Ideas sorted in a diversity and inclusion project based on recruitment actions versus internal cultural change.* |
| Impact versus effort grid | Assess ideas by placing them into one of the following four quadrants: 1. High Impact and High Effort; 2. High Impact and Low Effort; 3. Low Impact and High Effort; Low Impact and Low Effort. *HR example: Ideas are assessed for a large complex cultural change project and the team decide to start with some quick wins that sit in the High Impact and Low Effort quadrant.* |
| Assess against the business case | Assess ideas against pre-set business metric or value drivers, such as cost versus revenue, or cost versus impact. *HR example: Ideas are assessed on how to introduce and train people on a new HRIS (HR Information System) for the business.* |

After toggling alternative solutions and exploring innovative concepts, we then need to converge and prioritize which ideas should be taken through to prototyping and testing.

Handy methods include those listed in Table 4.4.

The ideate step also helps us decide on how to develop and deliver different slices of value to the end-customer once we move into the Agile ways of working loop. We do this by breaking the problem down into smaller chunks and prioritizing what will deliver the most value first, alongside the time, effort and investment needed to make this happen (Figure 4.5).

*Example*  The service development team at the airport now begin to ideate ways to get Barbara the Businesswoman and Mohomed the Dad to buy from the café when at the airport. The team choose two main ideas for each persona. For Barbara the Businesswoman they want to test installing lots of charging options as part of the seating facilities available, as well as installing small tables that would allow Barbara the Businesswoman to work while drinking coffee. For Mohomed the Dad, they want to try out themed

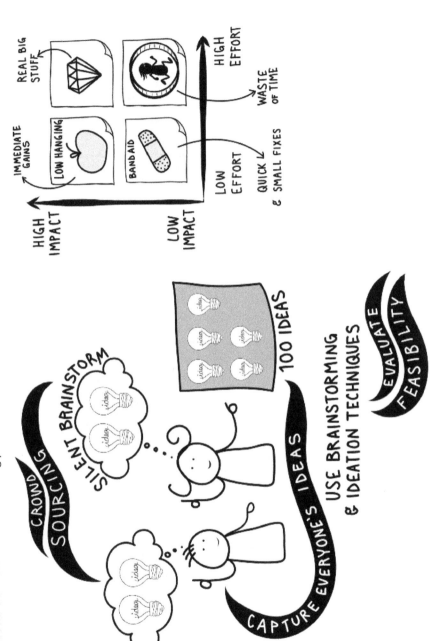

FIGURE 4.5   Ideation and evaluating possible solutions

drinks such as juices based on a popular children's film, as well as offer free kid activity packs when people buy a family meal deal. Each idea has been assessed in terms of cost versus projected sales.

## 6. PROTOTYPE

Prototyping is about quickly and cheaply making a concept real for the user to experience and test. We've seen teams use anything from cardboard cut-outs to Lego, plasticine, short plays, basic mock-ups of tech systems and simulations. In Agile, if we're not slightly embarrassed by the standard of our prototype, we've spent too long working on it. The idea is to quickly gain feedback on whether the idea works for the user and whether the concept should move into development. Indeed, prototyping is a great way to begin to validate whether an idea is possible in real life. There is also no limit on how many prototypes can be tested at the same time, and we encourage you to take several through to the test stage if time and resources permit.

The key is to keep the user in mind and continue to focus on how the prototype fixes the problem and solves the pain points identified for the end-customer. Aim to clearly define the hypothesis that is being tested and set necessary metrics to determine success.

Popular prototyping methods are listed in Table 4.5.

TABLE 4.5  Popular methods for the Prototype step

| Method | Tips |
| --- | --- |
| Mock-ups | Build an example model of the design using temporary or inexpensive materials.<br>*HR example: Create a webpage design for the new recruitment application process on paper and test it with example candidates.* |
| Prototyping | Construct an example of a new service or product using temporary or inexpensive materials.<br>*HR example: Build a Lego model of the new onboarding experience and talk a user through it while asking structured feedback questions along the way.* |
| A/B testing | Test two (or more) alternative solutions in parallel to assess which variant gets the best result.<br>*HR example: Ask one team to test peer feedback as part of their performance discussions and compare the results to those of a team that discusses performance as usual and without the peer feedback.* |

*(continued)*

TABLE 4.5  (Continued)

| Method | Tips |
|---|---|
| Acting out a service | Role-play a service experience or end-customer use of a product. *HR example: Team acts out a new way of discussing career development within the business in front of senior executives to get their buy-in.* |
| Pop-up service or store | Set up a pop-up, temporary store to probe the market and test product concepts. *HR example: Set up a pop-up stand in the office for people to test out a new ergonomic chair.* |
| Visualizing | Use storyboards or other visuals such as cartoons to describe a new service or product experience. *HR example: Present a storyboard to teams and leaders detailing a new approach to reward in the business.* |
| Fake door testing | Create a fake product or feature for people to select to test interest, for example a fake button on a webpage. *HR example: A fake button is added to the organization's intranet to see how many people want to offset 50% of their daily commute carbon footprint while the company offsets 50%. People are informed it is a test after selecting the button, and if the button gets a lot of hits the company will develop an integrated solution for the initiative.* |
| Wizard of Oz testing | Testing user interface logic without having a digital product, for example a person acting out what a piece of software would do and gathering user feedback. *HR example: Team acts out a new HRIS interface in front of selected employees.* |
| Real-user validation | For example, testing food products with real consumers or having focus groups watch a new streaming TV show. *HR example: Ask people to complete a new eLearning module and observe reactions.* |
| MVP | Build a minimum viable product that contains the least number of features required for it to work. *HR example: Use a basic peer feedback tool, built using Excel or a free online feedback tool, to test how people engage with peer feedback conversations and data, before designing a more advanced application to support the process.* |

*Example*  To prototype their ideas (Figure 4.6), the service development team decide to set up a temporary and low-cost version of the new seating layout that provides charging sockets and tables to test the ideas for Barbara the Businesswoman at two airports. For Mohomed the Dad they ask fellow teammates to bring their children to work on a certain day to assess what

FIGURE 4.6 Testing and validating

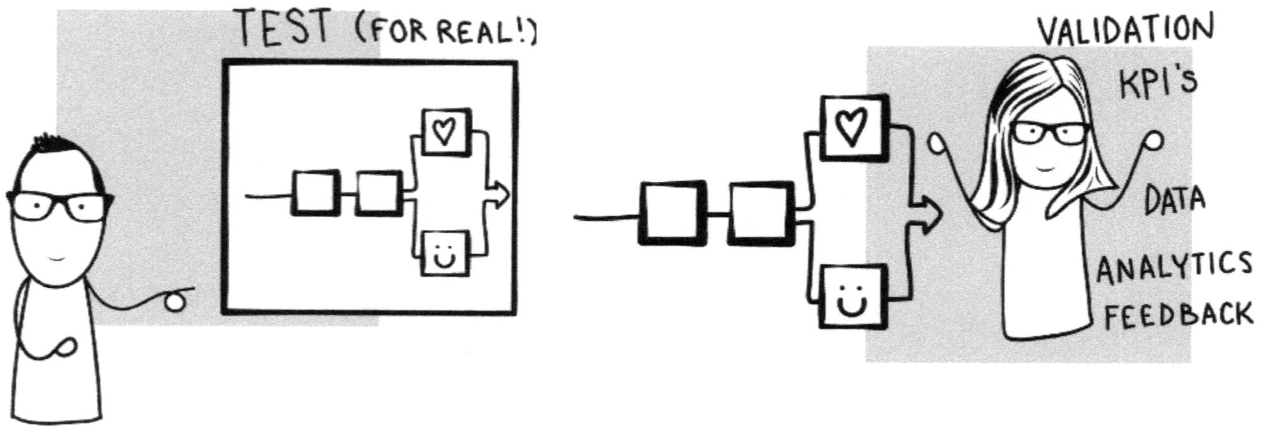

type of kids' drinks and activities packs they enjoy, and how best to promote these to the parents (all with appropriate health and safety policies covered!).

## 7. TEST

Testing is thinking like a scientist and being ready for an idea to fail or require further development. We are validating our MVP with real users and assessing the feedback and reactions against metrics and KPIs. Are our users truly delighted? Does it indeed solve their pain points? Is it a go or no go? We then use the feedback collected to turn our prototype into an MLP – (minimum lovable product). The user feedback also helps us decide if we:

- stop it there and don't develop the solution;
- run new experiments;
- begin to deliver incremental improvements to an existing service or product;
- commit to a full new build, particularly if designing a whole new product or service, delivered through incremental releases.

Often our testing methods reflect what resources we have at hand. Sometimes we don't have 20 real customers to test the product mock-up or we're unable to invite real customers into the office to try out the prototype because of the cost or time required. A great question when planning a testing session is: 'What is the easiest or smallest thing we can do to test our hypothesis?'

When validation is done properly, all the learning will be explicit, structured and measured. It's important that we're not mentally attached to our ideas and instead seek out the evidence on what works and what doesn't and challenge any confirmation bias.

*Example*  When testing their prototype for Barbara the Businesswoman, the team observe and record the different behaviours of this persona type and discover that more coffees are sold as a result, but that the users also remain working for a long time at the new tables and take up space that could be used by other customers. For the Mohomed the Dad prototypes, the team set up controlled taste-testing and product selection exercises for a kids' day held at the office, and discover that the kids love the juices but that the activity pack creates too much mess for the airport cafés to deal with on a daily basis. The team now decide to move only the successful prototypes into the development stage, and begin to build a backlog on how to install sockets and stand-up tables in a selection of cafés to further test this solution for Barbara the Businesswoman, as well as trial the introduction of juices at larger and more established airport cafés for Mohomed the Dad.

*Experiments versus pilots*    'Yes, but we already pilot' is the usual answer given by many in HR at this point, but experimentation and prototyping are vastly different from running a pilot. Too often a pilot in HR already represents a big investment of time and money.

If it's a management development programme, for instance, often the tender process has been decided, our top managers are in the room and the supplier is now expected to deliver. Even if the pilot feedback is poor, the programme isn't stopped and instead is tweaked and repackaged as much as possible, so that it can still be rolled out as scheduled.

For example, as part of a project to redesign performance and reward, an Agile HR team decided to test different ways to give and receive feedback, as well as the link between performance discussions and reward. To set this up, they asked different business teams to experiment with certain solutions. One experiment included an app-based tool that would help the teams share and discuss peer feedback. It was also initially assumed that everyone would love this solution because the organization was a tech-based business. The reality was quite different, with the teams hating the feedback app. It turned out that they didn't need an app to help them give feedback. What they needed was a safe space free from top-down performance ratings and bonus numbers to give feedback to each other openly.

In the past, this feedback app might have been rolled out to everyone in the business through a big-bang implementation as the new tech way to do performance. This has led to a lot of performance management processes being a direct product of the tech system that supports them, rather than the feedback conversation itself. The good thing in this case was that the Agile HR team could stop the experiment right there and openly discuss how this solution failed, and then use the learning gained to focus on the real problem and pain points for their customers. Here, this was the negative impact of bonus numbers and ratings on how people discussed performance feedback within their teams.

## Conclusion

As previously mentioned, design thinking is beneficial throughout the whole product development cycle, and many organizations now value service designers, user experience (UX) designers and user interface (UI) designers as vital talent. However, some companies still equate design thinking with randomly experimenting, rather than following a disciplined process. In these cases, the culture of experimentation is often left undefined, is not cultivated well and is conducted on a team level only, which often leads to confirmation bias and consensus.

A common Agile phrase is 'fail fast', but we believe a better concept to advocate is 'learn fast'. Using design thinking ensures that experiments remain incremental and small, in which we can afford failures. Failures (or learning) in these cases are reframed as successes because we rapidly validate if an idea or path is not worth pursuing. Viewed this way, design thinking should save a business a lot of time and money and help teams quickly discover how to delight their end-customer. Design thinking is a powerful tool for HR and helps us co-create user-friendly products and solutions directly with our people and the wider business. We'll demonstrate how by providing a step-by-step guide in Chapter 9.

---

KEY POINTS FOR HR PROFESSIONALS

- We encourage you to upskill in design thinking to build human-centric products and services that enrich the employee experience.

- Jump to Chapter 9 to explore a practical example of how to apply design thinking within HR.

- Design thinking is a collection of methodologies and tools that can be used at any stage in the product development and delivery cycle.

- The approach helps HR empathize with the employee experience, as well as validate the business value and feasibility of our product ideas and solutions.

- Design thinking guides HR in how to test and validate the products and services we create, to ensure we're delivering solutions that people not only need but that help them be awesome in their job.

Design thinking resources and tools

- Interaction Design Foundation, www.interaction-design.org/literature/topics/design-thinking

- Stanford University, d.school, https://dschool.stanford.edu/about

- The British Design Council, www.designcouncil.org.uk/

- d.school Bootcamp Bootleg toolkit, https://dschool.stanford.edu/resources/the-bootcamp-bootleg

# References

Brown, T (2019) Design Thinking, *IDEO* www.ideou.com/pages/design-thinking (archived at https://perma.cc/6EM4-36ZN)

Drucker, P (2017) The Peter F. Drucker Reader: Selected Articles from the Father of Modern Management Thinking, *Harvard Business Review Press* https://books.google.fi/books?id=gVo_DQAAQBAJ&printsec=frontcover&hl=fi&source=gbs_ge_summary_r&cad=0#v=onepage&q&f=false (archived at https://perma.cc/ELC7-G7CX)

HubSpot (2020) Culture Code, *HubSpot* https://cdn2.hubspot.net/hub/216938/file-24940534-pdf/docs/culturecode-v7-130320111259-phpapp02.pdf (archived at https://perma.cc/VTJ9-QW28)

Liedtka, J (2018) Why Design Thinking Works, *Harvard Business Review*, September–October https://hbr.org/2018/09/why-design-thinking-works (archived at https://perma.cc/5NAP-KZ85)

# 05

# Agile ways of working

## Introduction

In the previous chapter we explored how teams can start the innovation process by applying design thinking within their work. After following these steps and discovering a viable prototype, a business can then decide to move into full product development.

In this chapter we describe how a team develops and delivers a product through Agile ways of working. The chapter is a basic introduction to Agile methods within a business context and serves as a prerequisite to later chapters when we apply Agile within HR. We'll explore the basic theory that underpins Agile practices, drawing on examples from the digital product development domain and highlighting common Agile ways of working throughout.

Our aim is to help you begin to speak the language of Agile and understand why Agile teams and organizations work in a certain way. We recommend exploring beyond the business examples given and consider how Agile ways of working might look in your own HR work. This is a perfect warm-up to then exploring the practical and hands-on examples provided in the Agile for HR toolkit part of this book.

## Is Agile just a fad?

Upon meeting an Agile team for the first time, it can feel like we've stepped into a parallel universe where people work in a strange way and use intricate terminology for what seems like ordinary activities. Some HR professionals have noted that the language can feel distancing, and often label Agile as just another fad or 'ism' that will pass in a few years.

However, the Agile terminology is used for a reason. It consciously distinguishes Agile ways of working from the traditional, waterfall approach and describes the cyclical nature of the structured events, artefacts and roles that make up Agile. The terminology also reflects how teams that start working with Agile are often enthusiastic about the clarity and discipline achieved, as well as the continuous feedback received from stakeholders and the end-customer.

## Agile ways of working

To help bring the Agile ways of working to life, we'll explain each step by following the outline below:

1  Setting a product vision
2  Forming Agile development teams
3  Release planning and building a backlog of work
4  Working with a Definition of Done
5  Prioritizing the backlog
6  Self-organization and transparency
7  Agreeing when work is done
8  Using review and feedback to drive improvement
9  Adapting to change
10  Applying a cycle of continuous improvement
11  Closing an Agile project

It's also good to note that we've simplified the examples by always using the term 'product' to describe the deliverable. However, the deliverable could be a service, concept, process, or any combination of these terms to better describe your own business context.

### 1. Setting a product vision

Assuming the organization has conducted thorough innovation and design work, built a business case and decided to invest in full-scale product development, the next step is to create a product vision. This should feed off what the Agile team has discovered makes the end-customer love the product.

A great product vision is bold and unique. It attracts end-customers, investors and employees, and defines the reasons for the product to exist. It gives the team a bigger picture of what they are working on and why. It's the promise of value. Very few companies share their product vision statements, but by looking at well-known marketing slogans we can get a good idea of what this vision might have been. For example, the website for the iPhone 11 Pro indicates what types of commitment were made when starting to develop the product: 'Pushes the boundaries of what a smartphone can do. Welcome to the first iPhone powerful enough to be called Pro' (Apple, 2020).

A strong vision is needed to guide the Agile team through the complex and changing development process. It helps the team to remain focused on what truly matters and to disregard all other distracting noise.

## 2. Forming Agile development teams

Armed with a product vision, the business can now form a cross-functional development team which comprises all the necessary skills and capabilities to design and deliver the product. Useful questions to guide HR professionals when overseeing the formation of Agile development teams include:

- What are we developing and why?
- Who needs to be on the team to ensure end-to-end delivery, starting from design through to implementation?
- Who will be maintaining and supporting the product once released and should they be on the team or aligned in some way?
- What is our product dependent upon and what depends on it?
- Do we involve certain specialists from other areas of the business in some of the development steps?
- Can our team members realistically commit 100 per cent of their time to this project or should we try to work with a lower level of allocation?
- How do we include the capabilities of people whom we can't include in the team full-time but are essential to the design and delivery of the product?

There is no right or wrong way of assembling development teams. However, we recommend that the team members commit to the project full-time, so Agile is not an add-on to the day job.

### 3. Release planning and building a backlog of work

As we know, Agile is about delivering incremental value to the end-customer. Once the purpose and vision are clear, the project can be sliced into deliverable product increments, big chunks of work often called 'epics'. To do this, we consider which parts of the intended product could benefit the end-customers most, even if the whole product isn't yet completed. Also, is it possible to start selling something to the end-customer as a first version of the product and add in less important features later?

These epics are then placed into an overriding plan, creating a backlog of work. The team then considers the smaller bits of work needed to make each epic happen, which are called backlog items.

The backlog contains all the work that the team thinks it needs to do to deliver the product and is based on the best knowledge and information the team has at this moment. The backlog is made up of all the items potentially required to deliver the whole product. In the beginning these backlog items tend to be bigger chunks of work, described on a high level, but become more precise and detailed as the project progresses.

The team then considers which backlog items could be grouped together to deliver a slice of value to the end-customer. This process is called release planning and each version or increment of the product that is delivered is called a release. This constitutes a cycle of work within Agile, and the approach to release planning varies depending on which industry or domain the team might be working in.

For example, an e-commerce team might aim to release a new update to the web shop minute by minute (Figure 5.1). These minor releases do not

FIGURE 5.1   Release planning example

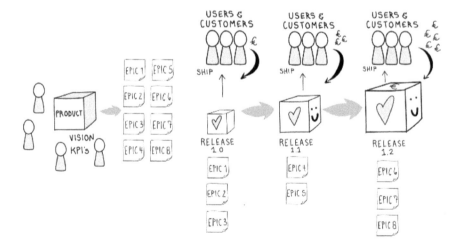

require a lot of preparation or involve new information for the users, who are able to continue shopping on the web shop despite the fact that a team has changed something on the site. In HR an equivalent example would be updating a recruitment website page, which could be released several times a day without disturbance to any possible candidates.

Unlike the web shop example, not all teams can release product increments continuously. Instead, several completed increments are combined into a larger release that is then delivered in one go.

---

EXAMPLE

The operating systems on our mobile phones always have a version number and we regularly receive version updates in order to access new features and fixes. It would irritate plenty of users if the development teams for the mobile operating system pushed out updates to our phones every day or indeed hourly. A similar release logic would also not work in HR when developing a recruitment process. For example, you could develop and test smaller bits but would need to wait to release a whole new section in one go. This is because releasing numerous changes to the recruitment process during the year would drive managers and teams crazy.

---

Releases must be valuable both for the end-customer and for the business. For example, releases can be defined and planned to gain access to a revenue stream, increase the user base or attract a new end-customer segment.

---

EXAMPLE

A good example is launching a new mobile app for loyal end-customers. A team would need to build in enough valuable and useful features, with significant user validation, before launching it. Additionally, a lot of marketing and support efforts would need to be undertaken before release. The team developing this new mobile app could choose to onboard existing loyal end-customers through the first release, by keeping it simple and including only the core features. The next release could include an in-app customer service chat, and a third release could include in-app purchases. Alternatively, releases can also be defined according to a certain user group (for example, teenagers), customer segment (such as small and medium businesses) or geography (for example, releasing in one location first, before a global release).

Release planning helps the team create a strategic product roadmap, rather than aiming to implement the whole product in one release. Agile development teams are skilled at assessing the various business cases for each release and choosing the most profitable or important product increment to be delivered first.

An Agile development team focuses on the product features that bring the most value to the company and the end-customer, thus avoiding time and effort wasted on low-value items. Agile is about delighting customers with early and frequent value delivery.

## 4. Working with a Definition of Done

A method called Definition of Done (DoD) ensures that the team remains aligned with the overarching product vision and the intended end-customer value, as well as the overall requirements and quality needs of the product (Figure 5.2). This enables the Agile development team to keep in mind the bigger picture while they focus on how to deliver smaller pieces of work.

Every bit of work the team finishes must be checked against the DoD, and only if it complies can it be marked as done. The DoD can include any requirement that helps the team deliver against necessary company policies or compliance needs, alongside the use of mandatory tools or practices within the business.

---

EXAMPLE

The team developing a new mobile app for loyal end-customers could include the following list of requirements in their DoD:

- Needs to be GDPR compliant – always check!

- Compatible with all mobile phone operating systems.

- Aligned with new brand guidelines, as approved by marketing.

---

FIGURE 5.2 DoD example

Once the release plan and DoD for the product are agreed, an Agile development team can move into prioritizing the backlog of work.

## 5. Prioritizing the backlog

To prioritize the backlog the team is guided by their release plan. Backlog items required for the next release come first, and less important backlog items will remain lower down. Agile development teams build their own prioritization criteria or methods, and some of our favourites are in Chapter 8. Once the backlog is prioritized, the team will focus on the first few items and start planning them on a more granular, task level, which details what needs to happen to get the item done.

It would be wrong to assume that Agile ways of working lack rules or sufficient planning. Indeed, Agile is an extremely disciplined method of working. Agile development teams undertake a lot of structured planning; however, unlike waterfall, this is done on a continuous basis, rather than detailing all the plans upfront at the start of the project. Agile planning is conducted in every work cycle, and results in the backlog being updated with any necessary changes.

This iterative Agile planning is called backlog refinement. Backlog refinement happens continuously, or during agreed backlog refinement meetings, and involves the team reprioritizing the various backlog items, introducing any new ones, as well as planning high-priority items in more detail (Figure 5.3).

Later in this chapter we'll explore how a team adapts to change through backlog refinement.

### TASK-LEVEL PLANNING

Only the higher-prioritized items in the backlog are planned in detail, to task level (Figure 5.4). This is because an Agile development team understands that changes will impact the project; thus, any lower-priority backlog items and corresponding tasks might not be needed, and it is a waste of effort to detail everything upfront. Once the team has broken down a backlog item into tasks, alongside who is responsible for what, everyone should be ready to begin the development work.

FIGURE 5.3  Backlog refinement and prioritization

FIGURE 5.4  Backlog item and tasks

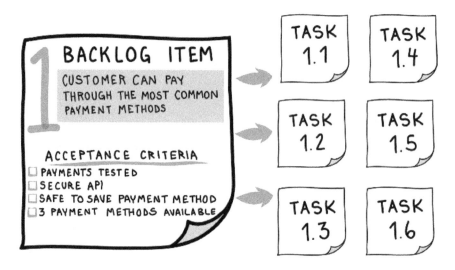

ACCEPTANCE CRITERIA

We've all experienced a situation where a delivery does not happen according to plan or expectations. Often the root causes are a misunderstanding of requirements and unclear specifications. Agile development teams have a great mechanism for avoiding these mistakes, called acceptance criteria, which are added to every backlog item. The acceptance criteria include the unique requirements for each backlog item, which must be fulfilled before the team considers a backlog item done. This helps the team know what they are building when working on each backlog item, as well as why and how it connects to the overriding product vision. Acceptance criteria are specified at a backlog item level, whereas the DoD is specified at the level of the whole project.

---

EXAMPLE

Returning to the example of the team developing a new mobile app for loyal end-customers, they may wish to include in-app purchases in a release. One of their backlog items is about building the necessary payment options into the app. To begin with, the team agrees to include three of the most used payment options on the market. Additionally, they agree that this item is considered done once they have tested that all the interfaces to banking platforms are secure and the user can save their preferred payment option.

---

## 6. Self-organization and transparency

Agile ways of working are made possible through self-organization and transparency. Everyone in the Agile development team should know exactly where the whole project is going, who is working on what, and which backlog items are coming up next.

### SELF-ORGANIZATION

Together the team agrees on who should do what and how to design and develop the product. No manager is needed to direct this work. Through self-organization and collaboration, Agile development teams direct all work, including how to solve problems, make decisions and explore alternative actions or choices (Figure 5.5). They also test and validate directly with the end-customer and adapt the plan based on the feedback collected.

### TRANSPARENCY

Agile development teams often use boards, such as the Scrum or Kanban boards that are discussed in Chapter 6, to visualize their backlog and track progress against the columns labelled Backlog, To Do, Doing, Done. Agile development teams use physical boards that are up on the wall in the office and the backlog items are represented by sticky notes. There are also digital tools, such as Trello and Jira, to support teams virtually.

FIGURE 5.5 Self-organization in action

Backlog items progress across the columns as follows:

- 'Backlog' to 'To Do' – when the items are pulled in for detailed planning.
- 'To Do' to 'Doing' – when the team starts to actually work on the item.
- 'Doing' to 'Done' – when the team has finished all the tasks, met the acceptance criteria for the item and checked the work against the DoD.

Starting with the highest-prioritized backlog item, the team aims to move each item into the Done column in order of priority. The team focuses on only a few items at a time, to avoid multitasking and overloading their capacity. The next upcoming backlog items are planned in detail to the task level and the low-priority items remain waiting on the backlog without details needed yet.

PULL-WORK SYSTEM
Self-organization and the pull-work system are probably the most powerful principles guiding Agile ways of working. Agile development teams don't

multitask and they work according to the motto, 'stop starting, start finishing'. The team commits to a certain amount of work in each cycle or limits the work in progress according to their real capacity (Figure 5.6). Only when the team has finished the previous and higher-priority items can they pull in new items. No one is pushing work on to the team, and instead they self-manage the amount and pace of work based on their capacity and skills.

## 7. Agreeing when work is done

The joy of seeing progress every day and moving items to the Done column is very energizing. To mark a backlog item as done (Figure 5.7), it must satisfy the following:

- All acceptance criteria on the backlog item are fulfilled.
- The item and deliverables are in line with the DoD for the whole product.
- The work is accepted by the product owner (a role we'll introduce in Chapter 6).

FIGURE 5.6  The pull-work system

FIGURE 5.7  When is something done?

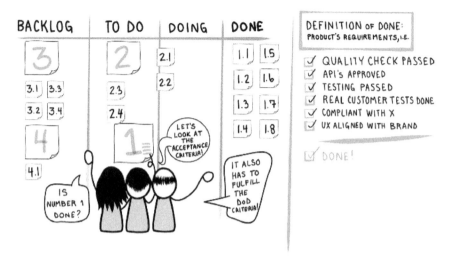

Items should not be counted as complete if not fully done. Any items that are not 100 per cent complete are considered unfinished and unable to deliver value to the end-customer or the business. This is a useful way of working that prevents HR professionals jumping too quickly on to the next task.

## 8. Using review and feedback to drive improvement

Once a product increment is ready, the team holds a review (also known as a demo or showcase) with the aim of assessing completed work. Through the review the team gathers feedback and recommendations regarding the product and uses this information to reflect on upcoming releases and clarify remaining backlog items. Often the review involves showcasing the work to end-customers or stakeholders with the aim of validating and assessing the value created and that the team is going in the right direction (Figure 5.8). The review often reveals unexpected findings that allow the team to adjust the backlog and overarching product vision. It's not uncommon for a team to realize that they have made a lot of assumptions about the user's behaviour, which are often proven wrong through the testing and validation stage.

FIGURE 5.8  Testing and validating through a review

EXAMPLE

Returning to our example of the team developing a new mobile app for loyal end-customers, the review session might involve the app prototyped on printed paper and showcased to stakeholders for immediate feedback, even before any digital development is undertaken. A later-stage demo could then include experiencing an early version of the in-app customer service chatbot feature.

Many Agile organizations arrange open-door demos, for anyone to join and give feedback on the developed product increments. Full releases are often showcased to analysts and selected end-customers first, to get their input before launching the release to a larger group of users. The review helps to continuously improve the product. There are also companies that pay people for testing and reviewing their products to ensure they receive valuable feedback from real end-customers (Razinski, 2019).

DESIGN THINKING DURING DEVELOPMENT

It's useful to note that Agile development teams use design thinking to prototype and test during the development work as well. The aim is to create fast feedback loops and constantly innovate on a feature level in relation to the different aspects and details of the product.

> EXAMPLE
>
> The team developing a new mobile app for loyal end-customers could test five different positions for the shopping cart button on a webpage or do a quick round of user interviews to ask where to place the in-app chatbot while undertaking the development work.

The design thinking and validation work combined with reviews ensures that the team are always focused on how to create a lovable and usable product.

## 9. Adapting to change

Through backlog refinement the team focuses on how to deliver value and removes wasteful items. Backlog refinement also helps the team keep track of the full project, by understanding all the dependencies, upcoming releases, individual backlog items and features. By undertaking frequent backlog refinement sessions, the team can adapt to all the necessary and important changes. For example, cycle time for backlog refinement can be as short as one week for digital product development teams. We find HR teams usually refine their backlog every 2–3 weeks.

Backlog refinement is continuous and can be undertaken at any time within the project cycle. This is to adjust the product backlog according to feedback, new requirements or changes impacting the project vision. Examples include:

- **Clarify vision or pivot.** The team might learn from feedback that what they're developing is not valuable for the end-customer and the whole project is going in the wrong direction. The team will need to update the vision or pivot in a new direction.

- **Reprioritization.** A backlog item increases in priority or an important dependency leads to the reprioritization of one or multiple items.

- **Adding or removing backlog items.** New discoveries may lead to adding new items now deemed important or removing items no longer necessary.

- **Adding features to backlog items.** The upcoming backlog items can be planned in more detail or specific features added to existing items not yet completed.

- **Removal of features from backlog items.** Non-valuable features could be removed from some backlog items.
- **Kill the project.** The whole project isn't worth pursuing anymore.

### FORECASTING PROGRESS

Agile development teams aim to maintain a sustainable workflow by not over-committing and attempting to deliver more than is realistic. How much work the team gets done within each cycle defines their velocity. By knowing the velocity of work and the remaining number of backlog items, the team can give estimates on when product increments or releases can be delivered (Figure 5.9).

Transparency in the progress, speed and capacity of Agile development teams enables an organization to better forecast results based on the true state of progress in real time rather than on wishful thinking.

FIGURE 5.9   Forecasting progress based on velocity

## 10. Applying a cycle of continuous improvement

Imagine the power of an organization that takes on thousands of self-directed improvements and adaptations across all their teams and units each year. Retrospectives form the basis to the Agile feedback loop and help build a learning organization, a goal pursued by HR for such a long time. Agile development teams are known for their never-ending quest to be better tomorrow than they are today, and continuous improvement is a vital element of the Agile mindset. As well as improving the product, which is considered the *what*, the team aims to improve *how* they work (Figure 5.10).

A retrospective, or retro, is a term for an event where the team explores how to continuously improve their performance. Through the retro the team aims to:

- acknowledge strengths and successes;
- remove blockers or impediments hindering the team's performance;
- identify how to further strengthen their performance and avoid any wasteful, non-value-adding work;
- improve their collaboration;
- agree on how to work with dependencies across the company;
- identify unresolved impediments and raise them in the right forum where they can be solved.

FIGURE 5.10  Team retrospectives

This means that Agile development teams are continuously developing their performance, which generally leads to an increase in team productivity, even over a short period of time. The best Agile organizations are disciplined in their approach to retrospectives and ensure these happen regularly across all levels of the business.

## 11. Closing an Agile project

It's important to understand when an Agile project has delivered a product that is good enough to bring the expected value. At this stage, and based on the success criteria set for the product vision, a development project should end. The approach avoids the long tail of working on non-value-adding features (Figure 5.11).

At this stage, the end-customer is satisfied, the product is considered good enough and the remaining backlog items are left undone. Adding any low-value features, details or finesses now wouldn't be a smart use of people's time or effort. The project is then closed, and the released product is handed

FIGURE 5.11  Avoid developing low-value features

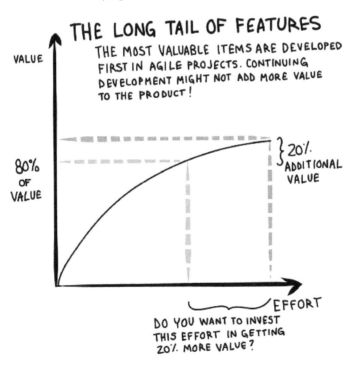

THE LONG TAIL OF FEATURES

VALUE

THE MOST VALUABLE ITEMS ARE DEVELOPED FIRST IN AGILE PROJECTS. CONTINUING DEVELOPMENT MIGHT NOT ADD MORE VALUE TO THE PRODUCT!

80% OF VALUE

20% ADDITIONAL VALUE

EFFORT

DO YOU WANT TO INVEST THIS EFFORT IN GETTING 20% MORE VALUE?

over to an operations or services team who are responsible for its ongoing support and maintenance. The team is now ready to move on, solve the next business problem and take up another product development project.

There is a huge efficiency potential for organizations that understand when to end projects or product development. HR professionals should remember the 20–80 rule (Pareto's principle), because usually 20 per cent of our features bring 80 per cent of the value to the end-customer and the business. It may not make sense to waste effort working on features after this point. Agile development teams never aim to finish the whole backlog, because they know the end-customer doesn't always need all the features it contained. When there is no more end-customer value to be gained, we stop.

## Conclusion

Through Agile ways of working we aim to deliver slices of value early and often to our end-customer. Agile development teams achieve this goal by embracing a feedback loop that helps them continually adapt and improve *what* they are working on as well as *how* they do it. Agile ways of working are powered through self-organization and transparency, which allow teams to solve problems and update their plans in direct response to end-customer feedback and changing circumstances. Agile is often misunderstood as working faster, but it's actually all about the speed of adaptation and improvement. It is this speed of change that ensures Agile organizations can deliver value to the end-customer at a much faster rate and deliver only what is actually needed.

KEY POINTS FOR HR PROFESSIONALS

- Agile ways of working include a lot of terms that you'll quickly become familiar with once you start using Agile practices.

- To understand how to redesign our people practices to support Agile, we must first appreciate how Agile teams work.

- You can apply most of the Agile practices covered in this chapter to your own HR projects and teams. We recommend attending a learning workshop to make it even more practical and relevant to your own context.

- Agile ways of working can greatly improve the efficiency of HR teams. By breaking down large projects and people initiatives into releasable slices of value, these can be tested and validated before being launched at scale.

- HR teams can also greatly benefit from applying the concept of *good enough* to release, with the idea that further iterations can continually improve the product or service instead of trying to perfect everything in one go.

## References

Apple (2020) Webpage for Apple iPhone 11 Pro, *Apple* www.apple.com/iphone-11-pro/ (archived at https://perma.cc/38AB-ZEUQ)

Razinski, S (2020) Get Paid to Test Products: 37 Ways to Become a Product Tester, *I'vetriedthat* https://ivetriedthat.com/get-paid-to-test-products (archived at https://perma.cc/S36V-DXVG)

www.scrumguides.org (archived at https://perma.cc/5F7B-WYTK)

# 06

# Scrum and Kanban

## Introduction

Scrum and Kanban are two of the most useful Agile frameworks for HR professionals to learn. While there are many Agile tools and techniques available, these two frameworks are great at helping HR teams bring every aspect of the Agile mindset to life. The practices contained within Scrum and Kanban have the potential to revolutionize HR results by helping us prioritize, design and deliver value to our internal customers. It's also essential for HR teams to understand these frameworks from an organizational design perspective so that we can better support Agile teams in the business. Only by embracing the same frameworks used within the organization can we truly appreciate the design needs of our people and create products and services that support Agile ways of working.

In this chapter we'll introduce the basics of Scrum and Kanban. This information also sets the foundations for the following chapters where we begin to apply these practices within HR. For anyone new to Agile, this chapter is essential reading that you may want to supplement with further study.

## Scrum

Scrum is the most popular Agile framework and is said to be 'the art of doing twice the work in half the time' (Sutherland, 2015). Scrum is a great framework to use when designing a product or delivering a project. Scrum began in software development and has a specific set of defined roles, events and artefacts. Approximately 70 per cent of all software development teams use Scrum (Sutherland, 2019), and it is considered one of the best frameworks to help teams manage changing requirements, achieve cross-team alignment and increase the speed of delivery (VersionOne, 2019). Since its inception Scrum has moved into a wide range of organizations and industries and is now seen in education (eduScrum, 2020), healthcare (Jonnalagadda *et al*, 2019), construction (Streule *et al*, 2016) and manufacturing (Justice, 2020).

---

WHAT THEY SAY

We delivered something in three weeks that usually takes this organization nine months.

Member of a Scrum team in HR that was developing a new learning academy for employees

---

Scrum was created in the 1990s by two people who also signed the Agile Manifesto, Jeff Sutherland and Ken Schwaber (Schwaber and Sutherland, 2017). Scrum is based on empirical process control and builds on the values of inspection, adaptation and transparency.

In Scrum, teams deliver increments of value within timeboxed periods called sprints. At the end of each sprint there should be a potentially releasable product increment that can be reviewed with end-customers and stakeholders to gather feedback on the value delivered. The Scrum framework is based on a 3-5-3 rule, with three roles, five events and three artefacts. Let's now review each of these elements.

## The three Scrum roles

### THE DEVELOPMENT TEAM

The development team consists of a group of people who have all the skills required to get the whole project done and deliver the intended value to the end-customer. This is a T-shaped team that we've mentioned previously, which holds a breadth of experience across multiple scenarios as well as the ability to deep dive into specific skills when needed. For example, a mechanical robotics development team might, for instance, consist of a designer, a mechanical engineer, an electrical engineer, a couple of software developers, a tester and a manufacturing specialist. Data suggests that a stable development team is more likely to continuously improve and realize higher velocity, and it's therefore recommended that all the team members work on the project full-time when using Scrum (Sutherland *et al*, 2014).

The development team self-organizes to decide *how* to get the job done and uses a transparent and prioritized backlog to manage their work. It can be inspiring to observe how a team using the Scrum framework begins to learn and grow together through the values of self-organization and transparency. We find that this can be quite a rapid transformation and that many teams start to achieve a high rate of velocity within a few sprints. However, we do recommend supporting teams using Scrum for the first time with additional coaching.

### THE PRODUCT OWNER

Translating the vision and purpose of a project into a prioritized backlog is the responsibility of the product owner (PO). The PO is the guardian of the backlog and responsible for realizing the value of the product being developed. While the development team owns the *how*, the PO is the owner of *what* needs to be delivered. The PO is a commercially focused role and a great PO will be passionate about the product they are delivering. The PO prioritizes the backlog by engaging in continuous conversations with the end-customers, as well as with the stakeholders and the development team. All work that is added to the backlog must go through the PO. Also, to ensure the PO and development team can always assess capacity and successfully track their delivery time, any non-development tasks, such as mandatory compliance training, should be added to the backlog. This ensures that the PO and development team can correctly estimate how much time it will take to get the backlog items done by the end of each sprint. The PO uses this information to track the overall release plan, as well as to manage stakeholder expectations on when things can be delivered.

At the end of each sprint, the PO is responsible for accepting the deliverables produced by the development team and assessing whether the work meets the acceptance criteria (see Chapter 5 for more detail). For example, the PO assesses whether the work achieved so far is delivering the value that is set out in the project vision. They're also looking to see if the work has been properly tested with users and meets the required quality, compliance or safety standards. For the Scrum framework to operate effectively, the PO needs to be able to make decisions on the go, without being subject to the delays of steering groups or approvals. For this reason, former business managers or client directors often make effective POs, because they already have good relationships with the end-customer and can conduct business-oriented prioritization discussions to identify the most valuable features for the development team to work on.

## SCRUM MASTER

If the PO is considered the guardian of the backlog, the Scrum master is considered the guardian of the Scrum framework and dedicates their time to helping the development team. This means that the Scrum master can play multiple roles and at times will be a coach, mentor, trainer and even protector of the team. The primary responsibility of the Scrum master is to help the team continually improve performance through coaching and facilitation. They also focus on how to remove impediments to enable the team to keep moving forward, as well as protect the team from outside disturbances. As such the Scrum master is considered a *servant leader* to the team. A Scrum master can be involved in a wide range of activities, such as escalating impediments to senior stakeholders to be resolved, helping align cross-team dependencies or facilitating a retrospectives to help the development team improve collaboration.

It's useful to note that Scrum does not define a line manager role. Indeed, the responsibilities and tasks that traditionally sat with a line manager are now divided across the three roles (PO, Scrum master and development team), which also hold each other accountable for the deliverables. When introducing the Scrum framework into organizations, we recommend spending time with the people involved, to map out the new expectations of existing line managers and whether the role needs to be redesigned or removed. See Chapter 15 for more information on how to approach this topic.

## The five Scrum events

The Scrum framework sets out five timeboxed events.

## SPRINTS

As mentioned above, sprints are timeboxed periods in which the team aims to deliver a certain amount of work. Sprints are consecutive, and each sprint essentially follows the Agile feedback loop of 'plan, do, check, act'. The length of a sprint ranges from 1–4 weeks, depending on the type of product that the team is working on as well as the response time required to adapt to changes. For example, a team working with digital products might need to work in one-week sprints to keep up with the pace of change in the market, whereas an HR team working on a performance management project might use four-week sprints because the product being developed requires a longer time for people to test the different solutions.

People often ask how long a sprint should be. The decision reflects multiple factors:

- What is a realistic time for delivering a potentially releasable product increment?

- What is the preferred frequency for feedback from the end-customer and stakeholders?

- How fast do we need to improve? For example, shorter sprints may help to lift performance by speeding up the cycle of continuous improvement.

- How much time does it make sense to allocate to the sprint events? Shorter sprints imply proportionally more time being allocated to the sprint events, such as planning and retrospectives (which we explain later), allowing for less development time.

### SPRINT PLANNING

Before every sprint, the Scrum team gathers to plan their work and decide how to deliver a releasable product increment within the timeboxed period. They create a sprint goal to guide the work and clarify expectations to ensure that everyone is clear on what to do in the sprint. The team then selects items from the backlog to form a sprint backlog, which is the work they will aim to deliver by the end of the sprint.

### DAILY SCRUM

Every day the development team and Scrum master meet for a timeboxed daily meeting of 15 minutes to review progress against the sprint goal and tackle any impediments that might be blocking their way. The PO can also participate. The daily scrum acts as a micro-level planning session where the team keeps track of tasks, progress and impediments and synchronizes dependencies. The aim is for a quick check-in to raise problems in real time and keep things moving.

### SPRINT REVIEW

At the end of each sprint, the development team, PO and Scrum master gather to review the potentially releasable product increment. Some reviews include stakeholders, sponsors or users. The aim is to check acceptance criteria and gather feedback from end-customers and stakeholders by showcasing the product increment. The sprint review results in a reprioritized backlog and guides the focus of the next sprint.

WHAT THEY SAY

OMG, we are showing an unfinished product to important people.

Said by a team member of an HR team using Scrum before their sprint review

When new to Scrum, it's good to help stakeholders understand the concept of a minimum viable product and that what they'll review at this stage might be far from perfect. This is particularly important if the stakeholders are used to seeing only the finished result. We find that HR teams can be fearful of showing people an unfinished product at the review stage, but how else will we know that we're on the right track? Indeed, most HR teams quickly discover that stakeholders welcome the opportunity to give this feedback early, and it helps them feel that they are co-creating the solution with us.

RETROSPECTIVE

While the sprint review focuses on how to improve the product being developed, the retrospective looks at what the team can do to improve how they work. Generally conducted by the Scrum master, the retrospective is a crucial mechanism to drive continuous improvement within Scrum. Development actions agreed in retrospectives often concern the processes and tools used by the team, as well as team relationships and how they collaborate (Dingsøyr *et al*, 2018). Discussions might cover things like, 'let's talk about issues in the daily Scrum, rather than send e-mails' or 'in every sprint, let's reconnect to the purpose and vision to stay on track'. Retrospectives are key moments that bring the Agile feedback loop to life and help drive a learning culture that strives to be better tomorrow than we are today.

## The three Scrum artefacts

PRODUCT BACKLOG

This is a list of all the things that the team might need to complete in order to deliver the project or product. The product vision guides the prioritization of the product backlog.

SPRINT BACKLOG

The sprint backlog represents the work that the team commits to getting done during the next timeboxed sprint. A Scrum board is used to visualize and track this work and is reset for every new sprint. Once a sprint backlog is decided, no new commitments should be made, and all new work is put on the overall product backlog to be reviewed and considered at the start of the following sprint. Also, if a team overcommits or realizes they've selected the wrong priorities, they still complete the sprint and then use the review and retrospective to assess why this happened and how to learn from the experience.

### INCREMENT

This is the sum of all the completed work achieved during a sprint, the value of which is combined with the work already achieved in earlier sprints.

### Scrum is a framework, not a rulebook

For Scrum to work well, it needs to be fully embraced as a holistic framework rather than just a collection of different activities and roles. The framework is like an ecosystem, where each element interconnects and depends on the others. If any part of the ecosystem becomes dysfunctional, the whole system deteriorates and only mediocre gains in performance and quality will be realized (Sutherland *et al*, 2009). The framework is built on the values of focus, openness, respect, commitment and courage, which are great guiding principles that help teams inspect how they're working and where they might need to improve. The Agile and Scrum community is also full of useful references and tools to help teams constantly improve, and we recommend jumping on the internet to find out more.

Scrum is also much more than just a method to manage projects, and many teams that think they're doing Scrum often miss out key elements. For example, it's common to hear of teams not having a PO in place or thinking it's OK for the PO and Scrum master to be the same person. In any of these situations, the teams will often fail, and this can have huge consequences for the successful adoption of Scrum and Agile within the organization. Handy questions to help test this include:

- Is the team delivering a potentially shippable increment by the end of each sprint?
- Can the PO make all the product decisions and quickly respond to customer needs?
- Is there one clear prioritized backlog for the team?
- Is the team protected from outside distractions or competing targets and are they able to focus 100 per cent of their time on the sprint work?

- Is the team T-shaped and able to get the work done without constantly needing help from elsewhere?

- Have the dependencies on other teams or functions been minimized, so that the team is not constantly impacted or slowed down by the work of others?

- Is the team trusted to self-organize and make their own decisions on how to get the work done?

If new to Scrum, we recommend fully committing to the whole framework and using the first few sprints to practise getting each element working well. Only then, and once the team feels confident and in control, should modifications be introduced to adapt the framework for the surrounding work environment. This is especially important for HR teams when they first try Scrum. For HR, the format of consecutive sprints is often best suited to projects where we innovate the design of new products, rather than maintaining business-as-usual processes or services; however, only by following the framework properly first do we know how to change it to improve performance.

## Kanban

When our work is more continuous in nature and doesn't easily fit within timeboxed sprints as outlined in Scrum, Kanban can be a useful framework to consider. Kanban supports an ongoing flow of work and looks at how to achieve an optimal level of efficiency by helping teams focus on the most important things and continuously improve their ways of working. The Kanban method is built on the principle of finishing work tasks before starting others, and constantly assesses the capacity of the team as well as the work in progress. To do this, the team uses a Kanban board to visualize their work and aims to reduce the time it takes to move a piece of work (like a backlog item) from start to finish. This constant focus on optimal workflow means that Kanban helps eliminate waste from the work system.

Kanban originated in Japan and was created by Taiichi Ohno when working with Lean principles and the Toyota production system in the 1970s (Ohno, 1988). In the early 2000s, David J Anderson started applying the principles within software development and in 2010 published The Kanban Method, which shapes many of the practices seen today (Kanban University, 2020).

## The Kanban board

While Kanban centres around the use of a board to make work transparent and allow the team to see the state of every piece of work simultaneously, it doesn't prescribe any specific practice and allows teams to shape their own ways of working. Overall, the Kanban framework helps to facilitate self-organization and the *pull*-based working system. The aim is to limit work in progress to an agreed amount and allow new pieces of work to be pulled in only once other items are finished. This approach helps teams to not over-commit or lose time attempting to multitask.

Often teams start with a basic Kanban board (Figure 6.1) and the columns of Backlog, To Do, Doing and Done. Then, based on the different aspects and nuances of their work, they may introduce new columns, work streams or ticketing systems. For example, an HR services team might use work streams to represent the different business units that they support, or begin to use coloured tickets to separate urgent work from BAU. These approaches could even be overlaid with new columns to separate work that has been reviewed in detail and prioritized from a bigger list that captures all the new work or requests coming in from the business. This means that the Kanban framework allows multiple products or services to be worked on at the same time as well as to cover different customer groups. For these reasons, a lot of HR teams find the Kanban framework useful; we'll explore more examples in Chapter 10.

FIGURE 6.1   Example Kanban board

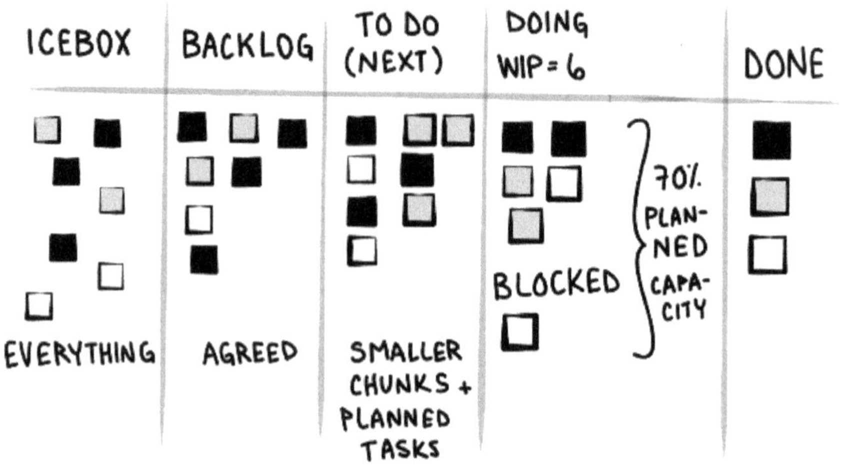

Some of the core principles that help guide the Kanban framework include:

- **Visualize** all work and understand dependencies by using either a physical or an electronic board.

- **Limit work in progress (WIP)** based on the true capacity of the team or organization, with the aim of reducing bottlenecks or clogging up of the system. By limiting the WIP, the most important work is finished first and more gets done overall (Kanban University, 2020).

- **Manage flow** to realize an optimal level of efficiency. This includes tracking all work with metrics and data to continuously assess performance (Kanban University, 2020). For example, a team might track data on how long it takes to move work from start to finish, the size of work, the number of items, what work gets blocked and why, as well as the percentage of urgent work versus BAU.

- **Agree ways of working** to help facilitate self-organization. For example, the team needs to know how the whole end-to-end process looks, what is required at each stage, how to assign team members to tasks and how to handle urgent requests coming in. The team should also know the constraints under which they work, such as budgets or cross-team dependencies. Additionally, the team should agree on what meetings are important to enhance the system, such as planning sessions, daily stand-ups or review discussions with end-customers and stakeholders.

- **Improve and evolve** by following the Lean principle of 'start where you are'. The team should continuously assess their pain points and iterate improvement actions.

## Conclusion

The Scrum and Kanban frameworks are both useful for HR teams wanting to improve their Agile working practices.

Scrum is great for innovation work and helps HR teams rapidly develop new products or services. It's particularly useful when it's possible to do part-releases and involve the internal customer in regular testing and validation activities. Scrum uses timeboxed events and specifically defines the roles and methods that teams should use. Within Scrum, all the work committed in a sprint needs to be finished by the end of the timeboxed period, with the aim of delivering a potentially releasable product increment. Only at the end of the sprint do teams assess what new work needs to be considered and what to prioritize for the next sprint.

Kanban centres around visualizing work on a board and allows flexibility in the methods that teams use to manage their workflow. The Kanban framework is often suited to work that is more continuous, such as HR services, operations or recruitment teams. It's also useful if the team has numerous dependencies across the business or needs to wait for responses from other areas. The key is to limit WIP at any one point in time and then seek ways to improve the flow and efficiency of how the work moves from start to finish. Often, we see that teams using Kanban also draw on some of the Scrum events, such as reviews and retrospectives, to further enhance the process and build an effective cadence of work.

---

KEY POINTS FOR HR PROFESSIONALS

- The only way to truly know how to use Scrum or Kanban is to give it a go!

- Both frameworks help to bring the Agile values and practices to life and can greatly improve how HR teams prioritize and manage their work.

- While Scrum is best suited to innovation and the development of new products and services, Kanban helps when the work is more continuous, such as the ongoing delivery and maintenance of an HR service.

- Sometimes just visualizing work and measuring how long it takes to get pieces of work done can greatly improve the efficiency and workflow within HR teams.

- The key to both Scrum and Kanban is working cross-functionally and collaborating with our internal customers.

---

# References

Dingsøyr, T et al (2018) Learning in the large – an exploratory study of retrospectives in large-scale Agile development, In *Agile Processes in Software Engineering and Extreme Programming*, ed J Garbajosa, X Wang and A Aguiar, XP 2018, Lecture Notes in Business Information Processing, vol 314, Springer, Cham

eduScrum (2020) Homepage, *eduScrum* https://eduscrum.nl/en (archived at https://perma.cc/3PGH-5JAY)

Jonnalagadda, K *et al* (2019) How Agile Is Powering Healthcare Innovation, *Bain & Company* www.bain.com/insights/how-agile-is-powering-healthcare-innovation/ (archived at https://perma.cc/AN78-KJSJ)

Justice, J (2020) Homepage, *Wikispeed* http://wikispeed.org (archived at https://perma.cc/MK5S-5DH9)

Kanban University (2020) Kanban: The Alternative Path to Agility, *Kanban University* www.kanban.university (archived at https://perma.cc/6G52-PCTK); https://edu.kanban.university/kanban-method (archived at https://perma.cc/5CFK-2PJK)

Ohno, T (1988) *Toyota Production System: Beyond large-scale production*, Productivity Press, Portland, OR

Schwaber, K and Sutherland, J (2017) *The Scrum Guide*, Scrum.org (archived at https://perma.cc/T9LR-XD93) www.scrumguides.org (archived at https://perma.cc/5F7B-WYTK)

Streule, T *et al* (2016) Implementation of Scrum in the construction industry, Creative Construction Conference 2016 (CCC 2016), 25–28 June

Sutherland, J (2015) *Scrum: The art of doing twice the work in half the time*, Random House Business Books, London

Sutherland, J (2019) *The Scrum Fieldbook: Faster performance. Better results. Starting now*, Random House, New York

Sutherland, J, Downey, S and Granvik, B (2009) Shock therapy: a bootstrap for hyper-productive scrum, 2009 Agile Conference, pp 69–73, IEEE, doi: 10.1109/AGILE.2009.28

Sutherland, J, Harrison, N and Riddle, J (2014) Teams that finish early accelerate faster: A pattern language for high performing scrum teams, 47th Hawaii International Conference on System Sciences, Waikoloa, HI, pp 4722–28

VersionOne (2019) 14th Annual State of Agile™ Report, *VersionOne* https://stateofagile.com/#ufh-c-473508-state-of-agile-report (archived at https://perma.cc/EH6L-DMFR)

# PART THREE

# Agile for HR toolkit

# 07

# Agile for HR: An introduction

Agile for HR looks at how HR can apply the Agile mindset and working methods *within our own* teams and projects. This Agile cycle of work can help HR become the value-adding function that we've always wished to be, rather than just a transactional service provider, and help us make evidence-based organizational change decisions. The Agile feedback loop and incremental development process also support the innovation of HR products and services and offer HR teams a way to start delivering value to the business at speed.

To support your learning, we've built an Agile for HR toolkit, full of practical examples, case studies and hands-on templates that can be applied back in the workplace.

The toolkit is built around the following topics:

- **Value and prioritization** (Chapter 8): how to manage the endless HR wish-list and deliver value to the business.
- **Co-creation** (Chapter 9): how to apply design thinking within HR and build great human-centric products and services *with* our people, rather than implementing solutions *on to* them.
- **Agile teams and operating models in HR** (Chapter 10): how Agile ways of working are reshaping the HR team model and helping us deliver a more end-to-end employee experience.
- **Thinking like a scientist** (Chapter 11): how to apply an evidence-based approach and make data-driven decisions.
- **Continuous improvement** (Chapter 12): how to use the Agile feedback loop to support learning and improve performance.

Throughout the toolkit it's important to remember that Agile for HR is about innovating within constraints. At all times HR needs to adhere to regulation and the compliance needs of the organization. It's also unlikely that HR teams will have the budget, time or capacity that we prefer and we will need to approach projects and people initiatives with pragmatism. However, in the past HR has tended to lead with the constraints, rather than first designing products and services that delight the user. To overcome this barrier, we advocate putting people before the process and encourage all HR professionals to follow a human-centric approach throughout their work.

Agile helps HR place the internal customer, our employees, at the heart of everything we do. The result is a cycle of work that drives high performance and enriches the employee experience. We hope this toolkit builds the confidence you need to get cracking and continually develop your Agile HR capability.

# 08

# Agile HR toolkit:
# Value and prioritization

## Introduction

While it's common for CEOs to talk about their people as their 'greatest asset', it's generally a struggle for HR to clearly articulate how our people practices and operations contribute to the bottom line. Despite HR's central purpose of helping an organization achieve competitive advantage through their people, we've often failed to demonstrate our impact beyond the processes that are delivered and end up being viewed as a cost centre rather than a generator of business growth.

Agile helps HR think and act more strategically, which has been a common goal for many HR leaders for some time. Bogged down by an endless to-do list and myriad processes, most HR teams crave the accolade of being seen as a value-adding function. In this chapter we'll look at how HR can build a strategic portfolio of work by using different definitions of customer and business value to guide their prioritization. We'll also share practical tools that assist HR teams in planning and scheduling what they will deliver to the organization week on week and explain where and why they should focus their time and effort. The goal is to help HR move beyond the never-ending strategic wish-list that plagues our profession and start to demonstrate our impact through a language that successfully combines the elements of both people and business.

# Defining value

As previously discussed, Agile is a mindset and method of working that is built around the concept of delivering value to the customer. Within HR this notion of value can be defined on multiple levels:

- **Strategic value.** Value is not just about helping the business achieve its strategic goals and delivering products to the end-customer. It is also how HR creates new value for the organization, in the form of a competitive advantage gained through high-performing teams, great leaders and the development of new capabilities, plus the impact of creative and innovative talent. Too often in the past HR leaders have needed to rely on HR processes to demonstrate business impact, such as how many training programmes people have attended or how many performance conversations are documented, rather than using data to display how HR's products and solutions directly contribute to the overall brand and bottom line. To do this, HR needs to be in sync with the business strategy and make proactive decisions on what they should focus on to better accelerate the business mission.

---

**HR TOP TIP**

Consider what strategic drivers are important and relevant to the business context:

- Business growth.
- Scaling up or down?
- Intended or planned mergers and acquisitions.
- First in market or a follower.
- More sales versus the need to save costs.
- Pay high for top talent versus build and develop a talent pool-based culture.

For example, the drivers for a high-growth start-up business might be:

- High-growth start-up mode.
- Aim is to win a big backer in the third and upcoming investment round.
- Need to double existing employee numbers to fuel growth.
- Overall goal is to scale and increase market share following recent product launch.

---

In this context, the strategic priorities for HR are to focus on recruitment and source and retain talent. They should look at ways to reward people for their contribution and connect them to the equity potential of the company. Another key focus is creating great working facilities, keeping people healthy while they work hard and start to harness a sense of belonging through community-building initiatives. The team decides it's not the right time to do a big employee engagement survey and instead focuses on small, short pulse surveys to gain feedback on immediate actions and results.

- **Enabler value.** This is how we help the business succeed day to day. This concept of value includes all the hygiene factors necessary to get the job done, such as a reliable payroll system or ergonomic chairs for people to sit on. Importantly, it's also about eliminating the waste that might exist in our processes, which can burden other parts of the business and stop them getting their own work done; for example, a heavily documented performance management process that requires managers and employees to rate numerous competencies and behaviours. While this process may have the intended goal of better shaping an annual performance conversation, the hours required to complete this task are a cost and waste to the wider business if the same result can be achieved through real-time performance conversations on the job. Indeed, a good indication is that if the HR team finds the task a pain to complete themselves, the wider business most certainly will!

HR TOP TIP

A great activity is to calculate the time it takes managers and employees to complete all the HR processes, such as performance management conversations and associated documentation, and then turn it into a cost or investment. If the investment is deemed necessary and it enables people to get the job done, then great. If it's not needed, however, we are essentially stealing time from people creating business value and it should be considered a waste created by HR.

- **Purpose-driven value.** To attract the talent necessary to gain a competitive advantage as well as build a loyal customer base for their products, organizations now need to become 'social enterprises' (Volini *et al*, 2019). These types of organization can combine the drive for profits and reviewing growth with a social mission that respects the environment and supports the health and equality of society. Being a social enterprise is more than just running a few corporate social responsibility campaigns. It involves building a trusted employee brand proposition that makes people want to work for the organization because they feel connected to a wider social purpose and can make a positive contribution to their community through their work.

---

**HR TOP TIP**

The need to build social enterprises was the number one trend highlighted by Deloitte in their 2019 Global Human Capital Trends report (Volini *et al*, 2019). It's becoming increasingly important for organizations to consider the impact of these factors both for their overall strategy and culture and for each of the people initiatives HR commit to. For example, we may find that by listing how an onboarding programme can connect with the organization's social purpose and vision, we are able to develop the main employee branding proposition to offer to new starters and even future recruits.

---

- **Employee value.** Intimately linked to building a purpose-driven brand is understanding the human element of work and the need to genuinely care for our employees. This need is captured through the human-centric approach of Agile HR and represents an opportunity where HR can add a lot of untapped value. Quite often, business leaders lack HR's experience in how to build a culture of belonging and an organizational design where people get excited by the work they do and who they work with. This goes beyond using a few motivational or engagement tools within the workplace and is about treating people as adults. The approach feeds off self-determination theory, which was formed by Ryan and Deci (2000) and made popular by Dan Pink, who used the theme of mastery, autonomy and purpose (Pink, 2011).

---

**HR TOP TIP**

In all situations we can consider the human impact. For example, an Agile HR professional saw a need to help leaders think in a human-centric way when a restructure was announced for their part of the business. To achieve this, the Agile HR professional invited the leaders to a meeting and asked them to create personas based on the main user groups that would be impacted by the upcoming restructure. They then mapped out the intended restructuring experience and assessed what the personas would do, think and feel at each stage along the journey. The result was eye-opening for the leaders and they subsequently compiled a backlog of actions to ensure that the people transitioning out of the teams were properly supported and also to have great conversations with the people who were staying.

- **End-customer value.** HR should never lose sight of the end-customer in our work. While HR's attention is naturally focused more on what we see as the immediate, internal customer, namely our employees and leaders, we need to assess how our activities and solutions impact the end-customer of the organization. For example, when HR looks at redesigning the onboarding programme and process, we generally focus on the new starter's experience and the interactions they have with fellow team members and managers, as well as the time it takes for them to start doing the job. However, what about their capacity to deliver to the end-customer? Often, we don't even let new starters engage directly with end-customers because they are not deemed ready yet, but is this always right and are there alternatives in how we set them up to work immediately with the end-customer? How do we ensure new starters know who our end-customers are, the needs and pain points they have, and the types of customer persona that marketing and product design use in the business? If we can then link the onboarding to results with the end-customer, such as an increase in sales, online engagement or faster time to delivery, we can begin to track the direct impact of the onboarding programme and process on the end-customer. With all our initiatives, it's crucial to map out how our HR processes and people practices help our internal customers get a better result with the end-customer and therefore lift business performance.

The HR value canvas is a one-page template that helps HR teams guide discussions and define value (Figure 8.1).

Finally, it's good to note that all these value drivers need to be weighed up against what is happening for the business and the wider market. It's also important for HR to challenge senior leaders and some of their default thinking when it comes to value. For example, often leaders want to focus

FIGURE 8.1  HR value canvas

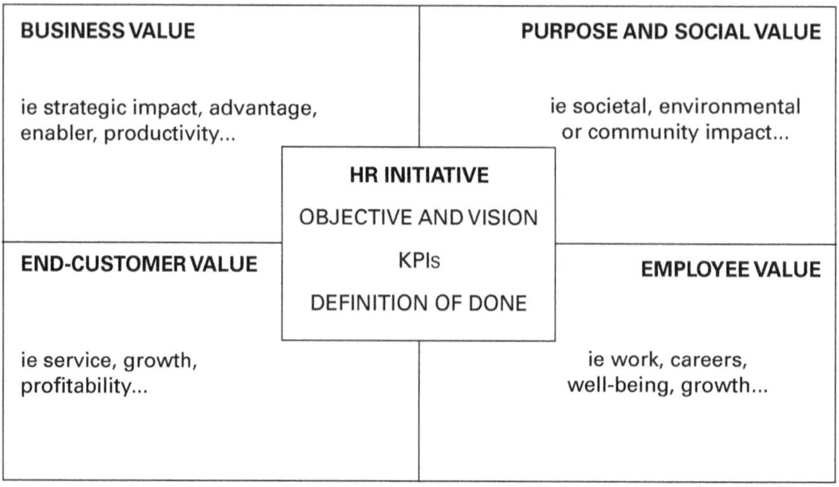

| BUSINESS VALUE | PURPOSE AND SOCIAL VALUE |
|---|---|
| ie strategic impact, advantage, enabler, productivity... | ie societal, environmental or community impact... |

**HR INITIATIVE**

OBJECTIVE AND VISION

KPIs

DEFINITION OF DONE

| END-CUSTOMER VALUE | EMPLOYEE VALUE |
|---|---|
| ie service, growth, profitability... | ie work, careers, well-being, growth... |

on short-term drivers linked to strategic value, generally at the cost of factors like employee value. Additionally, there might be a need to create a longer-term vision and roadmap for initiatives that sit in areas such as purpose-driven value. In these situations, it will be necessary to assess how to move elements of these longer-term plans forward at the same time as meeting short-term goals when managing the strategic portfolio of work.

## Building a strategic portfolio of work

It's often hard to know where to start when building the people strategy. Waiting for the wider business strategy to be ready first is generally too late and tends to lead to a reactive HR plan. Additionally, it's vital for employee needs to be considered from the start when formulating the organizational mission and goals. HR also can't just ask the business what they want without first offering some guidance, because otherwise the people strategy can end up too simplistic and lack some of the nuances that HR's experience in organizational development provides. Of course, HR also shouldn't just tell the business what the strategy is and push the plan out on to them without any consultation, in true waterfall fashion!

The limitation with all of these approaches is that they tend to view the people strategy as an end-game and a plan that should be produced on an annual basis. Instead, we encourage HR to role-model an Agile approach and view the formation of strategy as an ongoing dialogue with the wider business where we co-create the mission and goals on a continuous basis. The aim is to form an Agile HR strategic portfolio of work by following an evidence-based method that incorporates regular discussions and check-ins on business priorities, alongside an assessment of the external market, ongoing talent trends and end-customer information. We should also add to these data the regular collection of employee feedback and our own professional view on the development needs within the organization.

We recommend the following key steps on a quarterly basis to agree the high-level priorities with the wider business for the Agile HR portfolio of work. This ensures stakeholder buy-in and commitment for the main people initiatives, and the HR team can then use a weekly or monthly cadence to manage ongoing team-level backlogs and deliveries.

## Assess business priorities

HR needs to constantly update their holistic view on where the business is and what the priorities are for the next strategic period. Depending on the setup of the Agile HR team (see Chapter 10 for examples), the HR leader or business partners may take a lead in these discussions with the aim of bringing the information back to the team. Another option, depending upon the team model, is for the new role of HR product owner to have these types of conversation across the business. However, it's worth noting that in an effective Agile HR model, everyone seeks this information in their day-to-day work, continuously bringing it back for discussion and review.

The goal is to form a snapshot of the internal business environment. This includes check-ins with senior leaders, local managers, customer representatives, POs and other support teams like the project management office, tech and compliance. The following questions are a good guide to follow:

- What is our net promoter score and which customer segments are we going to focus on?
- What are our growth targets?
- What is the health of our product lines?
- What are the major product-related launches, changes or life-cycle decisions impacting the new strategic period in the business?
- What does the balance sheet look like and where do we need to save costs or make new investments?

- What are the big internal projects, such as technology updates or compliance process changes, that will impact the business over the coming strategic period?
- What organizational changes are planned, and why?

In all conversations, constantly assess priorities and ask questions such as: what is the most important initiative, and why? If forced to choose, what should be done first? It's vital that HR are armed with information that guides backlog prioritization and can articulate why certain decisions are made, as well as what HR are going after and what will have to wait for another time (Figure 8.2).

## Assess the people and culture landscape

It's crucial to construct an in-depth picture of the internal and external talent market, as well as to review all the available internal people data to

FIGURE 8.2    Domains impacting business priorities

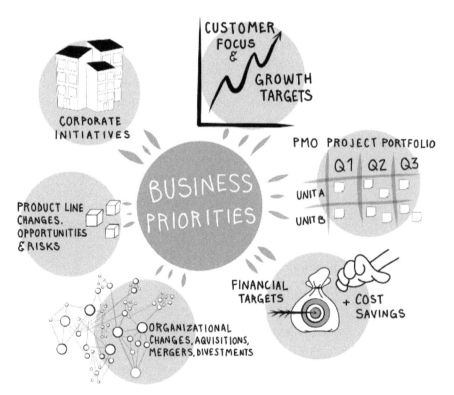

FIGURE 8.3  People and culture focus areas

assess the health of the organization and form a view on the current people and culture position (Figure 8.3).

Once HR has information concerning the business priorities, alongside a snapshot of the health of the organization and its people, we can conduct a SWOT analysis (invented in the 1960s by Albert Humphrey at Stanford Research Institute) on the strengths, weaknesses, opportunities and threats within the people strategy (Figure 8.4). For example, this might assess areas like talent acquisition, skills capability, employee net promoter scores and reward data, as well as diversity and inclusion and the employee brand proposition. Again, prioritization is vital here, and HR need to identify the biggest pain points alongside core strengths, to decide on the most important focus areas. Remember, we can never do it all and something will need to give.

## Offer insights

Data are only as good as the insights HR offers to the business. People analytics and HR metrics are huge growth areas in our profession, and we

FIGURE 8.4  SWOT analysis example

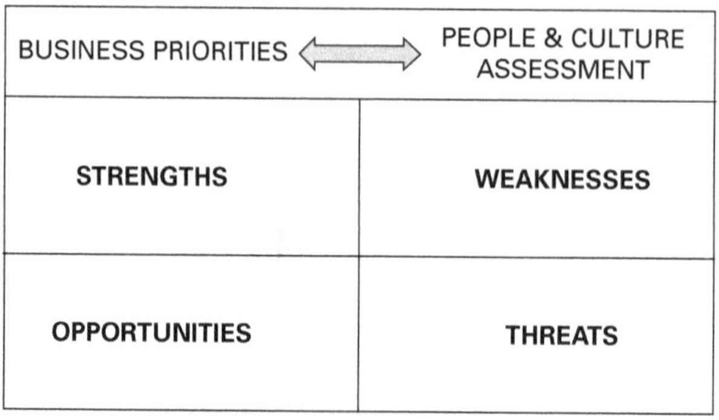

| BUSINESS PRIORITIES ⟺ | PEOPLE & CULTURE ASSESSMENT |
|---|---|
| STRENGTHS | WEAKNESSES |
| OPPORTUNITIES | THREATS |

Inspired by Albert Humphrey – Stanford Research Institute

encourage HR professionals to invest in strengthening their capabilities in this area. It's also useful to partner with other parts of the business that already have these skills, such as data scientists or finance. Using data to inform our position is very different from traditional HR reporting, where leadership teams reviewed backward-looking metrics such as headcount, absence levels and recruitment statistics. Instead, people analytics is about identifying the business challenges and potential pain points, alongside actionable ideas and suggestions on how these link with the business strategy. Look for how people metrics link to business activities and see what narrative this begins to form.

For example, HR may discover that 45 roles will be impacted over the coming quarter by technological change, and a shift in capabilities is required. Rather than jumping into solution mode, dig deeper first. What is the overall skills assessment of the people in these roles? What are the time, cost and effort to take different actions such as retrain, move roles or offer redundancies? Generally, the scenario that comes to light cannot be addressed with a generic solution. For example, HR may find that 15 people can easily move into new roles owing to their existing skills, while 10 have like-for-like skills and could work with the new technology, and another 10 may have the potential to retrain. Then, out of the remaining staff, five might already be a potential flight risk and another five might need to consider redundancy options.

Such findings should then be overlaid with business priorities. Does HR focus on this project in the next strategic quarter and if so, what elements are the most important to start first, and why? What is the risk if HR doesn't act this quarter? If HR doesn't have the capacity, can we still work on a few aspects of the project now to reduce this risk?

It's also important to look at how Agile can help HR manage risk and which slices of value can be delivered first. For this, we need to quickly validate whether certain things are indeed possible before fully committing large amounts of time and money, as well as break larger initiatives down into smaller, more manageable chunks to lower overall project risk.

### Co-create with stakeholders

As mentioned previously, strategy is a two-way process. We recommend forming a solid picture of the organization through the above steps and then inviting stakeholders and employee representatives to help prioritize the strategic initiatives. Often, it's useful to do this first within the HR team, using some of the prioritization methods outlined below. It's then easier to identify the gaps and different viewpoints when discussing the priorities with the business representatives (Figure 8.5).

It's also important to revisit our definition of value at this stage and understand which initiatives lead to a competitive advantage or end-customer benefit, as opposed to the initiatives that HR might need to just get done, such as an audit. These types of discussions help HR weigh up the non-negotiables versus the strategic goals versus the nice to haves. As we will see below, it may be necessary to rank the value of each and to develop a point system to assess what's in and what's out for that quarter. Remember

FIGURE 8.5  HR portfolio example

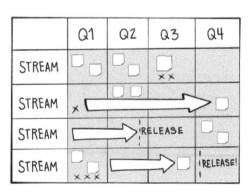

## HR PORTFOLIO ITEMS
### TO BE DEFINED WITH STAKEHOLDERS

**Programs**
**Projects**
**Initiatives**
**Go Do's**
**Requirements**
**Requests**
**Recommendations**

to keep in mind the capacity of the organization to receive releases of new products and solutions each quarter from HR. Is there space and time for the employees or managers to take on a behavioural change or new tech tool? How does this link into other support functions and can our efforts and releases be synced?

---

**WHAT THEY SAY**

I was really impressed yesterday with Megan's overview of the business. Without any involvement from my team or myself she was able to articulate our strategy and the focus for the next year. It is very refreshing to have an HR partner who is so supportive and understands our business.

Anonymous quote received from a business leader after their HR business partner applied the above business prioritization methods

---

Finally, all of this needs to be assessed against the true capability and capacity of the HR team. It's good to note that we're never able to operate at a capacity of 100 per cent and we suggest using a figure more like 70 per cent to account for holidays, sickness and business emergencies, as well as all the unplanned and unexpected work that impacts our sustainable (and healthy!) workflow. The power of no is very important in this discussion, and focusing on doing one thing well will deliver more value to the business than focusing on multiple things at the same time.

## Apply prioritization tools

There are many useful prioritization tools available to Agile HR teams. Let's review some of our favourites.

### RISK VERSUS VALUE GRID

This grid, shown in Figure 8.6, helps HR teams identify and manage project risk. Generally, the definition of risk used for the grid includes the *probability of the initiative failing*, for example the risk is higher for more complex projects, as well as the *consequences of the initiative not succeeding*, for example if not getting it done increased the compliance risk for a business. When using this grid, HR teams often jump on the initiatives identified as low risk and high value, as they're easier to get done. This is often at the

FIGURE 8.6  Risk versus value grid

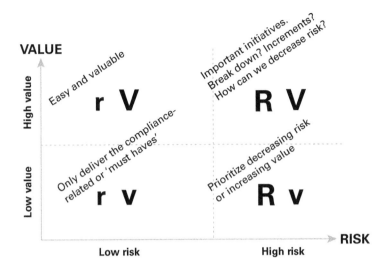

cost of leaving the high-risk and high-value initiatives to later, or attempting to do them all through one big implementation. As a remedy, we encourage HR professionals to review what sits in the high-risk and high-value box first, and aim to break these down into smaller, more manageable chunks of work.

### MOSCOW METHOD

MoSCoW (Figure 8.7) is great for prioritizing the features that need to be designed and delivered for a product or service (Richards, 2007). We have also seen it used effectively by HR teams to work with their stakeholders to prioritize and decide on things like which roles to hire given a certain budget or time period.

MoSCoW first identifies which features are the must-haves or non-negotiables, the absolute minimum to get the product or service functioning. Next, it identifies the should-haves, which are the features that make the product or service usable or likeable. From there, it identifies the could-have features that will help delight the users, though generally it will be impossible to deliver them all. Finally, MoSCoW identifies the features that simply don't add any value at this stage, and while these features should be periodically reviewed when requirements change, HR teams need to say no at this time.

FIGURE 8.7  MoSCoW method

Inspired by Dai Clegg – Dynamic Systems Development Method (DSDM), 1994

---

WHAT THEY SAY

The idea of product management isn't really in the HR books. It is about owning a product or thinking about an HR process as a product that people have to buy. It requires listening to your customers to help you develop something people actually like. A lot of this is now going to be transferred over to HR, the language is a bit clunky, but the practices are really starting to work.

Josh Bersin, Global Industry Analyst (Hellström, 2020)

---

EFFORT VERSUS IMPACT GRID

Most HR teams find this grid (Figure 8.8) easy to use and an effective method to determine what should be delivered given limited capacity and resources. Before using the grid, it's important to clearly define what impact and effort mean for the organizational context in which we work.

FIGURE 8.8  Effort versus impact grid

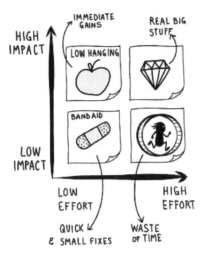

FIGURE 8.9  Value matrix

# THE VALUE MATRIX
## OR HOW TO DISCUSS INITIATIVES MORE OBJECTIVELY

| Initiatives / Unique value drivers | Growth | Employer brand | Securing finance | Attract talent | TOTAL |
|---|---|---|---|---|---|
| Automate recruitment | 10 | 8 | 8 | 9 | 35 |
| Employee survey | 3 | 5 | 6 | 5 | 19 |
| Recruit product owners | 8 | 3 | 10 | 10 | 31 |
| Restructure teams | 4 | 7 | 8 | 9 | 28 |
| Harmonize contracts | 6 | 2 | 6 | 9 | 23 |

RELATIVE POINTS          RELATIVE VALUE

VALUE MATRIX

The value matrix (Figure 8.9) is useful when HR teams need a system to compare the value of different initiatives and prioritize where to spend time and effort based on the overall value each delivers across the whole organization. The estimation is relative between the different initiatives, and thus not scientific, but it helps make the decisions more explicit and systematic. Remember that the value drivers should be updated according to the organizational context and that it always reflect a moment in time.

FIGURE 8.10   Forced ranking

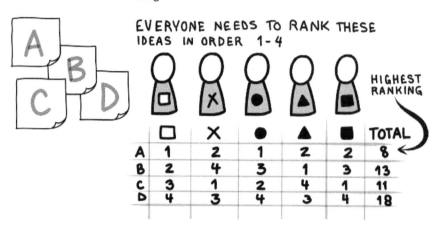

### FORCED RANKING

Forced ranking (Figure 8.10) is a useful sorting mechanism, which can be done using consensus or by inviting each person to rank the initiatives themselves first and then compare.

### BUBBLE SORTING

Bubble sorting (Figure 8.11) is the least objective method and invites HR teams to compare each new item to items already in the list. The prioritization is achieved through a mixture of discussion, what evidence is at hand and gut feeling.

Other useful prioritization tools include:

- **Dot voting** – where everyone gets the same number of dots and votes on the items they consider the most important.
- **Weighted dot voting** – where people who are domain experts get more dots than others and then vote.
- **Asking HiPPOs** – where we ask the highest paid person's opinion, which we generally advise to avoid but sometimes it's useful to weigh their views against HR's perspective.

## Sense-check the human element

We think it's vital always to keep this step in the process as a type of safety net to ensure that everything HR does has a human focus. Good questions to ask include:

- Does our strategy support our people before the process?

FIGURE 8.11    Bubble sorting

- Do we need to explore the human experience of specific initiatives further before committing to the project (see Chapter 9 for ideas on how)?
- Have we considered the moral and ethical implications of organizational change decisions and the impact on people's everyday life?

We like to think that by following an evidence-based method and truly co-creating the strategy using stakeholder and employee input, the human element will always be represented. However, it's always useful to play devil's advocate at this stage and challenge your thinking.

## Self-organize around agreed priorities

The outcome of all these steps is a clear roadmap on what HR will deliver and what we won't, and helps guide prioritization discussions over the coming quarter with the wider business and, more importantly, within our own team. For example, if HR needs to take immediate action to fix an unforeseen problem, like a social media reputation scare, the choices that need to be made on what HR will stop working on or postpone can be clearly articulated if the new piece of work is taken on (Figure 8.12).

FIGURE 8.12   Reprioritizing the HR portfolio of work

## Working with a backlog

At a strategic level, people initiatives and business-as-usual services are prioritized based on business value and visualized through a portfolio of work. This high-level vision then feeds directly into team-level and project-based backlogs, where decisions on how to get things done on a day-to-day basis are made by the teams. Transparency of information is central to these ways of working, and, as we saw in Chapter 5, work is pulled from the backlog by the team based on customer value, skills and capacity.

Many Agile HR teams who now use a prioritized backlog to manage their work talk about the credibility they've gained with the wider business as a result. By using a transparent and openly shared backlog, both senior stakeholders and employees can quickly gauge where an HR team is at and what their focus is. When combined with other Agile ceremonies like internal customer demos and planning sessions, everyone from the business should be able to track the choices being made on where and how HR spend their time.

Every HR initiative should also clearly state when it is done and what the expected outcome will be, ideally specified with associated metrics and KPIs where possible. HR teams should also integrate their main KPIs with business goals and ensure that these are based on outcomes rather than just activities. For example, rather than stating that HR will deliver five sales development training programmes next year, we instead set a goal to grow the strategic customer base by 10 per cent.

Definition of Done (DoD) is also a great conversation to have with the business when prioritizing. It's often surprising how much less they need in our products and services when we test essential requirements with people from the business. HR too often wants to design something that is perfect, when the business wants something that works. Agile HR also needs to embrace the Agile feedback loop to continuously validate the value being delivered and reassess ongoing backlogs. Once slices of value are ready, they should be reviewed with stakeholders and users, to ensure work is indeed done and to check whether any improvements and updates need to be added.

By working with backlogs, HR becomes much more concrete and action oriented, and we turn our often quite fluffy topics, like develop a growth mindset or develop leaders of the future, into actual tasks which are then assessed by the associated acceptance criteria and our DoD.

## Conclusion

By clearly defining the value that each people initiative and BAU service delivers to the organization and then using this to prioritize where HR spends their time and effort, we have an opportunity to revamp our profession into a value-adding function rather than a transactional service. We encourage you to try out the tools and techniques discussed in this chapter and begin to build effective methods that help turn our never-ending HR wish-list into targeted pieces of work that deliver a shared value across the business, to our people and to the end-customer.

KEY POINTS FOR HR PROFESSIONALS

- At a strategic level, people initiatives and BAU services are prioritized based on value and visualized through an HR portfolio of work.
- The HR portfolio of work then feeds directly into team-level and project-based backlogs, where decisions on how to get things done on a day-to-day basis are made by the teams.

- The value of the people initiatives and BAU services included in the HR portfolio of work should be assessed against the different value drivers of: strategic value, enabler value, purpose-driven value, employee value and end-customer value.

- The following seven steps will help HR teams prioritize their HR portfolio of work and guide team-level backlogs:

  o  Assess business properties.

  o  Assess the people and culture landscape.

  o  Offer insights.

  o  Co-create with stakeholders.

  o  Apply prioritization tools.

  o  Sense-check the human element.

  o  Self-organize around agreed priorities.

# References

Hellström, R (2020) Interview With Josh Bersin, Global Industry Analyst, 20 January  https://joshbersin.com/  (archived at https://perma.cc/92XC-JBHZ)

Pink, D (2011) *Drive: The surprising truth about what motivates us*, Riverhead Books, New York

Richards, K (2007) *Agile project management: Running PRINCE2 projects with DSDM Atern*, Office of Government Commerce. The Stationery Office, 31 July

Ryan, R M and Deci E L (2000) Self-determination theory and the facilitation of intrinsic motivation, social development, and well-being, *American Psychologist*, 55 (1), p 68

Volini, E *et al* (2019) 2019 Global Human Capital Trends, Introduction: Leading the Social Enterprise – Reinvent With a Human Focus, *Deloitte*, 11 April www2.deloitte.com/us/en/insights/focus/human-capital-trends/2019/leading-social-enterprise.html  (archived at https://perma.cc/W5DR-VGFP)

# 09

# Agile HR toolkit: Co-creation

## Introduction

Co-creation is about truly sharing the design of our HR products and services with the wider business and building solutions together, and draws directly on design thinking and the techniques discussed in Chapter 4. It helps HR professionals and teams clearly define the business challenges they need to solve and test possible solutions before fully committing to an organizational change project or service design. It's particularly useful when HR needs to tackle big, complex, workplace problems where the answers aren't clear yet, such as diversity and inclusion or well-being. Co-creation is also a powerful way to move beyond predefined HR processes, like performance management systems and competency frameworks, and totally rethink our approach to the design of people practices and the employee experience.

While we mainly look at co-creation through the lens of design thinking in this chapter, it's good to note that the process of co-creation can happen on multiple levels for Agile HR teams. Not only does co-creation help HR truly understand the employee experience, it also helps HR guide people through organizational change more successfully because they are literally in the change with us, testing and validating the outcomes. Instead of managing people through change, they now co-create it with HR. Additionally, co-creation happens as a result of people from the business working directly in our Agile HR teams, which we'll explore further in Chapter 10. The key message here is that co-creation is not about HR having all the answers or doing all the work ourselves.

---

WHAT THEY SAY

The answer is not Agile, unless you know what the problem is.

Tracey Waters, Director of People Experience, large media and telecommunications company (Dank, 2019)

## Design thinking in HR

If we start talking to people about workplace topics such as career development and salaries, many of the answers will be shaped by personal motivations and pre-held beliefs. These views lead to strong opinions or assumptions about how these HR activities should happen within a business setting. Design thinking helps HR move beyond these competing views and consider how to develop a contextual design that suits our specific organizational values. The methods also enable HR to empathize and understand the real experience people have at work.

Design thinking helps HR challenge ingrained thinking patterns and ensures that a workplace problem is properly investigated before diving into solution mode. For example, an HR team started to plan the redesign of a whole graduate programme because an initial review of the data showed a high proportion of new graduate hires opting out between the acceptance date and the start of the graduate programme. However, by conducting deeper user research and prototyping before committing to the redesign project, the team discovered that all that was needed to fix the problem was a phone call to the graduate from their new manager before the start date. This phone call helped to make the graduate feel nurtured and wanted, and thus more likely to turn up on the start date. By using a design thinking approach and testing a hypothesis first, they were able to create a simple and inexpensive solution that removed the need to design a whole new graduate programme.

To undertake a design thinking approach, we suggest engaging people in a timeboxed design sprint or incorporating these steps into the general Agile workflow. We've found the design sprint method can be very useful for HR teams who need to separate strategic work from BAU and rapidly validate ideas before committing to a larger project sprint or product development work. A design sprint can take many forms and can be a targeted five-day sprint or even take place over several weeks, depending on the size of the project and how much of their time team members are able to commit.

For example, a global company with over 50,000 people was in the middle of a huge organizational change project and needed to upskill a large portion of their workforce in digital and client consulting capability to deliver a new type of product offering to the end-customer. Based on the current pace of the project, it was going to take at least six months to design and agree the core elements if done traditionally through hierarchical decision making, committee meetings and siloed teams. Instead, the HR leader invited 12 people from across HR and the business to commit to a six-day design sprint, as well as ring fencing a few hours with selected people from the business for user interviews, testing and feedback. Following an Agile approach, the group used the six days to explore the business challenge, extensively research the user experience, brainstorm different ideas and then test and validate alternative solutions. A key win by the end of the sprint was that HR had a series of design principles and a core product outline to move into development work that had been approved by the executive board. This meant they had essentially streamlined six months of work and validated it with a wide part of the business in a fraction of the time.

## Applying design thinking to onboarding

We'll now showcase how design thinking can be applied within HR by working through an onboarding project for a successful mid-size technology company. The project is fictitious but comprises events we have encountered at some point on real-world projects. We chose onboarding because it's a common employee experience that HR needs to improve or redesign and is a good example of how HR needs to collaborate with other functions such as IT support, facilities and communications to enable an end-to-end internal customer journey. We'll follow each step outlined in Chapter 4, which we recommend for all Agile HR work, to demonstrate how different techniques can be used at each stage to define a problem and then rapidly test and validate solutions. We encourage you to consider, and perhaps even make notes as they read, how they can apply the templates and tools outlined below within their own workplace and role.

We'll be following the design thinking steps as outlined in Figure 9.1 (taken from Chapter 4).

### Onboarding example: Scenario

The onboarding project will take place at a mid-size technology company currently in a high-growth mode, having transformed from 700 employees to 1,500 over the last 3 years. Most employees are co-located at the same head office; however, the organization encourages flexible working arrangements and many work virtually each week. The business specializes in providing technical solutions to corporate clients, and offers cloud-based software applications and implementations, CRM integrations, commercial website

FIGURE 9.1  Design thinking and Agile development

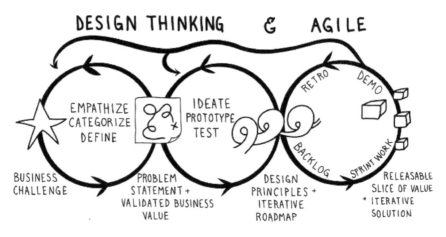

management and smaller digital tools linked to AI (artificial intelligence) and mobile applications. The current talent strategy is to pay above-market salaries to attract great talent, and they offer a range of benefits to suit a diverse mix of people, as well as a lot of attractive perks such as free lunches and bring your dog to the office. The business understands the importance of building a community of talent beyond traditional organizational boundaries and encourages employees to host meetups, tech workshops and conferences for both internal and external participants. Their mission is to prepare companies for the future through great technical solutions.

## Onboarding example: Design thinking steps

**A**  **Business challenge:** why do it in the first place?

**B**  **Empathize:** deep dive into the employee experience.

**C**  **Categorize:** discover the moments that matter.

**D**  **Define:** what is the problem we need to solve?

**E**  **Ideate:** brainstorm and challenge assumptions.

**F**  **Prototype:** bring prioritized solutions to life to test with real users.

**G**  **Test:** does it delight the customer and what slice of value will we deliver first?

We'll now work through each step, following the A–G sequence.

## A. ONBOARDING EXAMPLE: BUSINESS CHALLENGE

In this step we'll:

1 identify the problem – through an evidence-based method;

2 outline the business challenge – using a template;

3 gain sponsorship – for the subsequent design sprint.

*1. Identify the problem*    A recent employee pulse survey highlighted issues with the onboarding experience for new hires. Comments suggested that some people felt they didn't know what was expected of them when they joined, while others expressed frustration at not being able to find the right resources and connections, and felt they performed well below their potential in their first few months.

Other people data indicate that 20 per cent of new hires are leaving within the first six months, a statistically high number for the business and a real risk given the tough talent market and high salaries. Looking into the problem, the people analytics team report that this level of new hire turnover decreases the return on investment (ROI) for their talent acquisition strategy, as it takes 6–9 months for new hires to reach a high level of performance, and both recruitment costs and the return for the salaries paid to those who leave are not realized. There is also some anecdotal evidence that certain new hires have gone to a key competitor.

Additionally, the end-customer net promoter score (NPS) suggests that specific customer projects have been impacted by the early and frequent turnover of new hires. Team performance and velocity have also been negatively impacted, because existing employees take time out to recruit and mentor new hires – another indirect cost to the business. This situation has caused some negative team retrospective discussions and a few existing employees have expressed a preference not to be involved with the onboarding of new hires anymore.

The Agile HR team decided they have a potential onboarding problem and proposed a design sprint to further investigate the problem.

*2. Outline the business challenge*    Purpose: to gain buy-in for what the Agile HR team formulate as their business challenge to discuss with business stakeholders and senior leaders.

The business challenge template shown in Table 9.1 can be used to capture the business challenge and articulate the value it will bring to the business, end-customer and employees if we solve the problem.

TABLE 9.1  Business challenge template

| Business challenge | | |
|---|---|---|
| *Statement outlining the problem and the impact on the business (in the form of cost, risk and/or lost opportunity).* | | |
| Business value | End-customer value | Employee value |
| *The strategic business value realized if the problem is solved.* | *The value delivered to end-customer if the problem is solved.* | *The value delivered to employees if the problem is solved.* |
| Metrics | Metrics | Metrics |
| *How this will be measured.* | *How this will be measured.* | *How this will be measured.* |

Now, let's have a look at how we can use the business challenge template for the onboarding example (Table 9.2).

*3. Gain sponsorship*   The Agile HR team gains sponsorship to run a short, targeted design sprint as a result of their discussion on the business challenge. It's agreed that a temporary team made up of HR, IT and facilities, as well as a recent new hire and an Agile coach working within the business, will be formed to deliver the design sprint. A dedicated Scrum master and PO have also been identified, both of which will continue in the role if the project moves into the next phase of product development following the design sprint.

> ### HR TOP TIPS
> *Co-creation tips: Business challenge*
>
> - While HR professionals may recognize the onboarding example above, it's important to remember that every business challenge is unique and contextual, and that while we might think of some great immediate solutions, it's vital to explore facts and figures first.
> - It's crucial to connect our people and cultural initiatives with business metrics to gain the necessary investment and sponsorship – for example, we should move beyond simply analysing and reacting to the engagement survey, which was the starting point above, and instead build on this to formulate a clear outline of the problem and the subsequent impact on business success.

- To have a seat at the table we need to think like a scientist and use an evidence-based method to enrich our professional view with people data, business metrics and market research (learn more in Chapter 11).

- Co-creation helps HR understand the pain points of business leaders and teams and allows us to identify where a competitive advantage might be gained for the organization through a people and culture initiative.

TABLE 9.2  Using the business challenge template for the onboarding example

**Business challenge**

*Our onboarding experience is failing to delight our people and retain new hires.*

*Our current high turnover of new hires is negatively impacting business success through a lower end-customer NPS and a failure to realize ROI for our talent acquisition strategy.*

*By reducing the turnover of new hires by 50 per cent the business will save an estimated $ 1.3 million in costs related to salary loss, indirect and direct recruitment and onboarding costs, as well as reduced team performance.*

| Business value | End-customer value | Employee value |
|---|---|---|
| *ROI realized for the talent acquisition strategy and a decrease in the time it takes for new hires to achieve optimal performance positively impacts business results.* | *A great onboarding practice will delight the end-customer by maintaining expected delivery and performance levels, as well as boost innovation through fresh ideas.* | *New hires feel supported, able and excited to contribute immediately to team performance.* *Existing employees enjoy onboarding activities and seek them out as a form of on-the-job development and an important contribution to team performance.* |
| Metrics | Metrics | Metrics |
| *Quality of hire, customer feedback, time to performance, onboarding feedback and team feedback.* | *Forecasting accuracy (teams must be able to estimate the impact of onboarding on their velocity), end-customer feedback, product team feedback.* | *New hire retention, new hire feedback and recruitment referrals by existing employees.* |

## B. ONBOARDING EXAMPLE: EMPATHIZE

Next, we need to deep dive into the users' experiences and explore the problem from multiple perspectives.

In this step we'll:

1 conduct user interviews, using human-centred questions;

2 build user personas, using a template;

3 map the employee experience, using a template;

4 undertake early leaver research, to explore reasons for exiting;

5 observe, to assess people in action.

*1. User interviews*    The team discussed and brainstormed a collection of human-centred user interview questions to ask 25 real users about their onboarding experience. The users were a mixture of recent new starters, existing employees and people in roles such as Scrum masters and business leaders. The aim of the interviews was to explore the thoughts, emotions and motivations of the users to identify pain points, moments that matter and why people made certain choices or behaved in specific ways.

Example questions for a new hire user interview:

• What happened on your first day/week/month at the company?

• How did you feel at this time?

• What were the drivers behind these feelings?

• What made the biggest impact on you when you first joined the company?

• Why was this?

• What were the resources and connections you sought out when you first started to work in your new team?

• What support did you receive from your team members or buddy that made the biggest impact on you?

*2. Build user personas*    Through some initial user research, the team identify five key user types and build personas for the onboarding project, which are further validated by testing the information compiled in the real world with people who represent these internal customer groups.

The template shown in Figure 9.2 can be used to capture a persona profile.

Now, let's look at how we can use the persona profile for our onboarding example. Figure 9.3 shows a persona created for 'Sonia the New Hire Millennial'.

Figure 9.4 is a persona created for 'Stefan the Existing Employee'.

FIGURE 9.2  Persona template

**Persona Profile**

| Goals | Frustrations |
|---|---|
| 2 personal goals<br>Who do they want to be? | 2 challenges, roadblocks and pain points |

| Attributes | Needs |
|---|---|
| 3 keywords to describe personal characteristics | 2 needs in life<br>What's essential? |

**Name**
Fictionalize it

**Job**
Be specific

**Age**
Number not range

**Quote**
A short statement/saying that sums up their persona

**Personal background**
Mini life story

FIGURE 9.3  Persona profile for Sonia

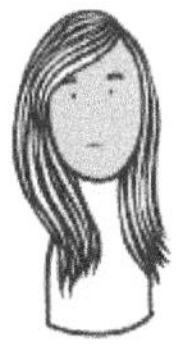

**Persona Profile**

| Goals | Frustrations |
|---|---|
| To own her own home by 30. To be a director by 35. | Rules that don't make sense to her. Boredom and repetition. Unfairness. |

| Attributes | Needs |
|---|---|
| Sociable, hardworking and values driven. | A sense of belonging to a team. To feel her work is making a difference. |

**Name**
Sonia

**Job**
UX designer

**Age**
26

**Quote**
Life is too short for bad design

**Personal background**
Moved to London last year and now shares a house with her flatmate, Gary, and his Shih Tzu, Milly. Sonia completed her Master's during her 2-year graduate programme at her previous company and is now excited about her first big career move.

FIGURE 9.4  Persona profile for Stefan

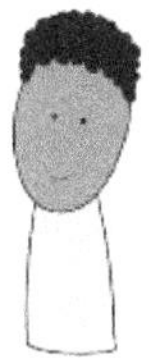

**Persona Profile**

| Goals | Frustrations |
|---|---|
| To be known for developing great teams. To become an Agile transformation coach. | People who aren't team players. Micro-management from senior leaders. |

| Attributes | Needs |
|---|---|
| People person, great listener and direct. | A sense of contributing to the wider organizational purpose and daily variety in his job. |

**Name**
Stefan

**Job**
Scrum master

**Age**
35

**Quote**
Agile is a way of life

**Personal background**
Been a Scrum master for the business for 3 years now and ready to take up his next role. Has received some great feedback in that time for onboarding new starters into the different teams across the organization.

*3. Map the employee experience*   To investigate the user experience further, the team mapped out the current onboarding journey for each of the five personas based on the feedback and information collected from the user interviews. The team also invited a group of people representing each persona type to validate the findings

The template shown in Figure 9.5 can be used to map the employee experience.

FIGURE 9.5  Journey mapping template

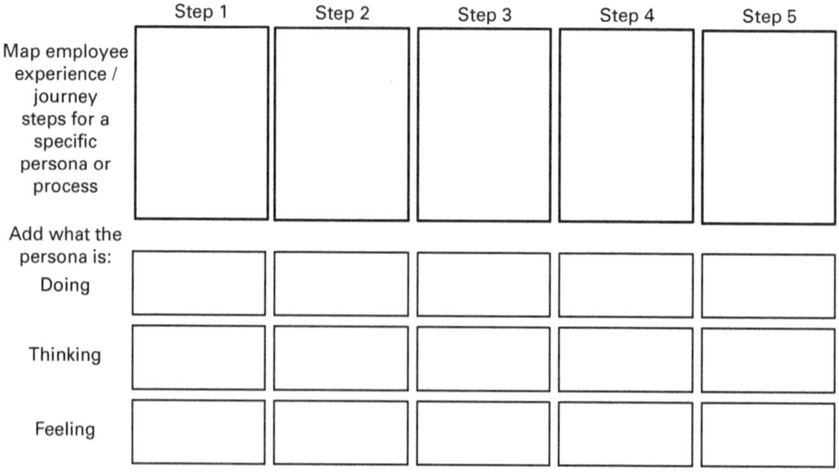

HR TOP TIP

Follow these steps when using the above template:

1  **Map out the process or journey steps**, for example the journey a new person has during their first week in the workplace. Record text in step 1, for example 'persona waits at reception for an hour when first arrives on day 1 because they're not correctly recorded on employee system', followed by step 2 etc.

2  After recording text for each step in the journey, explore the personas' experience using the **doing, thinking** and **feeling** boxes underneath, as follows:

a. Write text to describe what the persona is **doing** at each step in the journey. This needs to be in the form of an action, for example for step 1 the persona is 'sitting and waiting at reception'.

b. Once *all* the doing steps are completed, write text to describe what the persona is **thinking**, in the form of a question, at each step in the journey. For example, for step 1 the persona is thinking 'why don't they know I'm starting today?'

c. Once *all* thinking steps are completed, write text to describe what the persona is **feeling** at each step in the journey. For example, for step 1 the persona is feeling 'disappointed and frustrated'.

Once all the above steps are completed, we can now assess the full experience for this persona along the employee journey or process. We also suggest recording insights and ideas separately as they arise to review at the end.

*4. Early leaver research*    The team contacts 10 people who left the company within their first six months to gain alternative perspectives and challenge any pre-set assumptions about why people are leaving. To make it as easy as possible, they contacted people via LinkedIn and interviewed the first 10 that responded over video or phone.

*5. Observe*    Finally, to further challenge any pre-held beliefs, some of the design sprint team members spend a day observing new hires in action and record their findings against set criteria.

HR TOP TIPS
*Co-creation tips: Empathize*

- Remember, when we research the user's experience, we're looking for pain points, moments that matter and the problems to solve for our people and business.
- It's also about highlighting what is working well so that we can build on strengths.
- Personas are a great tool for HR because they help us move beyond the standard categories of 'employee' and 'manager' and get to know different groups of our workforce so that we can start to personalize our products and services.

- When working with personas, many HR professionals get worried about not capturing all the different and unique aspects of people, but we find that 8–10 personas are enough to cover the most important employee or user needs.

- Personas allow HR to capture the main differences and similarities between the different employee groups and make decisions on what features should be included first and what might need to wait until a later iteration.

- Challenge biases and ensure that the personas reflect a good level of diversity by covering different nationalities, cultures, religions, sexual orientations and physical abilities to test our employee experience from multiple perspectives.

- And... we urge you to test and validate all personas with *real* people! This can be done by showing the personas to people and asking, 'are your needs covered if we meet the needs set out in these personas?' Please note, they won't find a 100 per cent matching persona.

- Many Agile HR teams now use a library of personas to guide all their project work and to constantly sense-check the design of HR processes and systems.

- Once we've explored the current employee journey and experience, an HR team can use the same techniques to map out the ideal employee journey and experience on which to base the new design.

- The methods listed above are not new, with most marketing and design teams having used these techniques for some time now.

- Good empathizing skills are essential if HR is to understand and co-create a great employee experience. We encourage HR professionals to learn more by seeking out examples in other parts of the business or wider consumer market.

By the end of the empathize step, HR should have a solid and in-depth understanding of the problem and how this shapes different employee experiences across the business.

### C. ONBOARDING EXAMPLE: CATEGORIZE

Now, we need to sort and categorize all the information we've collected.
    In this step we'll:

1 collate the user research – and identify patterns;

2 discover moments that matter – to help us prioritize the most important problems to solve first.

*1. Collate the user research*   The team used a saturate and group method to help unpack all the user research, by placing all the relevant information up on a wall, followed by a discussion on the themes and patterns that emerged. Key findings included:

- It's assumed that new hires require an onboarding day where they get an overview of the business from all the different department heads, but most don't find this useful and are often overwhelmed by the information.

- It's also assumed that the intranet is the primary tool used to find resources, but new hires don't find it intuitive and tend to ask others for help instead.

- The team discover that the common approach taken in the organization is to rotate new hires across three different teams in their first six months, which helps people build a deeper understanding of how the organization works but also greatly unsettles team relationships.

- A positive is the strong cultural connection that new hires form with the organization's vision and purpose, which the team discovered begins at the recruitment stage and becomes stronger as the new starter onboards, and even people who left early still believed in the company's mission.

- Another find was the assumption that new hires are a 'blank sheet' and need to be educated and instructed, whereas many new starters felt they came equipped with great experience and knowledge from their previous roles, which wasn't always appreciated and sometimes remained untapped for the first few months.

*2. Discover moments that matter*   To discover the moments that matter for each persona in the onboarding experience, the team reviewed the journey steps they had recorded previously (using the employee journey map from Figure 9.5) and used a dot voting method, where each person placed three dot votes against the moment (or specific journey step) that they thought mattered the most for the persona (all three votes could go on one moment along the journey or be shared across several). Key moments identified included:

- For Sonia the New Hire Millennial the moments that matter are:
  - Day 2 when she's informed that her laptop won't be ready for another week and because there aren't enough spare desks where her team are based, she'll need to sit in a different area for a few days while it's sorted.

o   End of week 2 when Sonia starts to feel her previous experience isn't being appreciated by other team members and she could be contributing more.

- For Stefan the Existing Employee the moments that matter are:

o   End of week 4 when a new hire is rotated to a different team just as they're beginning to excel in their new role and contribute to team goals.

o   End of week 1 when Stefan has an opportunity to coach the new hire and further his own mentoring and coaching skills.

---

HR TOP TIPS
*Co-creation tips: Categorize*

- What we are trying to do here is find the most important problems within the overall employee experience that might influence business outcomes and people's behaviour.

- Be sure to tap into both quantitative and qualitative data to unpack all the relevant themes and patterns.

- In the categorize step we need to use critical thinking skills to challenge any assumptions held at the start of the design sprint, and truly immerse ourselves in the reality of the problem.

---

Categorize is a crucial step that allows HR to make evidence-based decisions and clearly justify why we should focus effort and time on specific organizational change projects.

### D. ONBOARDING EXAMPLE: DEFINE

Now that we've categorized our research and made sense of the findings, we need to clearly define the problem and begin to prioritize the key areas of focus.

In this step we'll:

1   formulate the problem statement – and validate the business value;

2   agree design principles – to guide future development work.

*1. Formulate the problem statement*   Based on all their findings so far and the metrics outlined in the initial business challenge, the team formulates a series of problem statements to showcase and discuss with business stakeholders and senior leaders.

TABLE 9.3  Problem statement template

| User | User need | Surprising insight |
|---|---|---|
| Name the user/ persona | Describe what they need | The surprising reason why they need this in their work and life |

TABLE 9.4  Using the problem statement template for the onboarding example

| User | User need | Surprising insight |
|---|---|---|
| Sonia the New Hire Millennial | Enabler: To be equipped with the right tools from day 1.Strategic: That fellow team members value my previous experience and skills when I join. | So that Sonia can delight the end-customer immediately in her job. As measured by team feedback, performance metrics and end-customer NPS. |
| Stefan the Existing Employee | Enabler: To strengthen his skills through the development of the new hires. Strategic: To achieve high team performance within a month when a new starter joins. | To get a kick out of developing others and celebrate great team results. As measured by team velocity, team feedback, performance metrics and end-customer NPS. |

For the onboarding example, the team has narrowed the scope and focused on the problem areas that hold the biggest potential impact for the business.

Now let's look at how we can use the problem statement template for the onboarding example (Table 9.4).

2. *Agree design principles*   The team also formulates the following design principles based on the themes identified in the user research and feedback received from business stakeholders. These design principles guide all future development work:

- Nurtures trust.
- Builds a community.
- Enables people to contribute to team performance immediately.

It's vital to ensure that HR has prioritized the most important problems to solve for the business in the define step, and the ones that will realize the most value once solved, before moving into ideation. That way, we know we're focusing our energy and efforts in the right area.

### E. ONBOARDING EXAMPLE: IDEATE

Now that we've identified the most important problems to solve for the business, we need to explore all the possible solutions through positive and interactive ideation.

In this step we'll:

1 brainstorm – to think out sides of the box;

2 assess ideas – using impact versus effort template;

3 identify slices of value – to assess where and what to prototype and test first.

*1. Brainstorm*    The team set up an ideation session and to encourage out of the box thinking they invite some example end-users to join them, as well as book a creative working space in another part of the office. The group begins with silent brainstorming where people write their ideas on sticky notes before sharing and discussing with others. They also challenge themselves to include ideas that have no budget constraints first, followed by ideas based on a very low budget.

**2. Assess ideas**   Once the team has sufficiently brainstormed, they need to converge on the best ideas to move into the prototype stage. The team can use the impact and effort grid to do this.

The impact versus effort grid template shown in Figure 9.6 can be used to assess ideas.

Now, let's look at how we can use the impact versus effort grid template for the onboarding example (Figure 9.7).

FIGURE 9.6   Impact versus effort grid

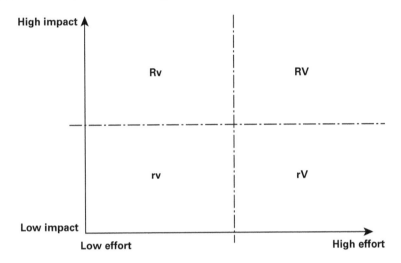

FIGURE 9.7   Impact versus effort grid: onboarding example

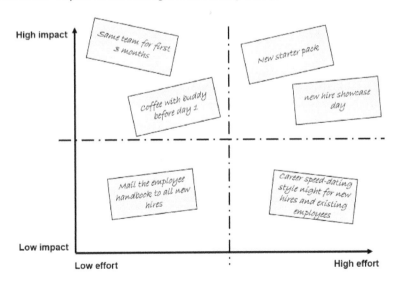

From Figure 9.7 and associated discussion, the team prioritizes the following ideas to prototype:

- **High impact and high effort** – designing and sourcing a new starter kit for new hires to receive at the start of day 1.
- **High impact and high effort** – organizing a new hire showcase day each quarter where new hires share their portfolios and skills, talk about personal interests and passions, and connect with existing employees who can offer support in the areas of the business where they want to develop knowledge further.
- **High impact and low effort** – new hires commit to the same team for the first three months before rotating.
- **High impact and low effort** – coffee meeting between buddy and new hire before day 1.

*3. Identify slices of value*   The team also starts to explore where best to start with the prototype based on what will deliver the most value first, as well as factors like capacity, resources and time available. For example, they explore whether to focus on just one role in the business first versus prototyping the solutions for the whole business straight away. Following much discussion, and reviewing the initial metrics from the business challenge, the team decides to prototype solutions for onboarding people in the product development area first, because this has the biggest potential impact on the end-customer and is the fastest-growing part of the business. They also decide to prioritize getting the new starter pack prototyped before spending time on team development, because this allows a new hire to begin work immediately.

---

HR TOP TIPS
*Co-creation tips: Ideate*

- Often, we find that HR overthinks the solution required and favours large programme roll-outs that are centrally designed, when great results can come from ideas that are simple and inexpensive to execute.
- We encourage HR professionals to open up the ideation session and invite people from across the business to contribute and participate in the brainstorm.

- Another great way to achieve this step is by hosting a hackathon event, where teams of volunteers sign up to design, prototype and test their best ideas within a set period, for example one day.

- Constraints are important when ideating. Sometimes we want to ideate with no constraints to push our thinking, while at other times it's useful to introduce parameters like budget and time to encourage people to truly think outside the box.

- Remember to use the other prioritization techniques outlined in the ideate step in Chapter 4.

Ideation should be a fun and energetic step that helps HR professionals break the problem down into achievable slices of value and land on a collection of possible solutions to prototype.

### F. ONBOARDING EXAMPLE: PROTOTYPE

Now we've got some great ideas, but will they work in reality? To find out, we move into the prototype step.

In this step we'll:

1 build prototypes – using different formats provided in Chapter 4.

*1. Build prototypes* Prototyping needs to be practical and the design will reflect how many users we can involve, as well as factors like time, capacity and budget. Based on these limitations, the team decided to create two prototypes that they could build quickly at almost no cost and showcase immediately, as well as two other prototypes that were more complex to design and required a bigger commitment from the wider business to test:

- **Mock-up/New starter pack** – they create a mock-up of the pack out of cardboard cut-outs and other craft materials to demonstrate to stakeholders and users. They also compile a report on related costs, procurement needs and design elements for the pack. While doing the mock-up they realize that everything, including the laptop, can fit into a backpack, which is also a great way to deliver it to the new starter on day 1. The team wonder whether this could even be couriered to the new starter before day 1, and cost this out as well, just in case.

- **Pop-up store/New hire showcase day** – new hires from the previous quarter are asked to self-organize and host a showcase meetup to share experiences and skills with team members, product owners and Scrum masters.

- **Storyboard/New hires committing to the same team for the first three months before rotating** – they storyboard the first three months of a new starter's experience in the same team to present through a short user and stakeholder demo.

- **Real-user validation/Coffee meeting between buddy and new hire before day 1** – they organize and plan five coffee meetings between buddies and new hires starting within the coming month.

---

HR TOP TIPS

*Co-creation tips: Prototype*

- Ditch the slide pack and aim to bring the idea to life by making it tangible and real for the user. This can be tricky though, because a lot of our HR solutions are experiences and linked to behavioural change rather than a physical product.

- For these reasons, we've found prototypes using role play or storyboarding can work well for HR design sprints as they help to place the solution in context.

- Ensure that we clearly define and document the hypothesis we want to test as we build the prototype.

- Prototyping actually helps us discover if something is possible or not, as illustrated in the above example when the team discovered that all the equipment in the new starter pack could fit into a backpack.

- We encourage HR professionals to build several prototypes to test at the same time and in different parts of the business.

- And remember – we should be slightly embarrassed by our prototype; if not, we've left it too late to test. it's not about being shiny and perfect. it's a prototype!

---

Often, less is more when it comes to prototyping and we're always surprised by the innovative and creative methods Agile HR teams use to bring their designs to life.

### G. ONBOARDING EXAMPLE: TEST

Now we need to test the prototype. It's good to note that testing is a distinct step, and not the same as prototyping. It's about thinking like a scientist to evaluate the impact of the solution created.

In this step we'll:

**1** test prototypes – against set criteria and hypothesis.

*1. Test prototypes*   The team test each of the prototypes listed above and assesses the results against the three areas of business value, end-customer value and employee value. The team also define a hypothesis to test for each prototype. Based on the user feedback and stakeholder input, they decide on the following:

- **High employee value/New starter pack** – tested against the hypothesis that new hires can start working immediately on day 1 with the right equipment. People loved it! Though senior leaders wanted to limit costs and set a specific budget for the initiative, it was decided to move this into development and that the team should spend a week iterating how the necessary equipment can be sourced and put together. The intention is then to trial it in the product development area for three months and assess results further. The courier idea was put on hold, owing to cost.

- **High business value/The newcomer meetup** – tested against the hypothesis that new hires were more connected to the business. This was considered a great success, and the new hires were keen to impress their new colleagues with an energetic meetup. In the meetup the new hires also used improvisation theatre to offer development ideas and constructive feedback about the organization and its culture, which received a lot of laughs, not to mention triggering a few debates afterwards. The learning from the event was that it should remain as a self-organizing activity for new hires, with the format left open each time. However, more people from beyond the immediate team members for new hires should be encouraged to attend, as well as senior leaders. For this reason, it should run for a maximum of 1.5 hours and a catering budget was also set.

- **Mixed end-customer value/New hires committing to a team for the first three months before rotating** – tested against the hypothesis that a new hire reached optimal performance faster by working in a permanent team. While the users who tested the prototype saw benefits in this organizational change, they were concerned about the impact on the need to move people around based on project and end-customer needs. As a result, the design sprint team was asked to ideate and prototype other potential solutions that could help the business teams develop relationships with new hires, as well as enable new hires to lead their own development, rather than rely on the Scrum masters.

- **Medium employee and business value/Coffee meeting between buddy and new hire before day 1** – tested against the hypothesis that a new hire was better equipped to start work immediately on day 1, the coffee meeting was seen as a great idea that was easy to make happen. While setting up the real-life coffee meetings the team discovered it's much easier to simply give the buddy the contact details of the new hire and let them arrange the meeting directly. All stakeholders agreed that the team should start with this initiative, as it was such a quick win, and then they could move on to the new starter kit in their prioritized backlog.

---

HR TOP TIPS
*Co-creation tips: Test*

- It's important to remember the Agile mantra that no product survives its first contact with a real user and be ready for tests to fail.
- Be conscious of the valuable time we ask from the users and stakeholders when we test prototypes and adjust the design accordingly – many solutions can be tested in a simple and inexpensive way and we should only involve a large number of people if the potential impact of the solution justifies the investment of time.
- Testing is all about validating our MVP (minimum viable product) which we can then build on further once we move into the development stage.
- Be sure to test the prototype with a diverse mix of users (this doesn't need to be a large number, but at least a few people that represent different user types), and seek out extreme views to challenge thinking, as their feedback will help to further develop the solution and turn it into an MLP (minimum lovable product).
- Both the users and designers learn the realities of the potential solution by testing, and some of the best solutions come from the feedback discussion as people further validate how to make something happen in the real world.
- Validate the tests against hypotheses, the metrics and the criteria established in the business challenge and problem statement stages.

By the end of the testing step HR needs to know… is it a go or a no go?

## Conclusion

Some HR professionals fear that design thinking is too time consuming, but we should keep in mind that testing ideas before expending significant resources will save a great deal of time, money and stress in the future. The true power of co-creation comes in the partnerships HR forges with our people and stakeholders when building solutions together, and the awesome feeling when an HR product or service delights our internal customers. There are lots of great design thinking tools available (as outlined in Chapter 4) and we encourage you to further develop these techniques by adding some of these methods to your Agile for HR toolbox.

---

KEY POINTS FOR HR PROFESSIONALS

- Co-creation happens on multiple levels:
- It's about using design thinking techniques to truly understand the employee experience and rapidly prototype and test solutions. It helps HR guide people through organizational change more successfully because they test and validate the decisions made. It's also about people from the wider business working directly in our Agile HR teams or as the users who test and validate the solutions.

- Design thinking helps HR challenge ingrained thinking patterns and ensures that a workplace problem is properly investigated before diving into solution mode.

- We suggest engaging people in a timeboxed *design sprint* to undertake the design thinking steps outlined in this chapter.

- Design thinking is not just an effective way of working, it can also be lots of fun and is a great way to energize the HR team.

- Remember, prototyping and testing are very different from running a pilot and we need to be ready to learn from the tests that fail just as much as the tests that succeed.

---

# Reference

Dank, N (2019) Interview with Tracey Waters, Director of People Experience at Sky, and Agile HR Pioneer [Blog], *The Agile HR Community*, 29 July www.agilehrcommunity.com/agilehr-community-blog/interview-with-tracey-waters-from-sky (archived at https://perma.cc/55WE-FX7P)

# 10

# Agile for HR toolkit: Agile teams and Agile HR operating models

## Introduction

When it comes to transforming the HR function, it's important to find a model of working that best suits our context and reflects our team size, composition, organizational values and types of employee. In this chapter, we'll explore different Agile HR operating models to help guide HR's approach, as well as offer ideas on how to get started. As mentioned before, it's crucial to view this as an evolutionary journey rather than a structural implementation, and to embrace each stage in the team development cycle as an opportunity to experiment and learn. It's definitely not about getting it right the first time, and even Agile HR teams that are several years into their transformation are still testing out new methods of how to collaborate and enhance performance.

The Agile evolution of the HR operating model is truly exciting for our profession. It heralds a new level of sophistication in how we partner and collaborate with the business because, as discussed in Chapter 9, we now co-create organizational change *with* our people, rather than implement our processes and products *on to* them. In this chapter we'll also look at this concept of how people from other parts of the business are becoming active members of our Agile HR teams and reshaping the operating model.

The emphasis on the customer experience in Agile is also leading some HR functions to explore how to build end-to-end accountability for their internal employee services. This approach is similar in design to how the business is structuring around end-to-end value streams, with the aim of delivering a product from conception through to the end-customer in a coordinated and seamless way. A key aspect of this evolution within HR is looking at how we deliver a more joined-up service that combines our work with other functions such as finance, marketing, IT support and facilities. The result would be a new way of working that has the potential to transform the whole concept of back-office support within organizations.

## End of the Ulrich model

For the past 20 years the Ulrich model has been synonymous with the functional design and structure of HR. Inspired by a strategic drive within business in the mid-1990s, and the aim of achieving competitive advantage by separating strategic work from administrative work, Dave Ulrich set out a vision on how this could look within HR through his book *Human Resource Champions* (Ulrich, 1996). Since then, structural interpretations of Ulrich's approach have led to most HR departments being characterized by a three-pillar model made up of strategic HR business partners facing into the business, centres of expertise housing HR topic specialists, and shared services overseeing transactional operations, which may even be outsourced.

Fuelled by the goals of efficiency and standardization, the Ulrich model helped to transform HR from a function based on personnel and administrative tasks into a department that was a more effective partner in talent attraction, development and management. The problem, however, is that the model hasn't seen HR become a true strategic partner, and as Ulrich himself now advocates, add value to the organization by helping to shape the future direction and capability of the business (Ulrich, 2018).

One of the main reasons why the Ulrich model limited HR's impact was the HR business partner bottleneck (Roper, 2016), which happened when delivering products and services into the organization. First, because the centres of expertise were not deemed client facing, they tended to design solutions in isolation from the wider business. It was then up to the HR business partners to implement these solutions, despite often not being involved in the actual design or holding the same level of expertise. This delivery model also led to large, company-wide roll-outs of new shiny HR products that sometimes took months to develop, without any real validation with the end-user until implementation.

Second, because business partners were generally aligned with the business structure and linked to individual functions, they often became frustrated by a sense of reinventing the wheel owing to the need to constantly react to real-time managerial issues, rather than solve the bigger, more strategic issues. This situation was often exacerbated by many HR business partners coming from a background of HR administration and advisory services, which meant they often found it hard to move beyond the operational side of the job and develop the strategic capability necessary to be successful.

Most of these problems can be attributed back to an HR operating model made up of lots of single-point topic owners, such as recruitment versus talent, or generalists versus specialists, and everyone owning an individual part of the overall strategic agenda. What was worse was that sometimes these structural silos harnessed negative power relationships and a 'get off my turf' mentality between different HR roles where people thought they owned certain HR topics or specific relationships with senior executives.

The impact of this disconnect between the different pillars of the Ulrich model was also evident in the shared services area. While these teams would administer most of the HR processes and systems, the ownership and therefore any potential redesign sat with the centres of expertise. This meant they were often unable to influence the delivery of their own work. Adding to this was the fact that shared services were customer facing and therefore often received most of the feedback from employees and managers on what needed to be improved when it came to the HR products and services. However, because this feedback wasn't usually tracked in a systematic way, they lacked the data or an ability to partner with the process owners to make the necessary process improvements.

Interestingly, the Ulrich model almost became a benchmark or an assumed best practice for all HR teams no matter their size or the goals of the function. For example, even small HR teams with fewer than 10 people would copy the model, and rather than whole teams owning different processes, it would fall to one person – a situation that often led to each person trying to get their own project done, though generally requiring the contribution of everyone in the team to achieve this, and as such there would be a lot of work happening but little progress made.

The good news is that Agile HR represents the end of the Ulrich model silos in HR. In the same way that Agile teams work in the business, Agile HR brings different HR specialisms and topic owners together in the form of multi-skilled and multi-functional teams. Now, HR roles like reward, recruitment, learning and development, and talent collaborate as a collective and tackle business problems in a holistic way, rather than through project groups made up of single-point topic owners. Also, instead of tasks being pushed down onto people as a result of predetermined roles or as dictated by a central centre of expertise, work is pulled by the team themselves, based on the definition of value and people's capability.

## Agile HR cadence

Another essential element of how Agile HR teams work is a new cadence or rhythm that they follow. Up until now, HR has primarily worked with an annual cycle, sometimes peppered with half-year or quarterly check-ins. Many of our processes, such as performance, reward and career development, also follow this annual timeframe and are increasingly out of touch with the shorter business cycles required for organizational agility. As shown in Chapter 5, the Agile feedback loop embraces a much shorter timeframe and asks HR teams to check in and re-plan at least monthly, with many teams working in one- or two-week cycles.

However, it would be wrong to assume that Agile HR teams match the same cadence and structure as Agile teams in software development. Instead, we tend to see Agile HR teams adapt the methods to better suit the type of work HR undertakes. For example, generally Agile HR teams use Kanban to visualize and manage everyday tasks because HR always has a certain amount of BAU to get done. Most then combine Kanban with short targeted sprints, using Scrum techniques and design thinking, to innovate, prototype and deliver strategic people initiatives. Agile HR teams also use daily stand-ups, but these are often more like daily operational check-ins, rather than a discussion focused on one specific project or sprint. Also Finally, while we recommend focusing on one strategic project at a time, Agile HR teams often work across several initiatives at the same time. This approach is also different from how Agile teams in software development tend to focus on the continuous development of only one product.

## Prioritization and transparency

As we've already learnt, Agile demands that HR leaders and teams ruthlessly prioritize and plan more than ever before. For example, Tracey Waters, Director of People Experience at a large media and telecommunications company (Dank, 2019a), feels she now applies far more precision and discipline in her Agile HR leadership role. Tracey talks about the need to pay attention to the mission and goals, as well as what to release and in what order. To do this, she constantly works with the product owners and Scrum masters in her teams to ensure both rigour of thought and clarity of direction. As Tracey explains, 'it can't be "let's just sprint"', and every piece of work needs to have a clear definition of value before being committed to the backlog.

In another Agile HR example, at a company called Sky Betting and Gaming, the team members talk about the power of saying no when prioritizing work, and that to truly deliver value it's important to clarify what HR won't be working on just as much as what they will (Dank, 2019b). This is often very challenging for HR teams to begin with, because HR always wants to make everyone happy and often ends up saying yes to everything on the wish-list.

Working transparently is also a big change for HR teams when embracing Agile. Up until now, a lot of HR work has been assumed to be secret or classified, and in some organizations HR even sat behind controlled-access security doors. While we don't advocate openly sharing details of a workplace grievance or employee complaint, most other HR work can be openly shared with the wider business. If there is something particularly sensitive, we advise using code names for the tasks that sit on the Kanban or Scrum board, but otherwise, by sharing what we are working on, HR becomes accepted as another part of the business, rather than being perceived as a secret, compliance-driven function.

## Agile HR release planning

Release planning is another area where we've seen the need for adapting Agile practices to the specific needs of HR. The main difference is that HR is generally able to update the people practices and systems in an organization only a couple of times a year, whereas many Agile teams in software development aim to release customer updates weekly or daily. The reasons are that HR product releases normally include a large amount of communication, the need to educate people, and they are generally linked to desired behavioural changes, which naturally take a period of time to achieve. For example, HR can't release an update to the performance management process every month because time is needed for people to adapt to the new way of communicating and giving feedback. Of course, some digital products that HR release, such as intranet pages or external recruitment websites, can be updated following a more continuous cycle, but most other products require a planned and managed release.

It's wise to also consider the impact HR releases have on the ability of other parts of the business to get their own work done. Some situations may be made worse if process changes or system updates are introduced at the same time as other support functions. It's not uncommon to hear business leaders say they can't get their 'real work' done because they're too busy implementing instructions or procedures issued by back-office teams. To ensure clarity and coordination for the business units receiving HR products, HR release planning therefore needs to be synced with other support teams, such as internal communications, compliance and IT support. It's also important to align HR releases with the business cycle and not overwhelm business teams during periods of high workload, for example during times when a high volume of end-customer sales is expected or when certain teams work towards set deadlines, like finance at the end of the tax year. This more coordinated approach to release planning is quite different from how HR has worked previously, but is a great way to ensure alignment with the working patterns and needs of the wider organization.

## New roles and skills

With the introduction of new ways of working comes the need to develop new roles and skills within Agile HR teams. The first aspect to consider is the impact of T-shaped people and teams, as set out in Chapter 5. In Agile HR, teams equate to people holding a breadth of organizational and HR topic experience, so they can work across a range of different business challenges, as well as developing specialisms that reflect experience, personal interests and acquired skills.

For instance, some team members begin to develop skills, such as coding, because they've had to previously source these skills from elsewhere and the team can work faster if the skill is in the team on a permanent basis. Additionally, Agile HR teams are hiring people with a different type of background, such as marketing or graphic design, to further strengthen the T-shape. However, it's not always necessary to have these specific skills in the Agile HR team on a permanent basis. Instead, some HR functions are building a community of specialists that they can tap into as and when the work demands (Ingham, 2019). This community might be sourced from the wider business but may also include freelancers and trusted suppliers from the wider economy. For example, we know of a team that invites market-leading experts to join timeboxed sprints on specific topics, such as a design thinking expert to help lead a career development design sprint or a marketing expert to contribute to an internal communications project.

As Agile HR teams evolve, we're starting to see HR professionals take up the roles of product owner, Scrum master or Agile coach. Indeed, people with an HR background often make great Scrum masters and Agile coaches in other parts of the business as well, owing to their interpersonal skills and ability to influence behavioural change. For example, the coaching and team development aspects of the HR business partner role lend themselves nicely to those of the Scrum master, and we're also seeing some HR business partners become a type of Agile coach and take a lead on the organizational design and development aspects of Agile transformation.

---

CASE STUDY
*Agile HR at Sky Betting and Gaming*

A great example of how Agile is evolving the skills and roles of HR professionals is a People Experience team at Sky Betting and Gaming. The team contains former HR business partners who now work together as an Agile squad and cover a wider remit of the organization, rather than operating as individuals serving just one function of the business. What they've discovered is they're able to deliver more value together and have a greater impact on the whole organization as a result. This outcome also helped some of the individuals overcome their initial concerns about losing their trusted relationships with the senior leaders and teams with whom they previously worked closely. Instead, they've found they now have more relationships across the business, and while they don't work as closely with some people day to day, they're enjoying opportunities that weren't available to them before, and are also building a more holistic knowledge of the overall business. The team also has a member with no HR background at all, who was previously an engineering manager in the Tech function. They've found that this person is an invaluable asset who has helped the team accelerate their Agile practices, despite not holding the same level of knowledge in the specific HR topics that the team covers. What is also interesting about the model at Sky Betting and Gaming is that they didn't achieve this structure immediately, and it reflects several years of iteration and testing. The case study demonstrates that it's important to view the design of an Agile HR operating model as constituting emergent change, and teams need to discover their own unique approach over time.

SOURCE Dank (2019b)

---

## Delivering end-to-end people experience

It's perhaps unsurprising to see the focus on customer centricity in Agile begin to also impact the shape of Agile HR teams and operating models. Similar to how brands are expressing the customer journey and mapping out end-to-end value chains for their products or services within the business, Agile HR looks at how to deliver a coordinated and interlinked service based on the employee journey. For example, how do we link up with other teams like IT, finance and communications to create a seamless experience for our people that not only enriches the experience of work but also helps people get the work done?

This trend has led to many HR teams beginning to use the title of People Experience as opposed to HR, with some social media posts now even expressing the term as #PX, in honour of its user experience (#UX) roots. This change is also linked to the goal of achieving competitive advantage through the culture and employee brand of the organization. These trends have led to some Agile HR teams now viewing people experience as their overall product, which they continuously improve for their internal customers by releasing features and updates across the whole people strategy, from onboarding and talent development through to topics like reward, employee benefits and corporate social responsibility.

For example, a UK-based bank has translated the approach they use within the business to design their end-customer journeys into HR, with the aim of delivering a more end-to-end employee experience. The organization has now mapped out 11 employee journeys and applied design thinking, alongside Agile working methods, to explore the pain points experienced by employees and to redesign the back-office processes to improve the overall journey. While some of these employee journeys include the more obvious topics such as performance and career development, they also include experiences like travel and expenses, which involve other support functions like finance aligning their processes with HR (Dank, 2019c).

---

WHAT THEY SAY

One of the things I've noticed during the last few years, and that I am finding out in the Josh Bersin Academy, is that HR was designed as a vertical profession where you were a compensation specialist, or a recruiter or a learning and development (L&D) specialist, or you were a business partner. Well, these roles are now becoming completely blurred in an Agile organization, where you are co-delivering a design to a business unit. You have to understand the horizontal part now. This is called the T-shaped professional development model, and it's great for the HR professional. HR gets to do more interesting things and learn new things, but HR also has to learn how to work as a pool of professionals and be pulled out of their day job or their normal role to participate in cross-functional project teams, just like they do in business.

Interview with Josh Bersin, Global Industry Analyst (Hellström, 2020)

## Challenges faced when building Agile HR teams

- **Business-as-usual versus strategic work.** As discussed above, generally HR needs to manage operational tasks and BAU work, like recruitment contracts or supporting quarterly salary reviews, as well as simultaneously delivering strategic business projects, like redesigning a performance management framework or building a new leadership development programme. It's not uncommon for Agile HR teams to become frustrated by the negative impact of BAU on their ability to focus on strategic work. To overcome this hurdle, we encourage teams to utilize a Kanban board, as described in more detail and shown in Figure 10.1 later in this chapter, and to visualize both BAU and strategic work together to better manage capacity and track where time is spent. Some teams start with just using Agile for their strategic work, and allow BAU to continue as normal, but this can create capacity issues over time, especially if it's not visualized on the same board. Figure 10.3 also offers ideas on how a team could divide up the time given by each team member for BAU and strategic work, which is particularly useful for small HR teams when they first start using Agile ways of working.

- **Agile 'on top of' the usual job.** Most HR teams start by applying Agile to a project and often create temporary Agile HR teams that may also include people from the business. However, if the team members are not released sufficiently from their existing day job, Agile will feel like something that is done 'on top of' their usual work. We recommend people committing at least 70 per cent of their time to an Agile project and keeping the number of people working across multiple Agile projects to a minimum. This is also a reason to run short, targeted sprints, so that people need to be released for only 1–2 weeks at a time, or certain days each week can be ring-fenced to work as a cohesive team (eg every Tuesday and Thursday for a month).

- **To Scrum or not to Scrum?** HR does not have a continuous flow of work that is directly linked to a specific product, like Agile software development teams. Thus, it's not always clear when and where to use Scrum in HR. Generally, HR can apply the Scrum framework to a project or people initiative but, as mentioned above, this may only be for a short period of time, or they find Kanban is a better option. Good questions to ask when considering the application of Scrum within HR are:

  o What are we developing and why?

  o Who needs to be on the team to realize an end-to-end delivery, from discovery work through to full release?

  o Who will be maintaining and supporting the product or solution once it is released and should they also be on the team (highly recommended)?

  o How can we realistically involve users when testing the solution?

  o Do we need full-time team members, or can people give a percentage of their time to the sprints?

  o What are the dependencies on other business areas, and do we only involve some people in certain sprints? For example, should compliance and legal be involved in a sprint dedicated to creating the policy components of a solution? Or should we only involve marketing in the sprint where we're branding the final materials?

  o Can our HR people realistically commit to five days a week or should we commit 2–3 days per week and allow other work to be achieved at the same time?

- **Starting with Agile projects versus committing to a structural change.** Starting Agile ways of working through projects generally means those not involved remain unchanged. This can create tension, particularly if these other HR roles or teams work in a more traditional way. It's important to set the Agile project up for success and consider things like dependencies, management reporting lines, existing KPIs and competing responsibilities. HR professionals need to consider how to structurally support Agile within HR and be ready to change the full operating model to ensure Agile is a success.

# Agile HR operating models

## Working with Kanban

Most Agile HR teams use Kanban to visualize and prioritize their work, as set out in Figure 10.1. As discussed earlier, Kanban helps HR achieve a sustainable workflow, aims to limit work in progress (WIP) and helps HR manage stakeholder expectations about what can be delivered at any one point in time. For example, Figure 10.1 has WIP set at six items of work, and nothing can move into the Doing column until an item moves into Done. Kanban is a great way for HR to visualize and manage BAU alongside their strategic work. Usually, the use of a Kanban board is further enhanced with practices borrowed from the Scrum framework, such as weekly or monthly team retrospectives, alongside showcases with stakeholders and employees to drive continuous improvement. Additionally, if something gets blocked, the team can decide if it's necessary to stop other work to fix the problem immediately, known as a 'swarm' in Agile.

Figure 10.2 demonstrates how a team can add work streams to the Kanban board to visualize and separate BAU from strategic work, and better understand how to allocate capacity and time.

## Delivering BAU plus strategic work

Figure 10.3 is an effective way to get started with Agile, especially for smaller HR teams. The approach helps to clearly separate BAU from strategic work and allocate capacity levels for each person in the team to both areas. To begin with, most teams leave the BAU and operative work as usual, and introduce an Agile cadence and ceremonies like retrospectives and customer show-

FIGURE 10.1  Example Kanban board

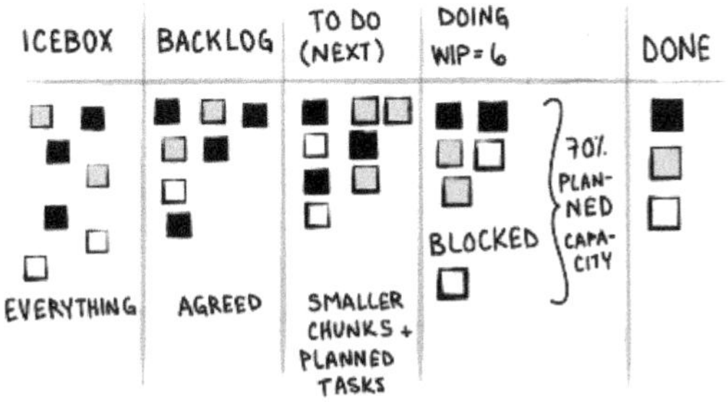

FIGURE 10.2  Kanban with a strategic and BAU stream

FIGURE 10.3  Capacity planning for BAU versus strategic teamwork

cases for the strategic work. We do, however, encourage all teams to look at how they manage and visualize their BAU work, and ideally to combine the two over time (similar to the Kanban board above), to better understand capacity and different skills requirements and to track team performance.

## Temporary people project squads

The formation of temporary people project squads, as shown in Figure 10.4, is another good way to start applying Agile to people initiatives within an

FIGURE 10.4  Temporary people project squad

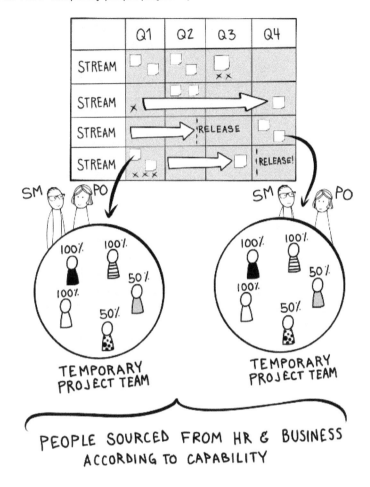

organization before a more permanent Agile HR operating model is created. The main idea is that a strategic list of people projects is agreed and prioritized based on stakeholder feedback and the assessment of value as outlined in Chapter 8. Then different people from across HR, such as HR business partners, compensation and benefits, and learning and development, form a temporary Agile HR team, with others sourced from the wider business to deliver a strategic project within a timeboxed period using Agile working methods. While we encourage HR teams to include people from the business in this approach, it is optional depending upon the organizational setup and level of Agile maturity within the business.

Furthermore, this model could be combined with a central Kanban board (like in Figure 10.1) that manages all of HR's work and the temporary people project squads are formed to deliver the strategic pieces of work that sit on the board. For example, a temporary people squad could be formed to undertake a design sprint for topics such as diversity and inclusion or career development. The BAU work that remains on the Kanban board is then completed by others in HR who are not part of that specific people squad, or people divide their capacity between the two areas and work a percentage of their time in a temporary people squad and a percentage of their time on BAU.

### Design sprint Agile HR teams

Like the previous model, Figure 10.5 is a useful way to introduce an Agile mindset and ways of working into HR and the wider business. We've also seen this work well for larger, more traditional organizations that are at the very beginning of their Agile transformational journey.

In this model a temporary Agile HR team is formed by sourcing people from across the business and HR to accelerate organizational transformational projects or people initiatives. The format is often a targeted, intense, almost hackathon-style, timeboxed period, such as five days. It generally reflects more of a design sprint, with the aim of quickly prototyping and validating key concepts or solutions that can then be worked on by various people across the HR function on a more BAU level.

FIGURE 10.5  Design sprint Agile HR teams

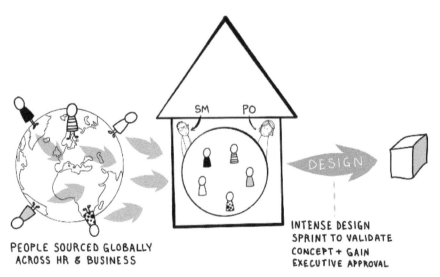

PEOPLE SOURCED GLOBALLY
ACROSS HR & BUSINESS

INTENSE DESIGN
SPRINT TO VALIDATE
CONCEPT + GAIN
EXECUTIVE APPROVAL

A key element of this design sprint approach is to have senior leaders as the users and internal customers that offer input and feedback. This is done to ensure that the concept or solution has been 'approved' and can subsequently be incorporated into standard project or BAU work after the sprint, without the need for further committees or proposal documents. In this way the model can help rapidly develop solutions to big complex workplace problems in non-Agile companies, and overcome the normal delay created by hierarchical approval steps within these types of organization. We've seen this model work well for a large global company that needed to accelerate a complex organizational change project linked to re-skilling their workforce.

## People experience squads

The model described in Figure 10.6 is more common once HR has worked with Agile for a while. This model is made up of people experience squads that are self-contained Agile HR teams delivering end-to-end solutions for either the whole business or a specific part of the organization. For example,

FIGURE 10.6  People experience squads

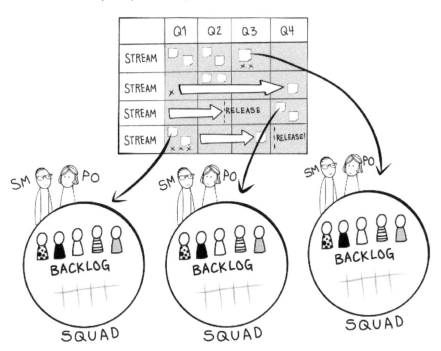

in larger organizations the people experience squad might deliver products and solutions for a specific user group or they might be aligned to different parts of the business such as product value chains, sub-brands or functional areas.

The squads focus on the people experience holistically and generally cover all HR topics like reward, talent, recognition, and learning and development in the same backlog. Sometimes, they may work alongside a separate HR operations team that covers administration and systems maintenance (though ideally the HR operational squad also uses Agile methods to manage workflow and deliver value). Generally, the squads contain around five people representing a mix of skills, from HR specialists to HR business partners, and they often invite external experts or people from other parts of the business to join specific sprints or contribute to certain pieces of work. If possible, the more permanent squad members regularly rotate between different people experience squads to develop new skills and experiences.

The squads use a Kanban board that combines BAU with strategic work, and ideally have a dedicated PO and Scrum master. To ensure good governance and coordination, a strategic portfolio of work sits above the squads to ensure aligned backlogs and consistency in what is being delivered across the organization. For example, the portfolio of work would set out the strategic priorities and overall definition of value that the people experience squads deliver against, and manage dependencies or potential conflicts between the different solutions designed for specific parts of the business. Alongside this, it would also ensure that the products and services are designed in such a way that they can be rolled out to the wider business later if value is validated for all employees. We also encourage the squads to come together for joint Agile events where possible. Regular portfolio and release-planning sessions and combined retrospectives would be particularly useful.

## People experience or culture as a product

Figure 10.7 is based on the concept of people experience or organizational culture representing the product that the Agile HR teams incrementally update and deliver to their internal customers. While some HR teams do this on a smaller scale owing to size, Figure 10.7 is an example of what is possible for a larger HR function.

FIGURE 10.7   People experience as a product

The people experience as a product model is based on four main components and reflects structures commonly seen in the wider business when an organization embraces Agile. The first component is made up of development teams, which are multi-skilled Agile HR teams that work on specific topics such as performance, career development and reward. These topics, also known as the features to the overall product, reflect a strategic and prioritized portfolio of work and will periodically change once certain value is delivered or strategic priorities shift. For example, the onboarding development team might cease and a new feature team focusing on diversity and inclusion might start, in response to a new strategic need within the business.

The development teams are made up of different skills from within HR, as well as people from the wider business who contribute on a temporary basis. The teams generally use the Scrum framework to collaborate and have a PO as well as a Scrum master or Agile coach. In this model, it's vital to coordinate and align the deliveries from the development teams, as well as manage release planning and co-dependencies.

The second component is a data and insights team that constantly listens across the organization to assess employee feedback and conducts research on people trends. This team tracks the impact of the value being delivered by the development teams, as well as recording upcoming needs and improvement areas to focus on.

The third component is an HR operations team, who oversee the maintenance of the products and services delivered by the development teams, alongside the general infrastructure required to run the day-to-day HR support of the business. This team also feeds off the portfolio of work and provides process improvement needs to the development teams. The input from the HR operations team on what products and services need to be developed, and why, is crucial as they will be maintaining the solutions once released.

The fourth component is a strategic HR team, which can contain HR business partners, as well as roles like Agile coaches that work across the organization. This team provides ongoing coaching and advice to the business and constantly informs the portfolio of work on the strategic needs of the organization and what is happening on the ground.

### One-person Agile HR

As we know, a one-person HR team often exists in small organizations or may come about because a certain location or brand operates independently of the global or parent business. As shown in Figure 10.8, in these cases we encourage the HR professional to embrace an Agile mindset and manage their workflow using a Kanban board. The strategic work can then be delivered through temporary Agile HR teams formed with other people from the business or perhaps the leadership team relevant to a specific part of the business. Often the people who join these temporary Agile HR teams allocate a certain percentage of their time for the work required, and the solo HR professional works as a type of PO for the temporary team. Where possible, we encourage HR professionals to also access support, in the form of Scrum masters or Agile coaches, from other parts of the business or the external talent market.

FIGURE 10.8 One-person Agile HR

STRATEGIC PEOPLE PROJECT TEAM FORMED TEMPORARILY TO SOLVE BIGGER PROBLEMS— COULD BE WITH LEADERSHIP TEAM OR PEOPLE ACROSS BUSINESS

## *No HR*

There is no reason why an HR function or team must permanently exist, especially within organizations that have developed in an Agile way from their inception, such as the tech start-ups and sociocracies discussed in Chapter 15. We also find that a lot of new start-ups manage their people initiatives in this way and especially while they remain smaller in size, and may then form an Agile HR or people experience squad once they grow and need to scale.

In this model (Figure 10.9) the operational elements of HR are generally outsourced, and a lot of the administrative tasks often covered by HR, such as sending a new employment contract or tracking holidays, are simply owned by the business teams and supported with various tech solutions. Next to this, a strategic portfolio of people initiatives is formed through stakeholder feedback and a definition of value. P Different people from across the business then volunteer to form a temporary Agile HR team to deliver the different projects as set out in this portfolio of work. The teams generally embrace a Scrum framework and ideally have a PO and Scrum master or Agile coach. Most of the time the team is made up of people who can volunteer only a percentage of their time and continue to do their 'day job' while working on the project.

FIGURE 10.9  No HR and temporary Agile HR squads

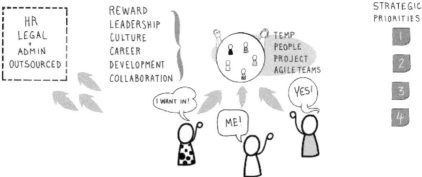

## Conclusion

The evolution of the Agile HR operating model reflects HR teams experimenting with different approaches with the aim of discovering their own unique style over time. What's great is that the Agile mindset guides us through this adventure by helping HR teams learn and grow through feedback loops and an incremental approach to development. It's also OK to feel unsure at the start and not have all the answers. We've found that just by getting started and truly working as a self-organizing team, many of the obstacles and uncertainties can be resolved together. We do, however, encourage all HR teams starting to work with Agile to seek support and tap into the great Agile coaching network that now exists across all industries.

---

### KEY POINTS FOR HR PROFESSIONALS

- The models explored in this chapter should always be viewed as a starting point rather than blueprints to follow, and we encourage all Agile HR teams to find a way of working that fits their organizational context and business needs.

- The best way to approach this emergent change is by viewing it as an opportunity to experiment and learn together.

- Excitingly, Agile HR heralds the end of the Ulrich model and traditional HR silos, by inviting HR professionals to build multi-skilled and T-shaped teams together with the business.

- Many of the Agile HR operating models are exploring how to deliver a more end-to-end employee experience, as well as aligning priorities and services with other parts of the business such as compliance, IT support and internal communications.

- While it's important for Agile HR teams to find their own style and way of working, the elements common to all teams include a new Agile cadence, prioritization through value, working transparently and the evolution of our HR roles and skills.

# References

Dank, N (2019a) Interview With Tracey Waters, Director of People Experience at Sky, and Agile HR Pioneer [Blog], *The Agile HR Community*, 29 July www.agilehrcommunity.com/agilehr-community-blog/interview-with-tracey-waters-from-sky (archived at https://perma.cc/8N3C-LTHW)

Dank, N (2019b) Sky Betting & Gaming Agile HR Transformation – Why They're Loving the Results, *The Agile HR Community*, 5 December https://youtu.be/metL1v47stE (archived at https://perma.cc/M3HK-MW85)

Dank, N (2019c) Interview with Jennie Jarmen, Group People Lab Product Owner at Lloyds Banking Group, 15 November

Ingham, J (2019) Beyond the Ulrich Model – HR in the People-Centric Organisation, *HR Magazine*, 1 November http://journal-download.co.uk/digitalmagazines/hr/HR01NOV2019/page_39.html (archived at https://perma.cc/U6VN-J9CN)

Hellström, R (2020) Interview with Josh Bersin, Global Industry Analyst, 20 January https://joshbersin.com/ (archived at https://perma.cc/JBT7-UQBN)

Roper, J (2016) Is the Ulrich Model Still Valid? *HR Magazine*, 22 August www.hrmagazine.co.uk/article-details/is-the-ulrich-model-still-valid (archived at https://perma.cc/D2YX-4Z2Z)

Ulrich, D (1996) *Human Resource Champions: The next agenda for adding value and delivering results*, Harvard Business Review Press, Brighton, MA

Ulrich, D (2018) Agility: The New Response to Dynamic Change, *LinkedIn Pulse*, 23 May www.linkedin.com/pulse/agility-new-response-dynamic-change-dave-ulrich (archived at https://perma.cc/KY8Z-MQ55)

# 11

# Agile for HR toolkit: Thinking like a scientist

## Introduction

To think like a scientist is to apply evidence-based practice to our HR work and make credible, commercially aware decisions in real time. As we've learnt already, the Agile feedback loop of plan, do, check, act helps to constantly drive data-based decisions by testing and validating directly with the end-customer. The aim is to know that something works before implementing it at scale. All the methods mentioned so far in this book, such as experimenting, prototyping and reviewing retrospectively, harness this evidence-based approach.

In the past, HR has often lacked the data and tools to inform our view and successfully contribute to the business discussion. At times, we've also been too easily influenced by the latest fad or quick-fix thinking and often relied on personal experience to make a workplace decision. Given the increased level of complexity and sheer volume of information within the modern organization, the need to apply an evidence-based approach is growing in importance. Furthermore, we're more likely to solve the problem, and thus make life a little easier, if we properly explore the evidence at hand rather than simply doing what we've done before, or worse, put the decision off until another time.

Excitingly, working in an evidence-based way has become easier for HR. With recent advancements in people analytics and technology, HR can now gather and assess different types of valuable data sources to inform their decisions. When they combine this with Agile ways of working, HR can start to truly justify their seat at the decision-making table within the business. To help you along this journey, we'll now explore how to start thinking like a scientist and begin to apply a more evidence-based approach to our work.

## Evidence-based practice

---

WHAT THEY SAY

You can't really work in HR if you don't feel comfortable with a spreadsheet, a little bit of statistics and some analysis.

Josh Bersin, Global Industry Analyst (Hellström, 2020)

---

Even without the direct influence of Agile ways of working, evidence-based practice has been gathering momentum within HR for some time. The Chartered Institute of Personnel and Development (CIPD), the leading body for HR in the UK, now includes the capability as a core component within their development roadmap for HR professionals. Key drivers behind the need to work in an evidence-based manner include the need to optimize our time, money and effort, but also the need to strengthen the commercial credibility of the HR profession.

As the CIPD explains, working evidence-based still requires an HR professional to draw on their experience in organizational design and development. However, to further strengthen this view, HR needs to also pull on people and organizational data, and stakeholder feedback, as well as scientific and academic sources (CIPD, 2019). Most importantly, HR should engage in critical thought to weigh up the validity and trustworthiness of the data presented, as well as separate opinion from fact and identify any personal or commercial interests at play. This means not just surveying more people, to get additional data, but investigating the data HR already has, and applying the Agile feedback loop when designing HR products and services.

Working evidence-based also helps HR better manage the opinions and expectations of our stakeholders, not mention the HiPPOs – highest paid person's opinion. For example, if a workplace project is undertaken as a result of opinion or assumption, it can be difficult to make subsequent decisions on the need to change direction or end the project if the benefits aren't being realized. Conversely, if the project is based on evidence and an Agile way of working, it's much easier to pivot because it is clear that the initial decision was based on what was known at the time and the change reflects what has been learnt since, and no egos are harmed in the process.

Evidence-based practices have also grown in importance for HR with the influx of people analytics technology. Indeed, some larger organizations are already employing teams of data scientists to drive this new approach within HR, and the ones who can't afford this are sourcing the capability through partners or tech applications that provide built-in analytics (Bersin, 2020).

What have been the barriers hindering HR's ability to work more evidence-based up until now?

- A current lack of capability in and experience of working with different data sources, as well as interpreting evidence and working with advanced people analytics.
- A reluctance within the HR profession to begin working with data, owing to inexperience with data privacy, data security and ethics in data science.
- Room for improvement in how we build an effective business case and connect people data with company performance and market outcomes.
- A tendency to favour myths, fads and truisms that influence the field of HR and organizational psychology, instead of following a scientific approach when faced with a business problem.

## Tips to get started

Let's now explore some of the basics of evidence-based practice and how we can begin to apply this type of thinking within our Agile HR work.

### Apply a holistic view

In the past, HR has tended to rely on one main metric, such as the results of an employee engagement survey, to propose certain actions or validate a decision. Instead, we encourage HR to draw on a wide range of data sources, which don't always have to be metrics and numbers and can also include academic research and stakeholder feedback, to build a more holistic picture of the business problem.

## Define a hypothesis

An important element of Agile ways of working is to test an assumption or idea. To do this scientifically, a clear and testable hypothesis must be established of what we think will happen and why. For example, 'if HR pre-screens applicants, we will source better candidates, as measured by the proportion of candidates approved by the team or manager'. Once we've established a decent, informed and documented hypothesis, the results can be measured systematically, and any unexpected outcomes tracked.

## Plan our research approach

It's important to plan our approach when gathering evidence and data for a business problem that HR wants to interrogate. At times, this might also include the need to access information that may initially appear hard to source. For example, most companies cannot use the healthcare data of their individual employees. However, it's usually possible to get anonymized data instead, and start researching aggregated events instead of singling out personal information. It's also useful to appreciate that different types of decision require differing levels of reliability and accuracy, depending on the potential impact of the solution and, of course, the associated risk of getting it wrong (Burns *et al*, 2011).

## Understand correlation and causation

Surprisingly, few HR professionals are familiar with the differences between causation and correlation. For example, when data indicate that the national levels of chocolate consumption correlate with a nation winning Nobel prizes (Messerli, 2012), it would be dangerous to assume that eating chocolate leads to more Nobel prizes (causation). If the results of an employee engagement survey correlate with the financial performance of a company, we can't automatically state that there is a direct causation (Levenson, 2015). To prove this, we need to apply additional data sources and explore different factors.

## Build partnerships

Most HR professionals appreciate the difference between qualitative and quantitative research methodologies and aim to draw on both to inform their view. However, to take the next step and apply mathematical approaches such as statistics, probabilities and sampling, it's useful (and powerful) to partner with a data scientist or analytics expert. While the expert speaks about sample sizes, data quality, algorithms and predictive values, HR professionals can more clearly articulate the people and organizational needs and ask the tricky questions necessary to build a coherent business case. The key to using data effectively is asking the right questions. This is the main starting point in data science and requires someone who can be an interpreter between the data scientists, the business, the HR practices and people data.

### Use control groups and randomization

Control groups and randomized research methods are commonly used within Agile product development and are great tools to help assess the impact of an HR initiative. For example, to successfully investigate if activity X influences Y, we need to also study groups that have experienced other activities, not just X, as well as groups where the activity didn't even happen. We can also randomly assign participants to different groups to further limit bias. A practical example is the current hype around the impact of mindfulness and meditation within the workplace. Many studies tend to focus only on the act of mindfulness and meditation itself, without comparing this to other activities such as exercise or drinking coffee, and often fail to randomly assign different interventions to the groups to further validate or disprove their hypothesis (Van Dam *et al*, 2018).

### Go to the source

When reading about popular science and areas like human and organizational psychology, we recommend assessing the credibility of the source before jumping on trends or using the information to support a workplace decision. Social media can now too easily popularize a scientific finding that often lacks substantial research or scientific validation. Learning to read research effectively is a great skill. First, read the abstract. Second, jump to the conclusion section at the end. Third, seek out information to confirm the accuracy and validity of the data provided. Fourth, look for peer reviews, listed research methods and further recommendations. Only then, if it sounds relevant, dive deeper into the study.

## Challenge bias

Many researchers, not to mention lay people, have a tendency towards confirmation bias, and favour evidence that supports their hypothesis or opinion. It's crucial to learn how to mitigate the impact of the many cognitive biases that could catch us out. Another example of bias is that of algorithm aversion, where we begin to doubt the credibility of an algorithm if there has been an error. Once an algorithm or forecast is working well, it can greatly accelerate workplace practices because it works much faster and more consistently than the human brain. However, if something leads a person to doubt its effectiveness, it can lead to a total rejection of using algorithms at all. This leads to the need for HR to get comfortable with working with algorithms and how to assess the data being used and decisions being made.

## Don't reinvent the wheel

Researchers around the world are sharing their findings on the many business-critical issues that organizations face. For example, it is quite easy to locate solutions such as a ready-to-be-deployed algorithm for optimizing the work schedules, or methods for predicting employee turnover (Talarico and Duque, 2015). A lot of time can be saved by conducting a literature review before jumping into the analysis.

## Start with the HR data we already have

It's common to hear of HR teams undertaking large data clean-up projects before starting to work with people analytics. However, as we've learnt, an Agile HR approach doesn't start with the available data, but rather the problem HR needs to solve. Additionally, once HR knows the right questions, we can evaluate the usefulness of the data we already have. Trying to get all the people data cleaned up and ready first serves only to slow HR down.

## Identify business cases through the numbers

An HR team does not need thousands of employees to harness the benefits of evidence-based practices or people analytics. Instead, it's often more useful to assess the numbers of events, such as sales transactions and customer service touchpoints. For example, a cinema wanted to explore whether the personality traits and behaviours of customer service employees could predict the sales figures for pre-film snacks. The study discovered a link between certain personality traits and higher sales figures, upon which they changed their recruitment pipeline to mirror the findings and saw a 1.2 per cent increase in the profit per customer as a result (Kruse, 2013). If HR begins to positively influence every sales transaction within a business through using people analytics, the impact will be massive.

### Learn the basics of AI

To ensure an ethical and transparent approach to using AI within the workplace, it's crucial that the technology is based on a human-led algorithmic and rule-based process, rather than left to the machine to decide. For example, HR needs to clearly demonstrate and document why one person might be hired over another and ensure that AI decisions do not contain any bias or result in unfair treatment.

---

**HR TOP TIP**

If a correlation is found, HR can start to explore whether predictions are possible. For example, an HR team at a department store wanted to determine two things through people analytics:

1   Was an accurate prediction of customer footfall possible, which in turn would impact employee scheduling?

2   Could a causality be proven between the number of customer service employees working within the store at any one point in time and the number of products customers might buy?

By partnering with data scientists and using readily available algorithms that were open sourced from scientific literature (Kabak *et al*, 2008; Talarico and Duque, 2015), the HR team could predict customer footfall and pinpoint the optimal level of employees to have in the store at the same time and thus potentially increase the number of products sold.

---

## Evidence-based storytelling

Learning to speak the language of business and building a narrative that connects the people side of business with company performance and end-customer results is a crucial skill that helps HR professionals work in a more evidence-based way. Rather than just presenting people metrics or HR reports, the aim is to explore the relationships between human behaviour and organizational design with business outcomes. To help, it's good to tailor the findings to an individual leader's business domain, as well as their people, end-customers and operations, rather than only presenting averages for the whole company.

Now, let's look at some examples of HR storytelling that aims to build a business narrative with the data to better guide workplace decisions.

---

HR TOP TIP

Let's compare alternative ways of presenting insights to a business leader through the following example.

From speaking HR

Thirty-five service technicians are retiring over the next two years. We should think about what to do together.

To speaking business

We will have 35 technicians retiring over the next two years:

1  We have investigated the capability risks here, and 30 per cent of the retirees possess hard-to-find skills in specific maintenance competencies, which will impact the servicing of products X and Y.

2  Through further research and discussions with the team managers, we estimate that the impact could be as large as a 20 per cent decrease in the service levels for products X and Y.

3  This could also directly impact the service level agreement with one of our strategic customers and create the risks of financial sanctions or a need to renegotiate contracts.

4  We recommend two routes for mitigating these risks:

   a. We've identified seven people who require only moderate training to become licensed in X and Y within the next six months.

   b. We've also identified two options for sourcing the talent externally to fill the potential capability gap.

5  Now let's explore what to do next together.

While we'll never know the exact future outcome, the aim is to build a story based on sound prediction and to explore different scenarios and possible results. This is exactly what the wider business does when assessing strategy and product design.

## From activity to impact

Traditionally, there has been a tendency to use activity-based metrics (often linked directly to KPIs) to assess the impact of our products and services. For example, 'how many people went to a training' or 'the ratio of employees that have a recorded development discussion'. A more powerful way to report on data is to assess and quantify the value our products and services bring to the organization, as we discussed in Chapter 8. Follow these steps to formulate an effective approach:

1  Evaluate whether the product or service is fit for purpose and is solving the actual problem, for example 'is a training workshop the right solution for this issue?'

2  Build in process metrics, like 'how efficient are we at bridging the capability gap?', as well as impact metrics, such as 'what is the evidence that the capability development has either positively or negatively changed business outcomes (eg sales, speed to market or a reduction in end-customer complaints)?'

For some of the people practices that are more difficult to put a number on, for example the impact of a leadership coaching programme, we recommend gathering narratives from across the business about what people have done as a result of the HR product or service. For example, collecting stories on the actions of leaders before and after the coaching programme, alongside a self-evaluation from the leaders themselves, as well as feedback and stories from the teams they work with. At times, some correlations can be made with employee engagement or the retention of people, but this can be difficult to associate to one activity alone, like a coaching programme, and the narrative helps build a more holistic picture. We encourage HR professionals to do this in modern and interesting ways as well, such as recording short videos with leaders and hosting storytelling events.

WHAT THEY SAY

What we have learnt in our people analytics programmes is that HR people
need help with:

- the scientific method of asking the right questions;
- interpreting the data correctly;
- explaining the answers, telling the stories;
- and making the data actionable.

This is a very sophisticated skill we're talking about, to interpret data and make
it meaningful and useful for people and not just producing a report and saying,
'hey look, here's a report'.

Josh Bersin, Global Industry Analyst

## Data-driven HR service design

Defining the data needed to assess and evolve our services requires a lot of
thought. We recommend building end-to-end processes from the very start,
where HR aims to solve business problems together with other functions
through a coordinated effort and a more holistic approach. This is linked to
the concept of continuously listening and assessing the full experience of
work, which we also discuss in Chapter 12.

For example, hiring and onboarding are great examples of services that
tend to involve teams from across the organization, such as facilities, IT
support, internal communications and finance. In these cases, and to design a
more end-to-end employee experience and challenge previous siloed working
practices, HR should establish methods to track the internal customer touchpoints, alongside activities like handovers, and processing and waiting times.

Let's explore some basic questions that can help HR professionals design
processes based on the data collected.

Process design questions:

- Which parts of the process are the users most or least satisfied with?
- What is the lead time between the user having the need and the provision
  of the service?
- What does the user feedback tell us at different touchpoints throughout
  the process?
- What is the work time spent on individual process steps?

- How much work time is spent by users on components that deliver value, as opposed to waiting or something not directly contributing to the creation of value (also known as process efficiency)?
- Which part of the process causes the most defects or mistakes?
- Where are the bottlenecks?

Value and impact questions:

- What are the impact and value of the process?
- What is the overall employee satisfaction level with the process?
- Which parts of the process should we develop next to positively influence user satisfaction levels or business impact?

---

### HR TOP TIP

A great case study comes from MUJI, and the need for its European flagship store to recruit nearly 100 people in a very short time. The targets for the project were:

1  to cut the lead time of the normal recruitment process from several months to a week;

2  to maintain high candidate experience satisfaction levels;

3  to recruit nearly 100 people;

4  to set up a new automated recruitment process;

5  for the project to cost less when done in-house compared to outsourcing the project to a recruitment agency instead.

To tackle the challenge an Agile HR team was set up, who began to explore the data currently held. This led to an introduction of automation at the beginning of the recruitment pipeline, which served to dramatically reduce the lead time from 1–2 months to 2–3 days from a candidate application being received to a suitable candidate being selected for a video interview.

The team also carefully crafted supportive messages throughout the automation process, which resulted in high candidate satisfaction levels about their experience and the speed of the service. Overall, by following an incremental development approach and co-creation, MUJI hired nearly 100 people on time and at less than half the price it would have cost to use a recruitment agency.

Peoplegeeks (2019)

# Conclusion

We don't need to be Google to build a strong and effective evidence-based approach within our own HR teams. By following scientific methods in how we gather and assess data, and supporting this with the Agile feedback loop, all HR professionals can guide their business in how to make better data-based decisions. We also recommend developing people analytics capability within HR teams or partnering with data scientists and experts to shift the profession to the next level of sophistication in this topic. Overall, the goal is to build effective business cases and research reports that connect people issues and employee value directly with business outcomes and end-customer results. By thinking like a scientist, HR can easily become a credible partner at the decision-making table.

---

KEY POINTS FOR HR PROFESSIONALS

- Working evidence-based and thinking like a scientist is an important component of Agile HR and can greatly improve the commercial credibility of the HR profession.

- Evidence-based practice draws on our professional experience and then strengthens this view by applying critical thought and assessing people and organizational data, and stakeholder feedback, as well as scientific and academic sources.

- Following an evidence-based approach helps us manage our HiPPOs and base organizational change on data-driven decisions.

- It's crucial to build an effective business case and connect people data with company performance and market outcomes.

- We encourage all HR professionals to develop their capabilities in people analytics and interpreting evidence, as well as to form partnerships with data science experts.

- Our recommendation is that HR should own employee-related analytics, caring for the ethical, sound, fair and transparent use of people data. If HR won't do this, someone else will own the domain, and there is a danger that they will not understand the compliance needs.

# References

Bersin, J (2020) Josh Bersin, Global Industry Analyst (www.joshbersin.com (archived at https://perma.cc/6VRD-P5JH)), interviewed by Riina Hellström for the book *Agile HR*, January 2020

Burns, P, Rohrich, R and Chung, K (2011) The levels of evidence and their role in evidence-based medicine, *Plastic Reconstructive Surgery*, **128** (1), pp 305–10

CIPD (2019) Evidence-Based Practice for Effective Decision-Making, CIPD, 26 February www.cipd.co.uk/knowledge/strategy/analytics/evidence-based-practice-factsheet (archived at https://perma.cc/BAR4-P8BX)

Hellström, R (2020) Interview with Dr Jeff Sutherland, Co-creator of Scrum, 7 January

Kabak, Ö *et al* (2008) Efficient shift scheduling in the retail sector through two-stage optimization, *European Journal of Operational Research*, **184**, pp 76–90

Kruse, K (2013) Think Traits Not Training: How AMC Theatres Increased Sales, Profits and Engagement, *Forbes*, February www.forbes.com/sites/kevinkruse/2013/02/14/employee-engagement-kenexa-amc/#1ca416945ac4 (archived at https://perma.cc/B57A-G9C9)

Levenson, A (2015) Employee Engagement Does Not Cause Performance, *LinkedIn* www.linkedin.com/pulse/employee-engagement-does-cause-performance-alec-levenson (archived at https://perma.cc/9MQS-YCVW)

Messerli, F (2012) Chocolate consumption, cognitive function, and Nobel laureates, *New England Journal of Medicine*, **367** (16), pp 1562–64

Peoplegeeks (2019) Case MUJI – Embracing the Change in Large-Scale Recruitment Process, *Peoplegeeks*, February https://peoplegeeks.net/2019/11/muji-embracing-the-change-in-large-scale-recruitment-process (archived at https://perma.cc/JH73-JSW5)

Talarico, L and Duque, P (2015) An optimization algorithm for the workplace management in a retail chain, *Computers and Industrial Engineering*, **82**, pp 65–77

Van Dam, N T *et al* (2018) Mind the hype: a critical evaluation and prescriptive agenda for research on mindfulness and meditation, *Perspectives on Psychological Science*, **13** (1), pp 36–61

# 12

# Agile for HR toolkit: Continuous improvement

## Introduction

Building learning organizations that can continuously improve through feedback loops and dialogue has long been a goal of HR leaders. Agile helps achieve this aim by linking the process of review and improvement directly with the business cycle and how we deliver value to the end-customer. The Agile activities of inspection and adaptation are powerful mechanisms that HR can use across the organization to help accelerate high performance.

In this chapter, we'll look at how Agile powers an environment of continuous improvement at the personal, team, organization and product levels. This happens throughout the business, but we'll look through the lens of HR and explore the different tools and techniques that HR can use to strengthen our own profession and skill set.

## Removing impediments

As we've explored already in this book, Agile as a way of working prioritizes the need to remove any impediment that might slow a team down or restrict the delivery of value to the end-customer. When practised well, the daily Scrum or team stand-up invites people to share the blockers and challenges that may potentially slow them down. These can be anything from a dependency on another team unable to deliver on time, through to an inter-team communication problem. The aim is to tackle these issues whenever possible on the same day and constantly free the teams from negative derailers.

Indeed, one company that operates a scaled Agile model across the whole organization runs consecutive stand-up meetings throughout the morning, starting at the team level and finishing with the executive level. While the focus is still to help teams solve their own problems through the dynamics of self-organization, any big blockers or large cross-team issues are dealt with on the same day by management teams who have the mandate to solve company-wide impediments. This way of working is a game changer and demonstrates how the role of a leader in an Agile organization becomes an 'impediment removalist' and is focused on helping the teams get on with the job, rather than delegating work to others.

This daily act of seeking out and removing impediments demonstrates the inbuilt mechanisms Agile offers a business to drive an ongoing process of continuous improvement. If an organization can also successfully harness an environment of trust, and support transparent feedback discussions across their network, it's possible to develop a strong sense of collective accountability and ownership around the goal to improve.

Learning how to improve also implies an ability to openly discuss failure and listen to the suggestions of others. As we've discussed previously, this means HR needs to operate from a place of trust and safety with our people. Facilitating this discussion and helping leaders and teams, not to mention ourselves, view failed experiments or missed targets as an invaluable learning experience becomes a core coaching activity for HR.

## Prioritizing improvements

All the methods discussed in this chapter will help individuals, teams and organizations uncover the improvements necessary to get better at what they do. However, there is no use highlighting improvements if we don't also prioritize and plan how these will be achieved. Just like all other work, it's rare that HR can get all the improvements that we want done, especially if HR needs to complete other design or development work at the same time.

The implication is that Agile HR teams need to add improvement work into their backlog alongside everything else and make choices about when and how these tasks can be completed. It's also useful to devise supporting mechanisms to ensure improvement work gets done. For example, some teams allocate a whole sprint to improvement work, while others dedicate a section of their Kanban board to track and complete improvement work alongside other tasks. Whatever approach suits the Agile HR team best, it's essential to find a rhythm that ensures all the most important improvements get done alongside the everyday work.

Let's now explore how to drive continuous improvement at the different levels of personal, team, organization and product within HR.

## Personal level

A lot of the Agile techniques discussed in this book can be used at an individual level to drive personal growth and learning. We use Kanban boards to manage our own to-do lists and there are numerous stories of people doing things like managing a house renovation or organizing a wedding using Scrum. Incorporating Agile tools into our everyday lives is a great way to bring the mindset alive and help to make the theory tangible and real.

We've compiled a list of personal learning actions that HR professionals can take to develop their Agile mindset.

### *Personal learning actions*

- **Gemba walk.** A Gemba walk (a Japanese term for stepping back from your daily tasks to observe how value is created) is a great way to learn from others and gain different perspectives on how to approach various Agile activities. Go and observe Agile teams in action. Ask to attend their stand-ups, customer reviews and retrospectives as a silent observer and then discuss insights and learnings with various team members afterwards.

- **Be a Scrum master.** As the Scrum master is the protector and facilitator of the Agile feedback loop, it is a great coaching role for HR professionals to try out, and not only strengthens general facilitation skills but challenges people to be objective listeners. HR professionals can also gain invaluable insights on team dynamics and organizational behaviour that help inform people strategy.

- **Personal Kanban.** Use a free tool like Trello to manage and prioritize your everyday work. Decide on your own value drivers and Definition of Done to guide your Agile cadence.

- **Personal retrospective.** Reflection is an essential part of the learning process. Use one of the many retrospective formats outlined below to run your own personal review session, and use the insights collected to inform your personal development roadmap.

- **Personal feedback.** Ask people you work with for improvement ideas and feedback on your own work. It's often useful to specify the deliverable you want to improve and seek concrete examples to help shape people's feedback.

- **Small-scale validation.** Whatever you are creating, aim to build a mock-up or draft version first, and seek feedback to further evolve your ideas. Test your MVP with 2–5 people and explore their reactions plus any improvement suggestions. Then use the feedback to iterate a second version.

- **Agile development roadmap.** Personal development should always be seen as an incremental process. Rarely can you develop all the skills or change all the desired behaviours you want overnight. You need to focus on one thing at a time to make it stick. Viewing different learning aims as epics, which you then break down into different actions and tasks contained within a learning backlog, is a powerful way to steer your development. We suggest mapping this out using a Kanban or Scrum board, and use timeboxed periods to track progress and review achievements.

- **Map your T-shape.** What does your own T-shape look like?

    o List your experiences and professional knowledge.
      – *What are the different situations you've dealt with over the years?*
      – *How have these experiences equipped you for business challenges ahead?*

    o List your specialist skills and the topics you feel most comfortable with.

    o Consider what's missing.
      – *How can you develop new skill sets to add to this list?*
      – *How could you link this skill development to different types of experience?*
      – *Now, go and seek these out.*

## Team level

Retrospectives are a powerful workplace tool and our main recommendation for supporting continuous improvement at the team level. While Agile actively incorporates the activity into a team's cycle of work, or each sprint, HR professionals can use retrospectives in multiple ways to facilitate organizational dialogue and tap into the employee experience. For example, HR can use a strategic retrospective to review the current people agenda or talent landscape with business leaders and stakeholders. Additionally, retrospectives are a great way to close a learning workshop or coaching session as they help participants structure their feedback in an objective and action-oriented way.

The aim of a retrospective is to build a safe space and facilitate collective storytelling on how the team experienced the last sprint or cycle of work. For this, people need to believe that what they discuss is confidential and stays within the team. As a collective, the team then decides what information and subsequent improvement points are shared with the wider organization. A nice pre-frame to help shape the conversation is 'regardless of what we discover, we understand and truly believe that everyone did the best job that they could, given what they knew at the time, their skills and abilities and the situation at hand' (Keith, 2001).

A retrospective delves into how people work as well as the tools used to get the work done. First, the activity encourages people to explore team dynamics and the behaviours displayed as well as the methods used to communicate and collaborate. Second, retrospectives assess the Agile tools and frameworks engaged by the team to get the job done, which can cover anything from how backlog items were written and presented, through to how velocity was measured and reported. For these types of conversations to be successful, it's crucial a retrospective doesn't become a blame game but moves people towards action-oriented discussions on why something has occurred and what can be done next to solve it. The facilitation skills of a Scrum master or Agile coach are thus essential, especially when teams are new or lack the maturity to explore these issues without an objective guide.

There are numerous books and online resources to help HR professionals craft a great retrospective. Most formats follow the five steps outlined by Derby and Larsen (2006):

1  **Set the scene.** State the intent and allow time for people to get into the zone.

2  **Gather data.** Encourage memories and build a shared view of what has happened.

3  **Generate insights.** Seek out patterns, trends and unexpected moments.

4  **Decide what to do.** Prioritize the most important issues to solve and plan tangible actions.

5  **Close.** Appreciate people's time and honesty, clarify next steps and revisit how the retrospective can be improved for next time.

For a good retrospective, we suggest lots of sticky notes, marker pens, timing devices and plenty of wall space. Most formats listed below also benefit from people undertaking silent brainstorming first, where they record their ideas and thoughts on sticky notes before moving into a group discussion.

### Common retrospective formats used by Agile teams

- **Lean coffee.** As the name suggests, this aims to invoke the feeling of meeting at a coffee shop for a friendly chat. People are asked to record the topics they want to discuss, which are grouped to capture any similarities and then prioritized using any preferred method (such as dot voting). Once ranked, set a timer and work through the topics one by one, for example allowing five minutes each. At the end of each timeboxed topic, people can indicate a preference to continue for another timed round on that same topic (thumbs up) or stop and move on to the next topic (thumbs down) (Lean Coffee, 2020).

- **Mad, sad and glad.** Ask people to consider what made them mad, sad and glad in the previous cycle of work and then share and discuss. It's often useful to invite people to place their individual comments on a wall or flipchart first, then gather insights and discuss the similarities, differences and reasons why (Derby and Larsen, 2006).

- **Sailboat or speedboat.** Draw a sailboat or speedboat on a flipchart. Next, explore the forces that pushed people forward, by placing sticky notes with people's comments on the sails or motor, or alternatively pulled them back, by placing sticky notes with people's comments on the anchor. You can also add things like storm clouds to explore challenges ahead and a sun for opportunities not yet taken (Hohmann, 2006).

- **Team satisfaction chart.** Feel free to use different criteria on each axis. One that works well is placing 'satisfaction in how we worked as a team' on the y-axis versus 'satisfaction with our result' on the x-axis. People place a sticky note to indicate where they sit between the two, and discuss differences and similarities and explore the reasons why (Andresen, 2017).

- **Feedback or ideas matrix.** Draw up a four-boxed grid that asks people to record their insights on:
  - what worked well (continue)
  - what didn't work well (change)
  - ideas and insights
  - appreciation (of something or person/s).

  Once done, ask them to add these sticky notes to the grid and group common themes. Depending upon time available, you can use a prioritization method to focus only on the most important topics or simply explore each topic one by one. It's generally advisable to time all these discussions, as they can become quite intense (Derby and Larsen, 2006).

- **Amazon or film review.** Ask each team member to write review of the previous cycle of work using a specific format, such as an Amazon or film review. They can even award stars, for example a rating out of five. Next, discuss insights. Other variations include 'tweet my sprint' or send a postcard from the previous sprint describing the experience (Baldauf, 2018).

- **Timeline or histogram.** Ask people to map out a timeline of events for the previous cycle of work. Once on the wall, you can add things like what people were doing, thinking and feeling, as well as influencing factors like events or different team roles. It's useful to use colour coding for your cards or sticky notes and aim to capture different perspectives rather than just consensus (Derby and Larsen, 2006).

> **HR TOP TIP**
>
> Retrospectives can be hugely influential and a catalyst for change. It's crucial to practise retrospectives regularly and build a safe space, as they can be quite emotional at times, with people showing vulnerabilities and sharing frustrations. For example, on a large Agile HR project made up of several small teams working together and using one overriding backlog for the product design, it took time to change behaviours and develop trust. Several sprints in, it became clear that tensions were developing between the teams owing to different views on what needed to be prioritized. When the retrospective happened, one team decided to go to their manager first to raise their concerns, who then came to the session complaining that certain views weren't being heard. This caused a huge reaction, not to mention disappointment, from the other teams, but it also helped to kick-start a discussion about why some people didn't feel comfortable about airing their concerns openly and how to collaborate better. While the retrospective itself was very intense, it represented a key moment when the teams started to trust Agile as a way of working and began to resolve cross-team dependencies themselves rather than escalating them whenever there was a problem.

## Organizational and product level

At the organizational level, continuous improvement invites HR to evolve beyond the exercise of tracking and monitoring employee engagement to that of building a continual listening strategy. Intimately linked with viewing employee experience as a product and perceiving our people as the internal customers, continual listening looks at how to orchestrate a cross-functional effort to collect and combine a wide range of data sources to enhance business performance (Stevens, 2018).

Interestingly, this means attempting to move away from the common situation where every function runs their own mini employee surveys, such as marketing to check brand awareness and HR to assess the perception of leadership, and aiming to achieve an aligned and coordinated approach to data collection. Also, rather than simply surveying more in the hope of capturing a greater amount of data, continual listening looks at how to tap into a variety of data sources. For example, combining the direct employee feedback collected through surveys with indirect feedback, which looks to what people say about the company through sources like social media, as well as inferred feedback, which tracks how people behave through actions like internal website clicks and calls made to HR services (Stevens, 2017).

Next, just as the business reviews their products with the end-customers, HR, alongside other support functions, should use these continual listening techniques to assess the needs, preferences and satisfaction levels of their people. Combining these data with design thinking steps can continually evolve and enhance the employee experience product. For example, by asking what the pain points for our internal customers are, we might then discover ways to solve these and subsequently raise business performance.

While some HR professionals reading this section might find this level of sophistication intimidating, many of us can simply start with the data we're already collecting. The key is to link the data directly to company performance and to team up with other functions to deliver a more coordinated approach. See Chapter 11 for more information on how to start thinking like a scientist.

Let's look at some of the useful organizational-level tools that HR professionals can use.

## Organization- and product-level feedback tools

- **Pulse checks, surveys and employee experience metrics.** Developments in cloud-based technology and mobile apps mean that HR is no longer tied to large employee engagement vendors who previously controlled the collection of data and reporting of feedback through heavy supply contracts. Instead, HR can now tap into a whole collection of lightweight products to track employee experience in real time. However, no matter what product you decide to use, make sure the questionnaires are kept brief, that the feedback is transparently shared and that people see actions taken as a result.
- **Immediate feedback questionnaires.** Ask people to complete a short feedback questionnaire immediately after they use an HR product or service. The data collected will help track service levels and satisfaction over time.
- **Digital and marketing tools.** Explore how best to use these tools to track HR products and services, as they can help monitor, for example:
  o click-through rates for specific websites;
  o dropout rates (such as people or candidates leaving a website page);
  o landing page engagement, using heatmap technology;
  o marketing metrics for internal communications (such as how many people open a newsletter e-mail).
- **Research into a specific topic, problem or need.** Apply a scientific method to inspect a business problem or people challenge with quantitative and qualitative data. Assess correlations and causality between business and

people data points with the aim of discovering root causes and the biggest impacting factors. To help in this area, we encourage HR teams to develop advanced analytics capabilities or to collaborate with other parts of the organization that have these skills.

- **Strategic retrospective.** Use a retrospective to conduct a strategic review of a people or organizational topic, such as the current state of health for the organization's talent portfolio. This is a great tool to use with senior leaders and can be very powerful when linked with other data sources and people metrics.

- **People analytic tools.** The opportunities and capabilities for the HR profession when it comes to people analytics are now exploding as next-generation technology enters the market. These tools mean we can now conduct things like network analysis, predictive retention mapping, talent mapping, and emotion and affect detection (for example of e-mail text), as well as risk and fraud prevention.

- **Agile maturity assessments.** There are numerous Agile maturity assessments available to help track organizational development and team dynamics. Use the data collected to start open and transparent discussions within the business on how to improve and to remove any impediments identified.

- **Crowdsourcing and co-creation.** Use crowdsourcing technology and video conferencing to reach a large number of people virtually and invite them to ideate, vote on decisions or discuss specific topics together. For example, one business ran an organization-wide strategy co-creation session by combining digital and face-to-face workshops. The initiative involved 400 people over a three-hour period and helped to generate immediate feedback on how the strategy was perceived and what was needed to make it stronger.

- **Regular internal customer reviews and showcases.** Many Agile HR teams hold regular internal customer feedback sessions with their people. While some teams link this to a specific project or initiative, many set up monthly or bi-monthly sessions with large sections of the business or even the whole organization, to review a collection of projects or initiatives at the same time. This approach can be an invaluable way to tap into regular feedback on what's working well and what to improve, as well as where to focus time and energy next.

- **Lean coffee with HR.** Using the format outlined in the retrospective section, some Agile HR teams run Lean coffee workshops with their people to unearth the most important issues faced within the business. This is also a great way to gather ideas and input on how to potentially solve the problems raised, as well as gain insights into employee experiences and general satisfaction levels.

## Conclusion

Too often we skip the project steps of review and reflection because we're short on time and too focused on the next thing to get done. This situation is particularly relevant for HR who focus much of their time on improving the wider organization, often at the expense of their own learning and team development. The Agile feedback loop naturally drives an environment of continuous improvement and it offers HR a pre-set business process that they can directly support to harness learning and improve performance. HR can add immense value in this area and use the coaching and facilitation skills we're known for to build psychological safety and help others learn.

---

KEY POINTS FOR HR PROFESSIONALS

- Agile can help HR professionals achieve their vision of building learning organizations.

- To support an environment of continuous improvement, it's important to embed the act of reviewing, reflection and improvement into the normal work cadence.

- Improvement work needs to be planned and added to the backlog like all other tasks, because only then do we have a chance of getting it done!

- HR professionals can play a vital coaching role within Agile organizations by facilitating retrospectives and review discussions.

- It's important to build a trusted space that helps people give and receive feedback.

- Use the techniques outlined in this chapter to personally learn and grow, an essential starting point to then help teams and the wider organization continuously improve.

# References

Andresen, J (2017) Erfolgreiche Retrospektiven: Ablauf, Regeln + Methodenbausteine, *Leanpub* https://leanpub.com/ErfolgreicheRetrospektiven (archived at https://perma.cc/AXU8-JF59)

Baldauf, C (2018) Retromat: Run great agile retrospectives, *Leanpub* http://leanpub.com/retromat-activities-for-agile-retrospectives (archived at https://perma.cc/BK55-4ZC6)

Derby, E and Larsen, D (2006) *Agile Retrospectives: Making good teams great*, Pragmatic Bookshelf

Hohmann, L (2006) *Innovation Games: Creating breakthrough products through collaborative play*, 1st edn, Addison-Wesley Professional, Boston, MA

Keith, N (2001) *Project Retrospectives: A handbook for team review*, Addison-Wesley, Boston, MA

Lean Coffee (2020) Lean Coffee Lives Here http://leancoffee.org (archived at https://perma.cc/KX6A-7NKL)

Stevens, L (2017) Three Basic Conditions for Employee Experience Success Using Data and People Analytics, *LinkedIn*, 29 August www.linkedin.com/pulse/three-basic-conditions-employee-experience-success-using-phd (archived at https://perma.cc/5A63-9MRH)

Stevens, L (2018) The 4 Guiding Principles of a Successful Continuous Listening Program, *LinkedIn*, 19 April www.linkedin.com/pulse/4-guiding-principles-successful-continuous-listening-program-phd (archived at https://perma.cc/9N99-P82R)

# PART FOUR

# HR for Agile

# 13

# HR for Agile: An introduction

HR for Agile looks at *our role in helping the organization* transform by embracing the Agile mindset and evolving our ways of working. While most organizations are seeking agility in response to an increasingly complex business environment, the reasons why will vary based on context and industry. The danger with Agile transformation is that some people mistakenly think it simply involves doing things faster, which fails to appreciate the profound behavioural change required to sustain Agile practices and realize the business benefits. HR for Agile builds on the knowledge and skills that already exist within the HR profession on how to guide organizational development and cultural change and modernizes these capabilities for the future of work.

To support your learning, this section will explore HR's role in Agile transformation, as well as how to redesign existing HR products and services to help make our people awesome and accelerate business agility.

The HR for Agile part is built around the following topics:

- **Co-creating the Agile vision** (Chapter 14): helping HR professionals answer the question of *why* it should adopt Agile and co-create a strong narrative across the organization to guide transformation and empower people to act.

- **Agile organizational design** (Chapter 15): exploring the two main pathways to Agile organizational design and how to scale Agile across large parts of the business or indeed the whole enterprise.

- **HR's role in Agile transformation** (Chapter 16): sharing all our tips, tricks and actionable ideas for how HR can play a crucial role in guiding organization-wide Agile transformation.

- **Agile HR products and services** (Chapter 17): offering a wide range of examples and case studies demonstrating how to use Agile HR to design great products and services in the areas of performance, reward and learning.

Throughout this part of the book, it's important to remember that Agile transformation can never be implemented *onto* people or introduced by following a predefined blueprint. At all times we need to consider the context in which we're operating, alongside the evolutionary nature of transformation. Rather than seeking an end-state, HR professionals should embrace the Agile values and use these principles to guide our work, not to mention the organizational and behavioural change that underpins Agile transformation.

# 14

# Co-creating the Agile vision

## Introduction

A deep understanding of the context in which an organization operates is required to skilfully adopt the Agile mindset and its corresponding frameworks across the business. Simply using a backlog or running a retrospective doesn't automatically make us Agile. To successfully define the speed and depth of Agile adoption demanded by a business, HR first needs to assess the context in which the organization operates.

This chapter will explore the different factors driving organizations towards Agile and help HR professionals answer the core question of *why Agile*, for a specific business context. We'll also share ideas on how to assess the maturity and ongoing development of Agile within an organization, and then use this information to help guide business-wide transformation.

For this discussion, our primary focus will be on traditional companies needing to reinvent their ways of working and embrace Agile, as this perspective currently dominates the public discourse around transformation. However, many of the examples discussed are also applicable to what we term 'Agile-by-nature' organizations, which have evolved from day one through Agile values and self-organizing networks and will be discussed in more detail in Chapter 15.

## Start with the 'why'

Lacking a blueprint for Agile transformation, every organization needs to answer the question of *why Agile* and build a narrative that empowers people to act and supports the cultural change required. To help HR professionals facilitate this conversation, let's explore the most common factors driving the need for Agile transformation within a business.

## Updating the operating model

Industries such as banking, travel and retail are currently facing a drastic need to digitize their products and services in response to changing end-customer needs. As discussed in the opening chapters, this dramatic change in customer behaviour sets an expectation of how a company should now operate. For example, with podcasts and audiobooks booming, a book publisher will soon be out of business if it doesn't adopt digital forms. Large-scale Agile transformation is necessary to support this digitalization and, given the competitive landscape, most business leaders want to see this update happen at speed.

---

**HR TOP TIP**

Organizations going through wide-scale digital transformation require an HR team that has strong knowledge of the Agile mindset and developing new organizational and operating models. HR will need to take a lead in re-skilling people in both Agile and digital capabilities. New roles will need to be defined, alongside the realignment of teams in to end customer-centric value streams. It also demands that recruitment is based on different profiles and cultural fit, as well as coaching leaders to role-model and sustain the new ways of working. In Chapter 16 we'll dive deeper into each of these as we explore HR's role in transformation.

---

## Scaling up a business

When an Agile start-up grows, it needs to scale operations for the next organizational phase. Often people have been running the day-to-day operations and sorting out situations to their best ability and intent, with freedom and very little bureaucracy. The decision-making and HR practices have been lightweight and undocumented. When scaling an Agile start-up, it's crucial to keep their culture alive while simultaneously introducing an element of standardization and structure for the sake of efficiency and enabling growth. The change perspective here is to create predictability and certainty where it makes sense and only standardize processes where it clearly helps people to succeed. At all times, the core values of self-organizing teams and transparency need to be maintained.

> **HR TOP TIP**
>
> When some HR professionals start working in this kind of company, we often hear them say things like: 'They are making the simplest mistakes, wasting so much time on reinventing the wheel. There are no processes in place!' However, because there is no structure, there is a tendency to overcompensate and introduce a lot of processes and systems. Less is often more when standardizing practices as a start-up scales, and we encourage HR professionals to experiment when designing these types of processes and systems, avoiding unnecessary bureaucracy. Chapter 8 includes great tools for the HR leader for prioritizing where to start.

## Growth of a new business

Expanding into a new market or geography is a challenge for any organization, as the cultural, political and contractual context may differ from what the business has worked with previously. In these situations, Agile ways of working can help the business deal with this complexity, and are therefore preferred over rigid, waterfall planning. There are so many unknowns when it comes to growing a new business that little can be planned upfront and an Agile operating model is advantageous.

> **HR TOP TIP**
>
> When growing a new business within an organization, HR will need to build the supporting people practices or prepare for acquisitions. For example, the first people recruited are crucial in laying the foundations of success, and the onboarding process needs to be flexible and ready to adapt as new demands in capabilities and skills arise. The situation may also require new local partnerships with freelancers and suppliers. This is a high-intensity, fast-paced environment, where surprises are guaranteed, and it's essential for HR to be upskilled in Agile to support this growth.

## Innovation

Many companies are installing innovation hubs or launching experimental start-ups to probe the market around new business ideas. For example, Volkswagen We is a start-up within the larger, more traditional enterprise, which is rethinking mobility and creating services that use the car as a platform. Recent initiatives include 'your trunk is your delivery address' and creating an ecosystem where car owners rent out the use of their car while it's normally parked and idle (Volkswagen, 2020). An Agile operating model is required to drive growth and innovation within these internal start-ups and help them continuously improve.

---

**HR TOP TIP**

HR often needs to work cross-functionally with teams like marketing, finance and facilities, to help the mini start-up or hub ramp up quickly and generate an engaging buzz that encourages innovation. For an HR professional, this environment may feel more like being in a team of entrepreneurs, solving problems as they arise and co-creating a physical and social environment that attracts creative professionals. Within the hub, an Agile HR approach will help to quickly evolve the existing people practices inherited from the parent organization into nimble, lightweight frameworks more supportive of innovation. In these situations, we need to be creative within our constraints, and often we demonstrate to the central HR team of the parent company that evolving the people practices enables freedom but doesn't lead to a compliance risk. Indeed, the HR team within the hub might need to act as a type of internal Agile sales representative, explaining the benefits to peers and colleagues still working within the traditional part of the parent organization. It's also important to combat the development of an 'us versus them' dynamic, which we explore further in Chapter 15.

---

## Lead time to market

Accelerating time to market is one of the main reasons for larger companies to adopt Agile. Often this means transforming a research and development (R&D) function to be much closer to the end-customer, both operationally and physically, but also mentally. The aim is to dramatically reduce the time it takes for products to reach the market, as well as lower the risk of failure when launching new products. For example, a digital product that has a two-year lead time from initiation to market is already considered old when it eventually hits the market. By introducing an Agile operating model, products can be developed quicker, new concepts validated earlier and the risk of designing products or features that end-customers don't want to pay for, is vastly reduced.

HR TOP TIP

In these scenarios, HR's primary goal is to aid the restructuring of teams to work more closely with the customer and harness collaboration between R&D and other parts of the business. Often this links to the next main driver we'll discuss below, where teams are realigned to form customer-centric value streams. This can be quite a challenge, given a lot of these teams may have worked in a siloed way previously, and people may feel overwhelmed or threatened by the new environment. For example, it might feel very uncomfortable to shift from working together in a homogenous team of engineers, working on the same tech and product for a long time, and then be asked to work in a cross-functional delivery team partnering with new business stakeholders and maybe even end-customers. The more we can co-create the new organizational structure directly with the people involved, the more chance it will stick. HR will also need to accelerate the development of new capabilities, not just in technical skills but also in areas like communications and understanding the customer.

## Customer-centric value streams

Many companies are attempting to realign their teams and infrastructure according to the *product* or *customer* instead of a process, geography or another type of silo. Customer relations are very complex, and customers may operate across many countries, receiving a different level of service depending on which party they are dealing with. Imagine a small company sorting out interrelated questions about their loans, insurances and future financing. They certainly don't want to be calling five people in a bank to get answers, just because the bank's internal organization structure does not allow collaboration around their problem as a whole. Think about an insurance provider moving from a process-optimized organization setup (1) to the customer-oriented organization setup (2):

Setup 1: Unit A offers car insurances, Unit B offers employee insurances, Unit C offers property insurances....

Setup 2: New Unit X offers all insurances to small companies, New Unit Y offers all insurances to individual consumers, New Unit Z serves multinational corporations in all of their insurance matters....

As a result, many organizations are realizing they need to simplify the customer journey and realign their teams and processes into end-to-end value streams. These changes usually involve large organization-wide restructuring programmes, including the introduction of new tech architecture, alongside a new type of understanding and awareness of the end-customer.

---

### HR TOP TIP

From an HR perspective, transforming into a customer-centric organization usually requires radical restructuring and the need to build new capabilities to support the new value streams. For example, HR might support development initiatives, especially for the sales and end-customer functions, as well as recruit new people in the areas of service design, customer relations and digital development. Everything from management lines and mandates, through to existing processes and systems, needs to be realigned around the customer-centric value streams. People often feel confused, maybe even threatened, and often HR needs to help people understand where they fit in. This can be particularly important for people who have owned specific processes up until now and who understand the challenges they face when restructuring, and we need to help them move forward despite not knowing all the details at the beginning.

These situations call on HR's experience in guiding organizational and behavioural change and often require HR to take the lead in activities like leadership coaching and running workshops to aid collaboration, as well as helping people through redundancy or significant job role changes. HR should take the lead in evaluating the investment required to successfully support the people side of the change, as business leaders might lack awareness of details such as how many learning workshops are required or the cost of Agile coaching, and fail to allocate an appropriate budget.

---

## Simplifying products, processes and systems

Another reason an organization may invest in Agile transformation is to simplify their tech infrastructure or product portfolio. This is particularly common for companies that have grown through acquisitions and mergers and may need to align hundreds of different IT systems and products that have been acquired over time. For example, many large traditional banks are embracing Agile to deliver these simplification programmes, both to streamline their product offering and to build the necessary tech infrastructure to support digitalization (Verbeek and Smith, 2019).

HR TOP TIP

Often, these situations require HR to partner closely with the IT leaders overseeing the transformation, as well as Agile consultants who might be hired to either support or lead the change. It's useful to note here that some Agile consultancies may push for the business to commit to a wider full-blown organizational change and suggest the implementation of a pre-set Agile organizational design model (see Chapter 15 for more information on these models). We recommend being cautious about buying a solution that sounds good on paper but isn't tailored to suit the specific context. Another important nuance to remember is that IT-focused Agile consultancies are seldom experienced in HR and people practices. In our experience, this can lead to frustrations with a perceived slow response from HR to evolve the policies and practices to enable Agility. Thus, there is a need to help guide the more nuanced elements of organizational and behavioural change, and work closely with the Agile consultants to ensure people practices, such as performance, reward and learning, begin to evolve at the same time (see Chapter 17 for ideas on how to approach this).

## Developing a people-centric culture

Incorporating Agile values and practices into an employee brand can be a strategic decision by some organizations wanting to build a healthy talent pipeline and be seen as a people-centric employer. The focus here is to attract talent through positive stories and narratives that promote innovative people practices through social media and other network forums. However, it's important to remember that any Agile branding of this nature needs to be authentic and reflect the true culture of the organization. Otherwise, the company will quickly experience a backlash on feedback forums such as Glassdoor or LinkedIn.

HR TOP TIP

In this context, HR professionals tend to focus on facilitating cultural and employer branding initiatives, as well as energizing their end-customers and network with inspiring stories from within the organization about how great it is to work there. Often the aim is to build a community that reaches beyond the company's employees, by inviting partners, end-customers and candidates to become active followers. A company like this might host a lot of meetups, having invested in an event space with the aim of being a trendsetter and thought leader. Professionals from these organizations tend to be in demand as speakers at business events and conferences, and HR should boost these activities as fantastic learning opportunities.

We suggest that many HR professionals will recognize at least one of the drivers listed above and may even be experiencing several at the same time within their organization. Whatever the reason is for the business to embrace Agile, forming a clear and concise narrative around *why* is crucial to support the transformation over the longer term. Where HR adds the most value is in supporting the human side of the change and ensuring the approach is inclusive and empathetic.

## Creating a strong vision

To clearly articulate the *why Agile* for an organization, HR professionals need to partner closely with the leaders and teams, and assess which drivers are relevant to this particular story and the wider business context in which the company operates. The reasons and direction need to be clear and understood across the whole organization. For example, a well-known bank appreciates the need to answer the question of 'why?' for every new part of the business or location that embraces Agile transformation. To support this, a global transformation team closely partners with the senior leaders of each new area embarking on an Agile change. One of the first steps is to run an Agile 'bootcamp' where the leadership team for the specific location or business area explores their own context and agrees together why their part of the company should go Agile. What's interesting is that the bootcamp not only helps to make the Agile transformation directly relevant for that part of the business, but helps to personalize the change so that each leader is able to explain the reasons why in their own words.

Once the reasons for embracing Agile are clear, the natural question is: 'Where do we start?' The more organic approach of letting Agile practices spread team by team in the organization often doesn't bring the intended business value, because the change remains just at a team level rather than creating cross-functional value streams. Given this scenario, it will be necessary to assess where best to start with the transformation, as well as the appropriate speed of change for the organization given the context. A transformation backlog needs to be formed to guide the investment of time, money and effort for the change.

### Strategic prioritization tools to guide Agile adoption

Every organization will need to build their own approach to strategically prioritize the transformation backlog, which generally involves assessing the readiness towards Agile across the different business units and functions.

The following tools can help HR professionals guide this process and support the business in identifying the best place to start with Agile and why, as well as how to begin restructuring teams and processes to form value streams within the organization.

RISK ANALYSIS

The risks associated with Agile transformation can be undertaken from two main perspectives:

1   What is the risk of *not* going Agile within the different units or functions? For example, what are the opportunity costs if particular areas of the business don't transform, based on the competitive landscape?

2   What is the risk of *going* Agile for the different units or functions? For example, would this type of organizational change potentially threaten revenue streams owing to the instability introduced or the large capability gap that may exist?

Rarely do organizations go all in for Agile, but instead they find that incrementally evolving the Agile culture and ways of working makes more sense. Indeed, we're even seeing the need for some companies to hit the pause button in order to further develop and support the Agile operating model introduced in business units already considered transformed, before expanding across the wider organization (Bajkowski, 2019).

AGILE MATURITY ASSESSMENTS

Agile maturity assessments are very useful in helping HR professional and leadership teams understand where to start with Agile and the ongoing development needs for different parts of the business.

There are several assessment tools available, and organizations can also use these as a basis to build their own. Most assessments measure how teams are using Agile ways of working and cover factors such as:

- Teams have clearly prioritized backlogs.
- POs have the power to make all product-related decisions.
- Incremental value is delivered each cycle.
- Impediments are systematically removed.
- The team is planning their own workload.
- Continuous improvement is undertaken each cycle.

Some assessments also recommend using the 12 principles for Agile software development as the basis, while others focus on one metric, for example how often the organization can release a functioning product increment (Hewett, 2017).

Another option is to assess Agile capability levels with the organization, such as:

- Release planning is done in each value stream.
- We have Agile metrics in place and can forecast progress.
- There is cross-team coordination.
- We have a company-wide impediment removal process.
- Management structures support Agile operations.
- Strategic-level prioritization is done by portfolio management.

It's useful to formulate a maturity assessment based on which Agile practices are most important, given the shape, pace and overall approach to the transformation. Agile maturity assessments can be used both before and during the transformation, or even once certain parts of the business are functioning well, to further improve the general culture and ways of working. The key is to co-create the assessment for your own organizational culture and values and to ensure that everyone involved can identify what and how to improve next.

### CULTURAL AND LEADERSHIP ASSESSMENTS

Cultural assessments are beneficial for assessing the readiness and different levels of acceptance for Agile transformation. This helps identify the teams who are already thinking and working in an Agile way, as well as who might be willing to be the next adopters. These assessments can help teams and people appreciate their existing mindset, and identify the level of support, training and coaching needed in order to feel safe to experiment with Agile and begin the necessary mindset shift. Agile leadership assessments are also useful to help people in managerial or senior-level roles evolve their behaviour and thinking. In a similar way, assessments that help explore the existing management structures and identify the type of thinking or processes, such as how decisions are made, can greatly help accelerate transformation; for example, assessing whether the current management structure is based on waterfall thinking or identifying the number of steering groups, sign-offs and approvals required to deliver end-customer value.

## It's about people, not implementation

As mentioned previously, many companies kick-start their Agile transformation by creating a pilot area or hub within the business. Often this is linked to IT or a digitalization programme. This can vary from a couple of teams experimenting with Agile through specific projects, with the freedom to test and learn, through to companies committing to large-scale transformation programmes that quickly span hundreds, if not thousands, of people.

Whatever the approach, it's crucial to involve all our people from the start, and work together on designing the purpose and vision, as well as engage in the assessments and prioritize where and how we can continue to strengthen the Agile mindset. Many ask how to best *implement* Agile, but this question fails to appreciate that Agile is not an implementation programme; instead it's about the people. This is also where HR can play an important role in supporting the successful adoption of Agile and help everyone across the organization live and breathe the Agile values as they transform.

# Change resistance

It's healthy to reframe the traditional concept of change management when considering how to approach Agile transformation. As mentioned above, Agile should not be seen as an implementation, and as such, HR doesn't need to *manage* people through the change. Instead, we aim to co-create the outcomes together, by creating a safe space to experiment and learn new ways to work that are better than before. The assumption made with regard to change resistance is that a necessary behavioural change is imposed onto another person, usually within a set deadline. This approach implies that someone else, often a senior leadership team or HR, has done the thinking and decided what is best for the individual, and thus removes important elements of the learning process associated with change (Davachi *et al*, 2010), such as:

- attention to the issue;
- reflection and making connections to existing thinking patterns;
- generation of new insights and learning;
- connecting emotions to the learning to make it stick;
- spacing, meaning that people require time and repetition to change behaviour.

A key danger that HR professionals should be aware of is when Agile transformation is brought into an organization using this type of forceful change management methodology, often in the format of tools and techniques only, and the need to first propagate an Agile mindset is forgotten. This can lead to confusion and cognitive dissonance, where teams might start to use Scrum or other Agile practices to do things faster, without appreciating the corresponding behavioural shift required. This approach often sets teams up to fail and can lead to situations where people think Agile doesn't work for them.

---

### LESSON

Let's consider the persona 'Walter Waterfall'. Walter is 43, a project manager within the medical systems industry, highly competent in compliance-driven product development. Walter has been dealing with governmental safety bodies and is respected among colleagues for his advice on compliance and regulations. Given his experience, Walter's project plans are well prepared and quite accurate in terms of budgets, resourcing and scheduling.

Imagine that Walter now sits in a strategy kick-off meeting where the CEO enthusiastically launches an Agile transformation programme. 'We're going Agile!' He listens to a pilot team talk about how they are doing 'sprints' and adapting the scope of their project every week. Walter thinks about the one-year lead time he requires for any government approvals. He is certain that this pilot team will forget caring about the documentation and preparations for regulatory matters. He is sensing risks all over the place with these 'Agile' ways of working. He also knows that the CEO lacks domain expertise in regulatory matters. Of course, Walter is 'change resistant' in this example, but in reality it reflects a relevant fear of failure. Indeed, Walter is doing the right thing in not swallowing the strategy that someone else has set, without asking questions and sensing the risks. Walter's behaviour leads to the 'planners' of change being frustrated that the 'receivers' of the change are not as enthusiastic as they hoped, and therefore he is called change resistant.

---

This is the way organizational change has been approached for many years, and we believe it reflects an outdated human view. Human beings are inherently adaptive and will change their behaviour *if it makes sense to them*. Naturally, people will raise concerns, but this simply represents how humans process change and begin to alter their behaviour. A top-down, mandated change agenda has a high risk of failing (Dikert *et al*, 2016) and only serves to build an environment that is fearful of the change because people are scared of making mistakes. Paradoxically, management resistance and the lack of executive support are considered two of the biggest blockers to achieving business agility (Dikert *et al*, 2016; Standish Group, 2019; VersionOne, 2019), which suggests that a modern, invitational approach to facilitating change is needed among leaders as much as it is among employees. We encourage HR professionals to move beyond the traditional change management approach and focus instead on how to build psychological safety across the organization to support the development and continuous growth of the Agile mindset.

## Conclusion

Evolving the operating model of an organization with Agile ways of working should be viewed by HR professionals as a continuous and ongoing cycle of adaptation and change. At all times, the business benefits of embracing Agile need to be assessed, and the reasons for 'going Agile' clearly articulated and understood by all involved. HR plays a crucial role in helping to co-create this vision across the organization and personalize the narrative for each individual. Just like Agile itself, there is no right model or best-practice roadmap to achieve business agility, and leaders can't just instruct it to happen from the top. Rather, we need to build a strong vision together and create a safe space for everyone to experiment, fail, succeed and, most of all, learn.

---

KEY POINTS FOR HR PROFESSIONALS

- An Agile HR professional requires strong business acumen to support leaders in creating a powerful vision and narrative for why the company is adopting Agile as an operating model. The story and vision are unique for each organization, and even for different units.

- Despite a strategic imperative to build the new operating model at speed, an organization can't transform everyone and everything at the same time. HR professionals can play an important role in supporting leaders in identifying where to start and prioritizing the transformation backlog.

- HR can help identify key individuals who will be important in leading and coaching others through organizational change, as well as build maturity assessments and metrics to track the change on a strategic level.

- Successful and lasting Agile transformation requires change to be created in a human-centric and invitational way.

- There are valid reasons why some people are resistant to Agile, and HR professionals can support them through the change by helping them understand the 'new' logic contained within Agile practices and invite them to identify how their responsibilities fit within the new structure and ways of working.

# References

Bajkowski, J (2019) ANZ's Boss Hits Pause Button on Massive Agile Expansion, *itnews*, 2 May www.itnews.com.au/news/anzs-boss-hits-pause-button-on-massive-agile-expansion-524529 (archived at https://perma.cc/SJA8-6JJ9)

Davachi, L *et al* (2010) Learning that lasts through AGES, *NeuroLeadership Journal*, **3**

Dikert, K, Paasivaara, M and Lassenius, C (2016) Challenges and success factors for large-scale agile transformations: a systematic literature review, *The Journal of Systems and Software*, **119**, pp 87–108

Hewett, D (2017) Welcome to the World's Simplest Agile Maturity Model, *Equal Experts*, 30 November www.equalexperts.com/blog/our-thinking/welcome-to-the-worlds-simplest-agile-maturity-model (archived at https://perma.cc/66NH-25VM)

Standish Group (2019) CHAOS Report, *Standish Group* www.standishgroup.com (archived at https://perma.cc/7GH5-FYC9)

Verbeek, H and Smith, I (2019) Benefits of simplification, *KPMG Frontiers in Finance*, Issue 61, October

VersionOne (2019) 14th Annual State of Agile™ Report, *VersionOne* https://stateofagile.com/#ufh-c-473508-state-of-agile-report (archived at https://perma.cc/Q3L5-9398)

Volkswagen (2020) Volkswagen We, *Volkswagen* www.volkswagen-we.com/en.html#/Start (archived at https://perma.cc/GK2T-ZXYN)

# 15

# Agile organizational design

## Introduction

As we've learnt, Agile is a team-based model. So, what happens if an organization needs more than one team to get the job done? What if we need 10, 50 or perhaps hundreds of teams coordinating to deliver value to the end-customer?

In this chapter, we'll explore the concept of Agile organizational design and how to scale the team-based model across large sections of the business or even the whole enterprise. We'll explore the tensions that arise between factors such as autonomy at the team level versus alignment across the business on the end-customer vision. We'll also look at how an organization ensures effective cross-team dependencies, integration and governance, when the main power of Agile stems from self-organization and rapid decision making. Unsurprisingly, there is no one-size-fits-all approach when designing an Agile enterprise, and we'll look at the most popular operating models beginning to emerge across industry as organizations seek new ways to collaborate and achieve business agility.

Understanding Agile organizational design is a new capability for HR that draws directly on experience in guiding enterprise-wide cultural and behavioural change. It's also an area where HR can add immense value to the business. Leaders and teams require credible partners to help them transform, and it's paramount that modern organizational design is led in a people-centric way.

## Designing Agile organizations

The different Agile organizational design models that we'll explore in this chapter are easy to understand on paper but hard to adopt gracefully and sustainably in the real world. It's important to remember that the main aim of business agility is to lift organizational performance and deliver more value to the end-customer. This means it's risky to rush into scaling Agile. The first focus should be at the team level and how we can produce more value with the same number of people, ideally in half the time. As Dr Jeff Sutherland points out, 'if the PO can double the value of the output (through prioritizing the backlog), and the Scrum Master can help the team double the performance (velocity), we have a team that is delivering four times the value' (Sutherland, 2019). The learning here is that we need to achieve an effective team model before we scale and thus start adding challenges into this mix. Otherwise, we only scale problems.

We've also found that there are two main evolutionary routes organizations can take to arrive at an Agile design. The first is what we term 'Agile-by-nature'. These organizations represent a growing collection of enterprises that generally don't even use the term Agile on a day-to-day basis because they've lived the values and practices from day one. The aim here is to scale an already innovative and human-centric culture as the business grows, as well as gain a healthy level of coordination and structure, while still enabling self-organization and creativity. For Agile-by-nature enterprises, protecting the 'start-up culture' or 'entrepreneurial spirit' is not only about gaining a strategic advantage, it's part of their very DNA.

The second main route is for a business that operates a more traditional, pyramid structure to transform into an Agile organization. This implies a very different evolutionary pathway to achieving business agility. In these situations, HR needs to guide the organization through a series of developmental stages to shift mindset and allow a new way of working to emerge over time. It's also important to align and integrate non-Agile parts of the business quite early on with the new Agile vision, even if these teams don't embrace everyday Agile working practices in the longer term.

We'll now explore these two different pathways and discuss the main themes that HR professionals need to be aware of when guiding the various design elements for these types of organization.

## Pathway one: Agile-by-nature

It's not hard to be inspired by recent examples of start-ups or community-based collectives founded on Agile and human-centric principles. Indeed, many of their founders are now seen as gurus of modern business and speak regularly at conferences. Journals like the *Harvard Business Review* and *Forbes* also frequently showcase the innovative people practices these organizations have developed, such as gender-neutral parental leave, unlimited holidays and openly transparent salary structures.

Many Agile-by-nature organizations are founded on concepts like the Danish company Pingala, which set out to design a company where people want to work for the rest of their professional lives and view their culture like a product (Pingala, 2020). Or put more simply, it's about creating a business where 'going to work on Monday should not piss you off' (Goodnews Finland, 2016), as beautifully expressed by the founder of the Finnish software company Vincit, now recognized as one of the best places to work in Europe.

HR professionals can learn a lot from these inspirational case studies. Based on the principles of self-organization and self-management, most are rethinking the purpose of business beyond traditional shareholder profit. Instead, these Agile-by-nature organizations are growing social enterprises where the well-being of both their people and the community is a cornerstone of their success. Here, it's not just about looking after your people in a paternal way; it's about understanding that a person brings their whole life to work and that employment is much more than 9-to-5. These trends are also beginning to reshape the infrastructure of these organizations, which increasingly reflect an ecosystem of interlinking parts, where people seek out connections and information based on the need to deliver value to the end-customer, rather than predetermined roles or hierarchical mandates (Figure 15.1).

To bring this to life, let's explore the common characteristics of Agile-by-nature organizations, alongside a few examples.

### *Culture of trust*

In these organizations the behaviour and actions of people are often grounded in the values of the brand, rather than following policies or instructional handbooks. The premise is to treat people like adults. Why hire talented people if we then just tell them what to do?

A well-referenced example is Buurtzorg, an elderly care services provider based in the Netherlands. With over 10,000 employees, Buurtzorg has

FIGURE 15.1  The Agile network

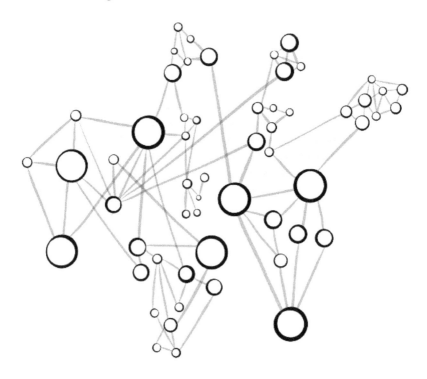

successfully scaled a self-organizing, nurse-led operating model into a highly profitable business that is even moving into new markets, such as Britain and Ireland. Within Buurtzorg, each self-organizing team essentially owns and runs the business for a specific geographical area. Each team undertakes both strategic and BAU tasks, and covers activities such as recruitment, workforce planning and capability development. The nurse-led teams are then supported by approximately 15 regional coaches and a small central-ized administration team that makes up only 8 per cent of all employees (compared to 25 per cent for most organizations), who manage core systems, payroll and other basic processes (Buurtzorg, 2020).

HR TOP TIP

Central to building a culture of trust is backing this sentiment with real words and actions. It's no use inviting people to make their own decisions within the workplace if they then can't even submit a travel expense without prior approval. HR professionals can take inspiration from Agile-by-nature enterprises and lead the way in building an environment of trust in all types of organization, through the way we write policy or design our processes. From dress codes that simply state 'wear what is appropriate' to entrusting teams with their own budget decisions, freeing people from low-level approvals and overly complicated procedures is a powerful way to display trust. What's more, in most situations these changes don't lead to the compliance breaches that are so often feared when the original policy is written. Most people want to and will do the right thing, especially when they believe in the purpose of an organization.

## Self-management

For people to self-organize, all essential information needs to be known and openly shared. As we have seen, Agile advocates using a range of techniques, such as visualization tools, backlogs and end-customer feedback, to constantly prioritize and make evidence-based decisions. Many organizations support this further through the development of sophisticated collaboration and communication frameworks. Great techniques to explore further include:

- non-violent communication (CNVC, 2020);
- work-out-loud peer networks (WOL, 2020);
- fierce conversations (Fierce, Inc, 2020);
- radical candour (Scott, 2020);
- advice-process (Bakke, 2013);
- consent decision making (Bockelbrink, Priest & David, 2020).

The level of organizational maturity required to achieve self-management should not be underestimated, and many organizations draw on specialist coaches or develop feedback champions to help facilitate outcomes. In saying that, people living by the consequences of their own decisions can be very motivating, and so blame is unnecessary if each person oversees their own actions and behaviours.

A great example is the Finnish national library, Oodi, which has developed a world-leading public space and service offering that attracts millions of tourists, not to mention corporate guests wanting to learn how they do it. Drawing on the principles of self-direction and nonviolent communication, anyone in their self-managing team of 52 people can make a decision that impacts the organization, with most made on the go. Larger problems and challenges are then raised either through team meetings or by gathering the whole organization together and using the format:

- *Thumb up*: For me it is good enough, go ahead.
- *Flat hand*: I have a concern, but as long as this concern is considered, go ahead. (Concerns are discussed.)
- *Thumb down*: I want to block this now; this is a no go, big risk, wrong timing.
- *Shrug*: I trust others who know more to make this decision; I empower others to decide.

The aim with this method is to make quick decisions that everyone in the group can commit to, without the need for full consensus or long drawn-out discussions (Norris, 2019). Another practice comes from the mid-sized tech company Futurice, which promotes a culture of self-direction, radical transparency and freedom. All decisions are fully transparent and shared with everyone across the organization. To do this, Futurice uses a tool called the '2×3 matrix', where any employee can make decisions as long as they deliver against the three dimensions of customers, company and employees, alongside the two time dimensions: today and in the future (Kantola, 2012).

Self-management does not automatically mean working without any hierarchy. Human beings often look towards leaders to help make decisions and assist in formulating vision and purpose. However, in Agile-by-nature organizations, there tend to be alternative forms of hierarchy to that of authority through position. Examples include representative voting systems and voluntary followership, where people choose their own leaders (Atkinson, 2015), as well as systems based on capability, effort and achievement (Gore, 2020). Of course, depending upon the ownership structure of an organization, shareholders or investors may have an influential impact, though some businesses have also aimed to shape this by forming cooperatives or designing option programmes that invite employees to become the main shareholders.

---

### HR TOP TIP

HR can help grow an environment of self-management within organizations by explicitly stating these behaviours in their values or in company artefacts such as culture codes and handbooks. The Hubspot Culture Code below is a great example of how company values can encapsulate an environment of trust and self-direction.

The Hubspot Culture Code

1  We are as maniacal about our metrics as our mission.

2  We obsess over customers, not competitors.

3  We are radically and uncomfortably transparent.

4  We give ourselves the autonomy to be awesome.

5  We are unreasonably selective about our peers.

6  We invest in individual mastery and market value.

7  We defy conventional 'wisdom' as it's often unwise.

8  We speak the truth and face the facts.

9  We believe in work+life, not work vs life.

10  We are a perpetual work in progress.

(Hubspot, 2013)

We suggest co-creating these types of organizational artefacts directly with your people and ensuring that the words capture the true meaning and essence of self-management for your specific culture and brand.

## Network

The foundations for these new operating models are networks of teams instead of hierarchical structures based on individual roles and ladders of authority. Networks are composed of small groups that are action oriented, where anyone can reach out and get in touch with another person to access the right information and move forward. To work effectively, networks require a shared purpose, which in Agile stems from the common goal of delivering value to the end-customer (Denning, 2018). Networks also pull directly on the strength of teams, because people find a sense of belonging and joint accountability to get things done together.

For example, the company Whole Foods is made up of a network of teams, each of which runs its own store and decides everything from pricing through to the recruitment of new team members (Burkus, 2016). Another good example is Sipgate in Germany, where self-managing teams take on tasks that traditionally fall to HR or the manager. At Sipgate the teams are directly responsible for actions such as recruitment and onboarding. They've also successfully created people practices and processes that are network based to remove the need for a manager, such as hosting three-way peer-to-peer feedback sessions to discuss people's performance (Mois, 2018).

---

HR TOP TIP

Facilitating the growth of networks becomes an important skill for the Agile HR leader. A great first step is to explicitly state that people have the freedom to discuss anything with anyone within a company code or values statement. This can help to encourage people to solve problems in real time through collaboration, rather than escalating them via management layers. Where possible, aim to limit the need for steering committees and written approval documents, especially for smaller decisions or ones that are under a certain budget. By harnessing the power of the network, HR professionals can greatly accelerate business performance.

---

## Servant leadership

In Agile, the team is the unit that delivers value to the end-customer, and all other roles, from the PO and Scrum master through to any business leaders, are subservient to the team. As we've seen, this generally leads to a much flatter organizational hierarchy or, in some cases, none at all. In many Agile-by-nature organizations, leadership can also become something that is distributed across many different roles, rather than tied to one in particular. Teams may even assign the tag of 'domain leader' to a certain person for a period, which then shifts to another person when a different type of expertise is required.

A famous example is Morning Star, a tomato-processing business that is entirely self-managing. Collaboration and coordination are built on two powerful principles: first, people should not use force or coercion against each other (meaning everything should be voluntary), and second, to honour the commitments you make to others (Hamel, 2011). As a result, Morning Star has no bosses, titles or promotions, and employees negotiate their responsibilities and even their salary with their peers (Kirkpatrick, 2018).

HR TOP TIP

In an Agile organization, HR plays an important role in coaching and developing leaders. A crucial mindset shift is supporting leaders to essentially let go and appreciate that they no longer need to provide all the answers because they can trust the Agile system instead. It's also important to consider the personality and cultural fit when recruiting servant leaders. Often, we're seeking out people skilled in coaching and enabling others, rather than experts in how the job is done. A lot of inspiration can be taken from Google's Oxygen project and how they identified the behaviours that helped a manager serve a team effectively. These included being a good coach, empowers team and doesn't micromanage, creates an inclusive and safe environment, and communicates a clear vision for collaboration (Google ReWork, 2020a).

## *Transparency*

Transparency is a core Agile value because it helps make everyone equal. In traditional, pyramid-style organizations, information often means power and is linked to positions of authority. As we've learnt, in Agile a lack of information slows us down. In Agile-by-nature organizations, transparent and visual information sits not only within the product or project backlog but across the whole business, which supports rapid and collective decision making as well as dialogue on opportunities and challenges that may lie ahead. It also encourages a diversity of thought, because everyone can contribute to the solution and so accelerate problem solving and performance. For example, some organizations allow anyone to make purchasing decisions with the knowledge that an inherent accountability exists within a transparent and openly visible system.

Transparency is also a great way to influence behavioural change. A good example is a medium-sized technology consultancy that made their sales pipeline and operations fully transparent. The result was immense, with people becoming more active, following up on customer leads and tracking market trends, as well as helping with the technical part of sales and even recommending projects to colleagues. In this case, information drove a sense of ownership and people were motivated to take on more responsibility because they were trusted with the customer data, including upcoming projects and opportunities.

Another great aspect of Agile-by-nature organizations' belief in transparency is that many publicly share their people frameworks, hacks and culture books. Indeed, most do this as a type of indirect brand awareness, confident that their culture drives a competitive advantage and attracts great talent. We encourage you to tap into this amazing open source, starting with some of the following:

- Hubspot's culture code, which took inspiration from the infamous Netflix SlideShare and is a great example of Agile values driving company culture (Hubspot, 2013);
- Netflix's hugely influential SlideShare (SlideShare, nd), which was the most ground-breaking insight into how to scale a successful Agile culture in Silicon Valley at the time (Nolen, 2014);
- Valve's uniquely different handbook, which takes the new employee on a journey (Valve Press, 2012);
- Beyond's award-winning and people-centric diversity and inclusion frameworks (Beyond, 2020);
- Google talks on YouTube, where you can learn from some of the biggest minds influencing society today (Talks at Google, 2020);
- ReWork, an amazing collection of practices, research and tools that are used internally by Google (Google ReWork, 2020b).

Remember, though, that we should never use these examples as blueprints but instead draw inspiration from these great ideas to help guide a design that is right for our own organizational context.

---

### HR TOP TIP

Witnessing teams solve problems together is magical, and a vital support mechanism is transparency of information. Even when the information is negative, if it's openly shared and discussed, people will tend to band together and take ownership to solve the problems faced. On the flipside, when only a limited amount of information is shared or none at all, people begin to mistrust the situation, even when it's positive. For example, being transparent about how salary and bonus decisions are made can dramatically shift people's acceptance of the process and why certain amounts are allocated.

## Protecting Agile-by-nature culture

The key challenge faced by many of these Agile-by-nature organizations is how to protect their great culture while they grow. Surprisingly, this often presents a need to introduce, *by choice*, standard processes to improve coordination or efficiency. Generally, this happens once the business grows beyond the ability for everyone to know each other personally. Another common reason is an unequal employee experience that can result from a mix of people practices being developed across the organization, such as different benefits or salary structures, because there was no one central team or mechanism aligning initiatives. Too often when this need for structure arises, we see HR professionals install unnecessary bureaucracy based on traditional best-practice thinking. Instead, we should see these moments as fantastic opportunities to embrace an Agile HR approach and co-create the solutions.

## Influential Agile-by-nature models

While some Agile-by-nature organizations draw inspiration from the Spotify model that we'll explore further shortly, many have been motivated by the frameworks and concepts presented through the *Teal movement*, *Sociocracy 3.0* and *Holacracy*. We've outlined the main elements for each below and encourage HR professionals to read more and explore different ways to enrich any organizational culture, not just Agile-by-nature.

### TEAL

Some of the examples referred to in this chapter are also included in Frederic Laloux's ground-breaking book *Reinventing Organizations*, as *Teal organizations*. Inspired by spirituality, integral theory and spiral dynamics, Laloux built a framework where humans, groups and organizations move through different stages of consciousness, each of which is symbolized by a specific colour. Teal represents the highest form of consciousness, where human interaction has evolved from an egocentric level into a world-centric dimension based on principles of self-management. Laloux describes Teal organizations as living entities oriented towards realizing their potential and driven through an evolutionary purpose, self-organization and wholeness at work (Laloux, 2014).

Based on Laloux's work, the Teal movement has begun to influence modern organizational development practices in important ways. The central themes of self-organization and self-management have encouraged people to seek new meaning in how and why we work and begin to redefine the purpose of an enterprise beyond that of shareholder profit.

SOCIOCRACY 3.0

Sociocracy 3.0 sets out seven principles to guide behaviour and, when made explicit, helps to evolve culture by raising people's consciousness about how they collaborate and adapt. The movement started in 2015 when James Priest and Bernhard Bockelbrink co-created a free learning resource that aimed to synthesize ideas sourced from the history of Sociocratic thought with Agile and Lean practices (Sociocracy 3.0, 2019).

---

LESSON

*THE SEVEN PRINCIPLES OF SOCIOCRACY 3.0*

- The Principle of Effectiveness: Devote time only to what brings you closer toward achieving your objectives.
- The Principle of Consent: Raise, seek out and resolve objections to decisions and actions.
- The Principle of Empiricism: Test all assumptions through experimentation and continuous revision.
- The Principle of Continuous Improvement: Change incrementally to accommodate steady empirical learning.
- The Principle of Equivalence: Involve people in making and evolving decisions that affect them.
- The Principle of Transparency: Make all information accessible to everyone in an organization, unless there is a reason for confidentiality.
- The Principle of Accountability: Respond when something is needed, do what you agreed to do, and take ownership for the course of the organization.

SOURCE Sociocracy 3.0 (2019)

---

Unlike other frameworks, Sociocracy 3.0 doesn't advocate a radical restructure but instead maps out a journey of continuous improvement that any enterprise can follow, be it a start-up, community body or large, networked business. Its collection of principle-based and independent patterns can be pulled on in different ways or adapted for various contexts to guide organizational development and design. We encourage you to delve deeper into Sociocracy 3.0 and learn more about the great frameworks.

HOLACRACY

Holacracy is a framework for decentralized management and governance, in which authority and decision making are distributed across the organization in the form of circles. Each circle is responsible for specific decisions and follows the detailed procedures set out in the Holacracy constitution, which guides everything from running a meeting to resolving conflict in a fair and democratic way (HolacracyOne, 2019). Throughout the organization, people take on certain roles and might contribute to several different circles as part of the governance structure. Zappos is probably the most well-known example of a company embracing Holacracy, with the aim of removing the layers between employees and the end-customer to enable 'faster and more creative decisions that improve customer satisfaction' (Zappos, nd).

## Not even Agile-by-nature is perfect

While these Agile-by-nature examples offer an uplifting vision for modern organizational development, they're not without their challenges, of course. For the many people who love the freedom a self-organizing environment offers, there are others who can feel pressured by self-managing peer groups. Also, despite the removal of managers, unhealthy influencers and social hierarchies can still develop if tension and conflict are not governed sufficiently (Spicer, 2018). The need for a high level of maturity and psychological safety is paramount, and to support this, HR professionals should build a coaching pool that can offer objective counsel.

We also see some people too quickly dismiss these organizational case studies because they tend to come from trendy tech companies and are sometimes too much of a stretch for more traditional organizations to even consider. However, it's important to see beyond the buzz that social media and magazine articles create over these examples of flat hierarchies or absence of managers, and to appreciate how the culture is a continuously evolving ecosystem within these enterprises. By creating a level of freedom for employees while still ensuring that all the necessary constraints and structures for quality and compliance are met, a fluid and adaptive organization can emerge and grow. The key point to remember is that Agile-by-nature organizations are never considered ready, but in a constant state of flux and development.

While it's possible to use many of the great ideas we've explored so far in this chapter to start a cultural change within any type of business, it might present too much of a mindset shift from our current starting point, especially for more traditional, pyramid-style organizations. To help with this alternative pathway, let's now look at how we scale Agile through transformation.

## Pathway two: Scaling Agile through transformation

Scaling Agile through transformation and shifting a whole legacy of hierarchical, top-down thinking (not Agile-by-nature) is a total game changer: the mindset shift required should never be underestimated. It's impossible to ask people to eradicate one operating system overnight and simply begin to self-organize instead. The path to Agile transformation is both evolutionary and contextual. We need to gradually and incrementally build up a new model of how we coordinate, align and govern across the business. The good thing is that HR professionals are not alone when it comes to Agile transformation: much can be learnt from the many organizations across the world that are now several years into their change journey, especially the Agile coaches and leaders who are now becoming seasoned experts.

In this section we'll explore how the organizational design and operating model begins to evolve when introducing and scaling Agile. We'll also review the common scaling models available and help HR professionals understand how and why they are used. This discussion then naturally leads into the next chapter, where we'll outline HR's role in Agile transformation and share all the hints and tips we've learnt up until this point in how to make scaling a success.

### Contextual and evolutionary design

As previously mentioned, the logic behind scaling Agile is not just about changing the organizational chart, flattening the hierarchy or adding more teams into the Agile model. The goal is to deliver more value to the end-customer, ideally in half the time. The holy grail of transformation is figuring out how to scale the Agile mindset and new ways of working, while simultaneously maintaining high performance and speed to the market.

An Agile organizational design cannot be implemented, it needs to *evolve*. Indeed, even the scaled models we'll look at are just starting points, and it will be necessary to adjust and fine-tune these operating models for each specific context. There are numerous narratives told in Agile coaching circles about companies rolling out a scaled model like a blueprint and trying to implement behavioural change through a business restructure. This approach is highly likely to fail, and what's worse, it can greatly harm people's perception of Agile and their subsequent willingness to embrace the mindset. Instead, research shows that customization and building a model that is fit for purpose are key success factors when it comes to Agile transformation (Dikert *et al*, 2016). It might seem obvious, but Agile transformation needs to be Agile in both its design and execution.

It's crucial that HR map out the different increments of change that we want our organization to experience and construct healthy feedback loops across the business to constantly assess where people's hearts and minds are at. Pace is also important, and while most senior leaders will want to follow an aggressive transformation agenda, there is a natural time lag in how behavioural and cultural change comes about, and HR professionals will need to help business leaders find the right balance.

That being said, it's also necessary to make significant structural changes from the outset if Agile transformation is to succeed. It's no use sending everyone to an Agile training if you're not ready to back this investment with actions such as redesigning the organizational structure, altering how you budget and asking managers to redefine their purpose and role. Many HR practices also fall into this category and we need to be ready to evolve our processes and systems from the beginning. When it comes to Agile transformation, Peter Drucker's famous saying, 'culture eats strategy for breakfast', is superseded by 'systems eat culture for lunch' (Honkonen, 2013). Ultimately, culture is what happens when no one is looking. It's far more powerful to influence the environment and structural boundaries that shape people's behaviour and how they collaborate rather than attempting to change the people themselves.

Experience and research suggest piloting Agile on a small scale first and learning from these experiments is a great way to kick-start transformation (Dikert *et al*, 2016). People who already see the value of Agile or perhaps have been testing Agile techniques in their own teams are great first movers. HR should help the teams involved share their successes, failures and learning to build awareness across the organization. The aim is to allow Agile ways of working to spread organically to where it makes the most sense, and early success stories can help create a curiosity and interest to try out these new ways of working.

HR can help to increase the successful adoption of Agile in these pilot teams by setting a strong mandate for the PO role, as well as explicitly stating which of the legacy processes the teams do *not* have to adhere to if they work Agile. For example, releasing the Agile teams from the annual performance management process or annual budgeting, and instead offering more lightweight practices, can greatly help reduce the conflicts created with traditional methods of working. Also ensure that only the PO, and not the line manager for example, can delegate tasks to the Agile team members and that all work goes through the backlog.

---

### WHAT THEY SAY

*Forbes* recently published an analysis of Agile transformations and found that 47 per cent of them failed. Eighty per cent of the people working with Agile transformation say they are using Scrum. MIT Sloan business schools did an analysis of the Agile transformation failures, and showed that 75 per cent of them were terminal, meaning the company went out of business, either going bankrupt or was acquired.

This isn't just another organization change. The executives need to give transformations their full attention. The reason for these failures is primarily keeping traditional management structures up and running when trying to manage Agile. So, executives and management need to understand, if they stay with the waterfall mindset, their Agile transformation is going to fail, and when it fails, they have a 75 per cent probability of failing big time. Executives need to go personally through a transformation in the way they approach their business and in the way they approach working with people. If C-level is serious about this, and the future of their company is dependent on executing this right, they really have to know how this works and then start to roll this out and learn as they are doing it.

Jeff Sutherland, 2020

---

### The inevitable hybrid

In reality, most organizations host a dual operating model for a long time, perhaps forever, when they scale. In a hybrid model, parts of the organization continue using the traditional waterfall practices or hierarchy, while other parts embrace Agile. This situation often arises when a large IT programme decides to support their roll-out with a specific scaling model, or an innovation hub starts using design thinking and Kanban to accelerate results. A hybrid model also results from it being unclear whether teams such as auditing, finance and compliance should embrace Agile ways of working when the transformation begins. As already discussed, we think it's crucial for these teams to also understand Agile and how it impacts their responsibilities, but these functions are often less likely to use Agile practices day to day.

Dual operating models can have unwanted consequences. While an experimental approach is recommended to get Agile started, it also carries a risk of quickly creating an 'us Agilists' vs 'those waterfall people' culture. This can isolate the Agile teams, and essentially create a company within a company that the wider organization may reject. We begin to hear statements like 'the rest of the organization doesn't understand us' or 'the leaders have no idea what we are doing'. To limit this, it's crucial for all teams aligned with the pilot teams to understand the Agile mindset and discuss why the organization is experimenting with Agile and what it hopes to achieve. In turn, the Agile pilot teams need to accept and acknowledge how their ways of working impact other parts of the business, and be willing to patiently onboard stakeholders as well as openly discuss tensions and collaborate to fix alignment and coordination problems as they arise.

Most organizations need to establish a supporting system for the hybrid model, and evolve management practices, governance and decision-making structures to serve both the traditional and Agile parts of the enterprise. Again, this means preparing to service a one-size-doesn't-fit-all environment. For example, a business might need to design two different budgeting processes as well as test out new methods of how to reward people as they create a fit-for-purpose organizational design.

Another good example of how a hybrid model develops is when we turn to the role of the manager. As teams begin to self-organize and the PO delegates work into the backlog, the traditional role of the line manager becomes blurred. The danger here is attempting to overlay an existing hierarchy onto the newly emerging Agile organizational design. In some cases, we have even heard executives and HR professionals answer this question with 'everyone must have a line manager, because the global HR tech system is built that way'. Instead, we need to determine what value a managerial role brings to the new structure.

In an Agile environment the role of the line manager often shifts to that of a coach and facilitator helping to align people with the end-customer vision, as well as solving dependencies and removing impediments. Additionally, we've seen line managers take a lead on important customer relationships rather than continue in their existing position. In all these examples, maintaining an open and transparent dialogue with the people transitioning is crucial to help them self-select and evolve their own role within the business. It's also good to note that some countries have legislative requirements on what constitutes a line manager role.

Finally, we might also need to educate our end-customers or suppliers on Agile when we start transforming, to counter the development of yet another type of hybrid. For instance, if our external stakeholders are used to working primarily with waterfall practices, such as a fixed scope, schedule and cost, embracing an Agile and adaptive approach may seem risky at first. Increasingly, we're seeing organizations use a form of Agile contracting to guide their end-customers and suppliers through the incremental development process.

---

**HR TOP TIP**

There will always be tensions between the waterfall world and the Agile world. Acknowledging these tensions and hosting forums where people can discuss and co-create solutions are essential. It can be truly magical when we find ways to collaborate and partner, rather than just collide. HR professionals can add immense value by helping to facilitate these conversations.

---

### Guaranteed fail

When scaling, some organizations tend to implement Agile teams into their existing waterfall structure without support or clearly defining the purpose of both. This can create a lot of unnecessary tension and is a sure way for Agile transformation to fail. Common signs include:

- **Agile as an add-on to an existing team structure.** Happens when a company has not understood the organizational design principles of Agile. Rather than people being allocated fully to cross-functional Agile teams, they continue to participate in numerous projects across the business, each with its own line manager or product owner.

- **PO plus manager delegates work.** Generally occurs when a manager fails to appreciate the role of the PO and working with a backlog or they continue to have their own targets to deliver that sit separately from the work being done by the Agile team. In both cases, the manager continues to delegate work to the members of the Agile team and disrupts the flow of work.

- **'Push and pray'.** Takes place when there are too many projects occurring simultaneously and work is not prioritized according to value at a strategic level. Different senior leaders have their own 'turf' and push projects onto teams based on their own annual bonus targets, without a realistic view of the true capacity and lead times required for the development work. This 'push and pray it will be done' approach can block agility and clog up the flow of work in the organization.

- **Micro-management through Agile.** Occurs when senior leaders implement backlogs and detailed planning, with the aim of strict micro-management, believing that managers can push more work through Agile and forgetting that true power comes from self-organizing teams.

---

HR TOP TIP

It is common for managers and POs to clash when Agile is first introduced. Useful methods to help resolve this problem include:

- agreeing that all work goes through the PO who prioritizes the tasks into the team's backlog, regardless of whether it relates to the Agile development work or not, and has the right to decline;

- hosting a forum to handle prioritization conflicts and competing targets;

- curtailing the line manager's ability to delegate anything to team members by restructuring or redefining roles;

- if team members cannot commit 100 per cent, defining a clear percentage of capacity for each member of the Agile team to focus on external 'own department work', for example one day per week.

---

## Common scaling models

There are several existing frameworks for scaling Agile that help organizations build the required governance, alignment and mandates to solve cross-team dependencies and achieve a good level of coordination. We believe every HR professional should be familiar with the most common Agile scaling frameworks and understand why and how they are used. To help, we'll introduce the basics of the four main models of Scaled Agile Framework (SAFe), Scrum at Scale (S@S), Large Scale Scrum (LeSS) and the Spotify model from an organizational design perspective.

### SCALED AGILE FRAMEWORK – SAFE

SAFe is the leading framework for scaling Agile and the most used model for large transformations or product development initiatives. The framework is robust and ensures strong governance across the whole organization, starting from the strategic portfolio level and flowing down to the different Agile teams.

SAFe is primarily structured around a 'release train', which is an aggregate of teams all working towards the same product (Figure 15.2). The goal is to deliver a shippable increment of value within a timeboxed period of 10 one-week sprints, called a programme increment. To ensure coordination and alignment, SAFe advocates a common cadence and big-room planning session (with the whole release train) every 10 weeks. Here, teams define their backlogs for the upcoming period, coordinate dependencies, deepen their understanding of the vision and map out deliverables together. Over 100 people can be in the room for this standardized two-day planning event, which happens four times a year. At the team level, Scrum is the main framework embraced, while Kanban is primarily used at the strategic portfolio level.

SAFe is a highly blueprinted framework and prescribes an implementation roadmap to successfully reach enterprise agility. It also offers best practices to follow, including an 'HR Playbook for SAFe implementation'.

FIGURE 15.2  Scaled Agile release trains

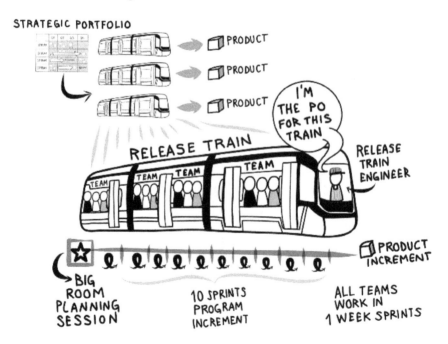

## HR TOP TIPS

- The SAFe framework offers a strong method for governance, alongside portfolio and programme-level prioritization, and herein lies the danger – some leaders like its prescriptiveness and HR should challenge if it's the right cultural fit and whether the leaders are ready to support the behavioural change required.

- The model is very structured and is based on clearly defined roles.

- From an organizational development perspective, the framework is more directive than evolutionary, and can be implemented one 'release train' at a time.

- The model introduces new roles such as 'release train engineer' or a 'portfolio manager' and it will be important to consider how these roles link into existing salary bands, position evaluations and accountabilities.

- By providing a pre-set design of what the model should look like and advocating clearly defined roadmaps for implementation, as well as defining the teams' scope of work for 10 weeks, SAFe has been criticized by some Agilists as being too blueprinted and commercial (Jefferies, 2014).

- The SAFe HR playbook (Priller and Richards, 2018) is pretty light but offers some direction in how to approach the supporting organizational development.

## SCRUM AT SCALE – S@S

Scrum at Scale or S@S is the new scaled framework launched in 2018 by the father of Scrum, Dr Jeff Sutherland. S@S is based on the fundamental principles of Scrum and draws from concepts contained in complex adaptive systems theory, game theory and Dr Sutherland's own work in biology. It is an evolutionary framework built for continuous improvement rather than a blueprint for implementation. For this, S@S creates a 'reference model' of a well-functioning Scrum team, which is then fractally copied across the organization (Figure 15.3). At all times, performance should remain stable, or indeed increase, as new teams are onboarded into the model.

However, the focal point for S@S is to scale not the number of people but the value of delivery. Sometimes 3 well-functioning teams do a better job than 10 teams owing to the increased demands on coordination. As such, S@S advocates scaling only when the data show it will lift performance and deliver more value.

FIGURE 15.3   Example of an S@S organizational model

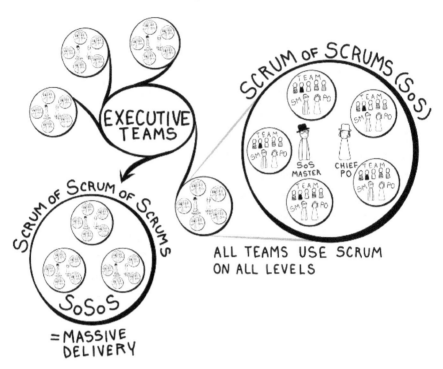

The idea behind S@S is that we only need to learn the basic Scrum framework to then scale the model across the whole organization. There are two sides of accountabilities for S@S:

- The **'what and when'** is delivered through the PO cycle. Work is prioritized and coordinated at a strategic level by an executive Scrum team, and then flows through to each team via the chief POs and team-level POs.

- The **'How?'** is delivered through the Scrum master cycle. The team-level Scrum master helps remove impediments and develop ways of working. This flows up to the Scrum of Scrum masters that aims to coordinate the same things at a larger, organizational level. The final level is the executive action team, which can influence corporate processes and structures as well as remove any impediments that are escalated all the way up. Importantly, the executive action team also use Scrum to ensure they walk the talk advocated to others.

> **HR TOP TIPS**
>
> - The model is fractal, with everyone embracing Scrum at all levels of the organization.
> - HR professionals need to support the creation of the Scrum team reference model before scaling, which also implies the redesign of the supporting people practices.
> - An important detail here is that the Scrum teams may use different cadences according to what makes sense to them, and we may need to design people practices that support some teams with one-week sprints as well as others with four-week sprints.
> - The model can scale from a couple of teams to the whole enterprise.
> - When scaling across bigger value streams, the executive team is actively leading the change themselves, through either the PO side (what and when) or the Scrum master side (structural changes and culture).
> - Senior leaders use Scrum as their main method of working, alongside everyone else, and will require appropriate coaching and support.

## THE 'SPOTIFY MODEL'

Almost every Agile conference over the past decade had one if not several people from Spotify, talking about their journey and sharing insights on their organizational design (Kniberg and Ivarsson, 2012). The model represented a snapshot in time for Spotify in 2012, rather than any pre-set organizational design, and gained popularity because the company was rapidly becoming synonymous with disruption and the ability to scale innovative methods across thousands of employees and several international locations. The fact that it was never meant to be an Agile operating model is a key point, and one that still mystifies many at Spotify, as organizations around the world continue to use it as the basis to their design (Kniberg, 2018).

Sitting at its core are autonomous Agile teams, known as squads, that work as independent units or, as Spotify likes to see it, mini start-ups (Figure 15.4). Each unit self-organizes, and decides which Agile tools to use, with the aim of designing, developing, testing and releasing products directly to the end-customer. These ways of working are summarized through their slogan of 'think it, build it, ship it, tweak it' (Kniberg and Ivarsson, 2012).

FIGURE 15.4  Tribes and squads

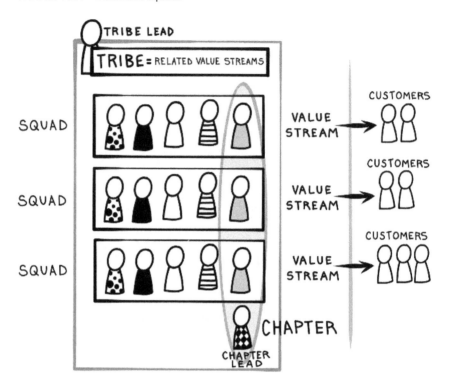

To further drive innovation, the squads can dedicate 10 per cent of their time to 'hack days', and work on any new ideas they want to test out. Some teams do a hack day every two weeks, while others save the time up and run a whole hack week.

Each squad has a PO, and can also access an Agile coach, who acts as a type of Scrum master and helps to evolve ways of working and run activities such as retrospectives. A collection of squads working on the same related product area, such as a mobile interface or playlist app, is called a tribe. Tribes are viewed as a type of 'incubator' for the mini start-ups. These follow the 'Dunbar number' theory, which limits the number of people a human can realistically know and socially interact with to 100. It is at the tribal level that issues like cross-squad dependencies, governance and alignment are worked out, usually by using the 'scrum of scrums' concept seen in the S@S model above. Generally, each tribe also has a leader.

Perhaps the most interesting component of the Spotify model for HR professionals is the concept of guilds and chapters. Acting as a type of glue for the organization, these collectives ensure good communication and the development of capabilities. A chapter is a capability group, for people with the same skill, for example testing, that sits within each multi-skilled squad to discuss shared challenges and maintain quality. A chapter lead also helps this collective further strengthen their specific skills. A guild is more organic and usually works across the whole organization as a community of practice. Here, people with the same interest, for example keen followers of AI technology, come together through regular events to grow the body of knowledge for the company.

---

HR TOP TIPS

- The Spotify model is essentially a matrix, which even they acknowledge, but what makes it unique is the logic of value delivery through autonomous, self-organizing squads with access to direct end-customer feedback.

- Spotify's true differentiator is the beauty of their culture, which isn't visible in the organizational model and instead reflects a huge investment in developing great collaborative patterns and a strong set of values to guide behaviour.

- Despite Spotify stating it is not a model, and they themselves have since evolved beyond the design, many companies have followed this structure to scale Agile, and indeed several prestigious consultancies now present it like a blueprint for Agile transformation.

- The HR team at Spotify shares a great public blog from which HR professionals can learn about the cultural initiatives and hacks used within the company (Spotify, 2020).

---

## LARGE SCALE SCRUM – LESS

The LeSS model works on the principle of 'one team Scrum' and was formulated by the idea of taking what works so well on a team level and scaling it up for large product development initiatives. The model can work with just a few teams as well as be scaled up for thousands of people. Within LeSS, all teams work on the same product and from a single overriding backlog. For this there is one PO, as well as one overriding Definition of Done and one Potentially Shippable Product Increment at the end of the one same sprint that all the teams contribute to.

Where the model differs slightly from the core Scrum framework is at the planning stage. Here, the teams have two levels of sprint planning. The first is a multi-team planning session with the PO, where the teams pull the product features they will focus on for the sprint. This is followed by a second planning session, which happens at the individual team level. The teams also undertake a joint backlog refinement session to check in and continuously improve during the sprint, often directly with the end-customer. At the end of the sprint, all the teams come together for a large sprint review, which is likened to a 'bazaar' or 'science fair'. An overall retrospective then follows, through which the teams explore how to improve the overall system, before focusing on individual team dynamics via their own team-level retrospective (LeSS, 2020).

---

### HR TOP TIPS

- LeSS always works on the principle of delivering one integrated product increment at the end of each sprint, even if multiple teams contribute to this output.

- There are no assigned coordinators in the model, and teams are responsible for aligning and resolving cross-team dependencies themselves.

- During the mid-sprint backlog refinement session, the teams often check in with the actual users and end-customers, rather than with the PO (Dawson, 2017).

- LeSS focuses on how an organization can strip away the rules, habits and processes that limit people's behaviour and results, and on how to continually simplify the culture towards LeSS principles.

- LeSS aims to co-create a supporting and evolving culture of continuous improvement.

- The model itself is seen as the minimum starting point, from which teams can take ownership, gain a holistic product view and optimize the organizational design for value delivery and flexibility.

- LeSS tends to be applied within an IT environment and is particularly suited to large, technical programmes or product development.

---

While the above list of scaling models is by no means exhaustive, we hope the discussion demonstrates how each design supports different outcomes and the need to weigh up the benefits and potential pitfalls of each when supporting Agile transformation. For example, SAFe may provide a business with strong governance and backlog alignment, while the Spotify model may be best suited if the goal is to innovate rapidly. Our aim is for you to feel comfortable in asking great questions, challenging leaders' thinking when necessary and truly helping organizations co-create a design that suits their own unique context. Furthermore, it's important to appreciate the different models in order to understand the systemic structures and processes, such as budgeting and planning as well as our own HR services, that are required to enable their success.

It's also good to note that if an HR professional begins to work within a specific model, because it has been selected or was already in operation when they joined, it's important to help make the model a success no matter their personal preferences. For each model, different people practices will be more relevant. For example, a team-based performance framework may be less suited to the SAFe model because everyone works within a train and it might be beneficial to lift to consider the train holistically when exploring how to set up performance and reward. However, a team-based performance framework might be more successful in a Spotify model, where the teams work as autonomous squads. The way to find out is to test these ideas with your people.

## Conclusion

Agility is not about the end-state, it is an evolutionary journey. Whether it forms the basis of an Agile-by-nature organization or guides the transformation of a traditional business, the Agile operating model will never be fully ready. Organizational development will be a continuous improvement quest, balancing structure and governance to ensure stability on the one hand, while on the other enabling agility and adaptation to respond to end-customer needs. Agile can be scaled by evolving an organizational design to fit the purpose, context and desired pace of transformation. HR has a central role in making all of this happen successfully, which we'll explore in the next chapter.

KEY POINTS FOR HR PROFESSIONALS

- The goal of Agile organizational design is to scale the team-based model across large sections of the business or even the whole enterprise.

- Understanding Agile organizational design is a new capability for HR that draws directly on our experience in guiding enterprise-wide cultural and behavioural change.

- When guiding Agile organizational design, HR needs to constantly navigate the tension between an alignment of vision and governance across the organization and autonomy and self-organization at the team level.

- There are two main evolutionary routes that organizations can take to arrive at an Agile design:

  o Agile-by-nature – comprising organizations that have lived the Agile values and practices from day one;

  o Agile transformation – comprising organizations that need to transform away from a traditional, pyramid structure.

- Designing healthy and successful Agile organizations should always be viewed as a journey, rather than an end-state, and, just like Agile itself, continually evolves.

# References

Atkinson, D (2015) Executives and Managers Should All Be Elected, *TechCrunch*, 21 July https://techcrunch.com/2015/07/21/executives-and-managers-should-all-be-elected/?guccounter=1 (archived at https://perma.cc/Z3CY-T2TJ)

Bakke, D (2013) *The Decision Maker: Unlock the potential of everyone in your organization, one decision at a time*, Pear Press, Seattle, WA

Beyond (2020) The Belong Frameworks, *Beyond* https://frameworks.bynd.com (archived at https://perma.cc/PA8T-QP3P)

Bockelbrink, B, Priest, J and David, L (2020) Sociocracy 3.0, *S3* https://sociocracy30.org/the-details/principles/ (archived at https://perma.cc/8ZNM-MLRA)(https://sociocracy30.org/ (archived at https://perma.cc/9G9P-PNSX))

Burkus, D (2016) Why Whole Foods Builds Its Entire Business on Teams, *Forbes* www.forbes.com/sites/davidburkus/2016/06/08/why-whole-foods-build-their-entire-business-on-teams/#47eb14df3fa1 (archived at https://perma.cc/HM4X-AK62)

Buurtzorg (2020) Homepage, *Buurtzorg* www.buurtzorg.com/about-us/
our-organisation (archived at https://perma.cc/3QUD-GABL)

CNVC (2020) Homepage, *Center for Nonviolent Communication* www.cnvc.org
(archived at https://perma.cc/SM92-7UL7)

Dawson (2017) Introduction to LeSS (Large-Scale Scrum), YouTube, 17 September
www.youtube.com/watch?v=1BZf_Oa7W94 (archived at https://perma.cc/
VL43-T2ZK)

Denning, S (2018) *The Age of Agile: How smart companies are transforming the
way work gets done*, American Management Association, New York

Dikert, K, Paasivaara, M and Lassenius, C (2016) Challenges and success factors
for large-scale agile transformations: a systematic literature review, *Journal of
Systems and Software*, **119**, September, pp 87–108

Fierce, Inc (2020) Homepage, *Fierce, Inc* https://fierceinc.com (archived at https://
perma.cc/KC7U-3XJC)

Goodnews Finland (2016) Vincit: From Bankruptcy to Europe's Best Workplace,
*Goodnews Finland*, 23 November www.goodnewsfinland.com/feature/vincit-
bankruptcy-europes-best-workplace (archived at https://perma.cc/9S6R-8YWP)

Google ReWork (2020a) Guide: Identify What Makes a Great Manager, *Google
ReWork* https://rework.withgoogle.com/guides/managers-identify-what-makes-
a-great-manager/steps/learn-about-googles-manager-research (archived at
https://perma.cc/GWQ9-Z45E)

Google ReWork (2020b) Guides, *Google ReWork* https://rework.withgoogle.com/
guides (archived at https://perma.cc/5VFM-NXPJ)

Gore (2020) Working at Gore, *Gore* www.gore.com/about/working-at-gore
(archived at https://perma.cc/8XKN-RJEY)

Hamel, G (2011) First, Let's Fire All the Managers, *Harvard Business Review*,
December https://hbr.org/2011/12/first-lets-fire-all-the-managers (archived at
https://perma.cc/PA9C-KC4J)

HolacracyOne (2019) Evolve Your Organization, *Holacracy* www.holacracy.org
(archived at https://perma.cc/RA4N-AQES)

Honkonen, S (2013) System Eats Culture for Lunch [Blog], 14 November  https://
blog.samihonkonen.com/system-eats-culture-for-lunch-623c9dfff25f (archived
at https://perma.cc/EUU6-A2PG)

Hubspot (2013) The HubSpot Culture Code, SlideShare www.slideshare.net/
HubSpot/the-hubspot-culture-code-creating-a-company-we-love (archived at
https://perma.cc/ZNN7-6ZUW)

Jeffries, R (2014) SAFe – Good But Not Good Enough, *Ron Jeffries*, 27 February
https://ronjeffries.com/xprog/articles/safe-good-but-not-good-enough (archived
at https://perma.cc/57JC-Z5FP)

Kantola, E (2012) Decision making at Futurice [Blog], 7 May www.futurice.com/
blog/decision-making-at-futurice (archived at https://perma.cc/2YQM-6APV)

Kirkpatrick, D (2018) Keynote – Futurework: Managing Complexity With Simplicity – Doug Kirkpatrick, YouTube, 30 October m/watch?v= WF3Lloyp-xc&list=PLe-GNgMqRelw1-EESqgD2HMh 5uDdRtTkH&index=3 (archived at https://perma.cc/R4B8-YHNN)

Kniberg, H (2018) Twitter post, Twitter https://twitter.com/henrikkniberg/status/1000997890934816768 (archived at https://perma.cc/EKK4-FZG4)

Kniberg, H and Ivarsson, A (2012) Scaling Agile @ Spotify with Tribes, Squads, Chapters & Guilds [Blog], October https://blog.crisp.se/wp-content/uploads/2012/11/SpotifyScaling.pdf (archived at https://perma.cc/S5PB-KEEP)

Laloux, F (2014) *Reinventing Organizations: A guide to creating organizations inspired by the next stage of human consciousnes*s, Nelson Parker, Millis, MA

LeSS (2020) LeSS Framework, *LeSS* https://less.works/less/framework/index.html (archived at https://perma.cc/E56E-HD5T)

Mois, T (2018) Sipgate's Agile Transformation, *Agile 42*, 16 August www.agile42.com/en/blog/2018/08/16/sipgate-agile-transformation/ (archived at https://perma.cc/86YJ-SSRE)

Nolen, R (2014) Netflix Culture: Freedom & Responsibility, LinkedIn Slideshare, 23 June www.slideshare.net/nolensan/netflixorganizationalculture-131001173045phpapp02 (archived at https://perma.cc/VS4E-PCQW)

Norris, L (2019) Laura Norris: Oodi – The New Way of Working [Video of live talk], *Helsinki City Library*, July www.kirjastokaista.fi/en/laura-norris-oodi-the-new-way-of-working (archived at https://perma.cc/N66N-CK6D)

Pingala (2020) Pingala – When Culture Is Your Product (Case Study Taken From 'The Responsive Leader' by Erik Korsvik Østergaard) https://pingala.eu/en/pingala-when-culture-is-your-product (archived at https://perma.cc/85UZ-ZQJ7)

Priller, L and Richards, M (2018) An HR Playbook for a Successful SAFe Implementation [Blog], *Scaled Agile*, 25 April  www.scaledagileframework.com/guidance-an-hr-playbook-for-a-successful-safe-implementation (archived at https://perma.cc/TM93-2QL2)

Scott, K (2020) *Radical Candor* www.radicalcandor.com (archived at https://perma.cc/7LS5-MU8Z)

SlideShare (nd) Netflix Culture: Freedom & Responsibility www.slideshare.net/nolensan/netflixorganizationalculture-131001173045phpapp02 (archived at https://perma.cc/VS4E-PCQW)

Sociocracy 3.0 (2019) Sociocracy 3.0 – A Practical Guide, 27 June https://patterns.sociocracy30.org/introduction.html (archived at https://perma.cc/K36U-2SCD)

Spicer, A (2018) No Bosses, No Managers: The Truth Behind The 'Flat Hierarchy' Facade, *The Guardian*, 30 July www.theguardian.com/commentisfree/2018/jul/30/no-bosses-managers-flat-hierachy-workplace-tech-hollywood (archived at https://perma.cc/D9U8-GUCL)

Spotify (2020) HR Blog, Spotify https://hrblog.spotify.com (archived at https://perma.cc/2VUA-EFJG)

Sutherland, J (2019) Scrum at Scale Training live event, Boston, MA

Talks at Google (2020) Talks at Google, YouTube www.youtube.com/channel/UCbmNph6atAoGfqLoCL_duAg (archived at https://perma.cc/M5J3-M2G3)

Valve Press (2012) Handbook for New Employees, *Valve Corporation*, March https://steamcdn-a.akamaihd.net/apps/valve/Valve_NewEmployeeHandbook.pdf (archived at https://perma.cc/HX2M-CZXZ)

WOL (2020) Working Out Loud https://workingoutloud.com (archived at https://perma.cc/T3FT-RZM6)

Zappos (nd) Zappos Insights, *Zappos* www.zapposinsights.com/about/holacracy (archived at https://perma.cc/G5ND-WRT5)

# 16

# HR's role in Agile transformation

## Introduction

It's time for HR to be a strategic partner in guiding organizational-wide Agile transformation. As we've come in appreciate, Agile is all about people, and the HR domains of culture, talent development and organizational design are crucial components in all business transformation. By closely collaborating with leaders and teams, as well as having roles like Agile coaches, HR has a fantastic opportunity to co-create the necessary changes in people practices, such as performance and reward, which are crucial in supporting the success of transformation.

In this chapter we'll explore the important role HR plays in Agile transformation. We'll primarily look through the lens of a traditional company seeking to reinvent their operating model by embracing Agile ways of working. However, many points made here are also applicable to what we call Agile-by-nature organizations, which have developed through Agile values from day one. As discussed throughout this book, there is no one recipe or blueprint for how to guide Agile transformation, and HR needs to view this change as an evolutionary journey that is unique for each organization. To help HR professionals get started or accelerate an existing organizational change project, this chapter contains tips, tricks and actionable suggestions that we've learnt over the years we've spent leading and participating in Agile transformation work.

## Be a transformational leader

It's important for HR professionals to lead the people component by being on the transformation team from the start and to help leaders guide an empathetic and behavioural-based approach to the organizational change required. HR's role in the transformation team is crucial, because the systemic structures of existing management and people processes may quickly create blockers to Agile ways of working if they are not evolved alongside the behavioural change taking place at the team level.

---

HR TOP TIPS

- The first thing HR needs to focus on is evolving the performance management and reward system to reflect the team-based, self-managed and cyclical nature of Agile. Sometimes these changes require negotiation and trade-offs with a central team or corporate HR and may therefore require more time to do it successfully. Check out Chapter 17 for ideas on where to start.

- Despite often starting in IT, Agile transformation should not be perceived as only an IT change. This is a human behavioural change, impacting everyone across all levels of the company. HR professionals skilled in people strategy and organizational design and development are great at catalyzing these changes. This is an opportunity to co-create solutions with our people and embrace our central role in building the future of work. HR shouldn't be on the sidelines waiting for a seat at any table. There are more and more examples of HR professionals taking on the role of Agile transformation leads for the whole business. This is hugely exciting for our profession.

---

## Ensure leaders understand Agile

To ensure that a transformation initiative leads to lasting change, it's essential that the people responsible for leading the vision and enabling the organizational design understand what Agile means holistically. Numerous times we've spoken to executive teams who say, 'we're already Agile', because they know some teams are using Scrum within their units. However, following a two-day hands-on learning experience, exploring the Agile mindset and assessing their own readiness, most realize how far reaching the change is for their business to become a truly Agile organization. We therefore recommend creating opportunities for leaders to learn and experience Agile first-hand. Executive sponsorship is a key success factor for Agile transformations, as highlighted by various Agile surveys such as the annual State of Agile Report (VersionOne, 2019) or the CHAOS Report (Standish Group, 2019). These findings also concur with research on Agile transformation (Dikert *et al*, 2016).

HR TOP TIPS

- Invite executive teams to participate in silent brainstorming on what they believe Agile means. We're often surprised by how different the answers can be, even within companies that are already working with Agile methods.

- Book at least two days for an initial executive learning workshop. Ensure the facilitators are experienced in dealing with senior stakeholders and have actually trained executive teams to maximize the impact and likelihood of motivating leaders to act. Start facilitating honest and open retrospectives with executive teams, so that they too embrace the Agile feedback loop and explore how to continuously improve together.

## Understand the mindset before the practices

The focus of the Agile transformation should be on how to evolve people's belief systems and thinking patterns to then guide their sense making. Sometimes organizations approach Agile transformation like a technical implementation and begin to adopt the Agile work practices while ignoring the core values that drive the methods. As we explored in Chapter 3, it all starts with mindset, which in itself will encourage people to seek new learning and start to experiment with Agile practices.

HR TOP TIPS

- Create a narrative around what is happening for the end-customer and the value the company is creating for them. Discuss where business agility is needed and where it's not.

- Invite people to experience the difference between waterfall and Agile ways of working, for example an exercise where people solve a complex problem using waterfall methodologies. Be sure to assign a manager to oversee the whole activity and introduce changes along the way. Then repeat the exercise, but this time invite the group to self-organize and apply Agile practices. Then facilitate a discussion on the insights, benefits and pitfalls of both approaches.

- Avoid placing waterfall and Agile against each other as different parts of the organization begin to transform. Explicitly state that people haven't been doing anything wrong up until now. Agile is a way of navigating complexity and delivering value to the end-customer in an environment of constant change, whereas waterfall is still useful for projects involving a high level of certainty or repeatability.

## Own the change

While external coaches and consultants can provide useful guidance and advice on how to start applying Agile practices, the true mindset and culture shift takes place at the human level. The aim is to build a sustainable, long-term change, and it's important for HR to upskill their own teams and other supporting roles, to own the change agenda internally and ensure Agile becomes intertwined with everyday actions.

---

HR TOP TIPS

- Help choose consultants who work with the ideology of building internal capability and a *do it yourself* approach, thus avoiding change tailing off when the consultants leave.

- Maintain a continuous onboarding and handover plan from any consultants to the internal transformation team or leads. Then good consultants will leave without any pain, knowing the client can lead the change themselves.

- Secure funding for organic change activities such as learning events, external guest speakers and for hosting face-to-face sessions such as planning meetings or reviews.

- Ensure funding for people to participate in Agile conferences or other events where the early adopters and Agile coaches can look for inspiration and ideas on next steps.

- Offer space and snacks for internal Agile events, like hackathons and Lean coffee meetups. Often, this type of funding increases as the Agile transformation spreads, when teams and coaches become more active and the learning more self-directed, and it's useful to anticipate this need.

---

## Get to know different scaling models

As we covered in Chapter 15, there are many different models to help organizations scale Agile. It's important that HR professionals become familiar with each of these models in order to follow, support or challenge the thinking of senior leaders or consultants. Although transformation is an evolutionary and contextual adventure, the target organizational design and operating model will dictate the choice of the corresponding scaling model.

---

HR TOP TIPS

- Before scaling Agile, first help coaches and leaders ensure the practices work really well on a smaller scale or team level. This provides a learning opportunity for everyone in the organization, using insights gained to guide the wider transformation.

- Organize a learning experience that allows decision makers to explore different scaled Agile models and discuss the pros and cons of each.

- Look for a good fit to your organization, but keep in mind that Agile transformation is never simple and straightforward.

---

## Agile transformation should be Agile

As we've explored previously, Agile cannot be implemented simply by following a predetermined plan. We therefore recommend applying the same Agile practices advocated across the organization to the transformation itself. Use backlogs to prioritize actions and engage in activities like retrospectives and reviews to continuously improve the organizational change roadmap. Also support the organic nature of Agile transformation by encouraging people to experiment with new ways of working, form learning networks and share information across teams.

---

HR TOP TIPS

- One of the risks with transformation is that people understand the concept of agility in different ways (Dikert *et al*, 2016), so it's useful to co-create common Agile terminology.

- Co-create what a minimum viable common Agile approach might look like within the organization.

- Refrain from instructing everyone to use a specific Agile methodology... that is not Agile.

- Start leading the transformation by using Agile practices, for example mapping out a transformation release plan and working according to a cadence.

- Use the ideology that everything is transparent unless there is a specific legal reason for it not to be.

---

## Lead transformation through a backlog

We recommend setting up a transformation backlog in collaboration with the change team, Agile coaches and senior leaders to guide all work. This helps people appreciate that leading change takes a lot of time, and requires collaboration, cross-team syncing and communication. We recommend using a visible and transparent backlog, instead of meeting minutes or e-mails, to make leading the change practical and more tangible.

---

HR TOP TIPS

- Be concrete and specific when working on the core transformation team. For example, a backlog item saying 'draft new team compositions' is not specific enough. Instead, create acceptance criteria for the transformation backlog items, such as 'every vice president co-creates with mid managers and at least 10 team members a draft of the new customer-centric team composition'. We find this greatly helps to make it clear that each leader needs to *do* something.

- It's important that everyone knows when a backlog item is considered to be done. To help with this, it's important that less specific items, such as 'communicate about X', 'run a strategy workshop' or 'create psychological safety', are broken down into more concrete items. Then, define clear acceptance criteria to ensure everyone is clear on who does what and by when. This can be particularly useful to leaders who are often used to talking about these topics at a higher, more theoretical level.

---

## Measure the transformation and be transparent about tensions

Agile maturity and cultural assessments can offer insightful data that help guide transformation. For example, are teams successfully adopting Agile values, practices and principles? Which tools and methods do they prefer? What challenges are they facing when adopting Agile? See Chapter 14 for more information on these assessments.

---

HR TOP TIPS

- Share the results of Agile maturity and cultural assessments with the wider HR team to ensure that other HR initiatives are also in sync with the transformation.

- Encourage early adopter teams to share their experiences with a wider audience.

- Keep track of any tensions that arise between Agile and waterfall, and offer coaching and support. Regardless of the scope of the transformation, there will always be tensions at these interfaces. For example, we've seen R&D units embrace Agile, without helping their business counterparts responsible for customer relations and sales understand why they should also actively participate in product development with the end-customers. These tensions will shift according to how the company is solving impediments, onboarding more people into the Agile teams or agreeing how to collaborate.

## Prepare for new roles

Agile transformation creates new roles in the organization, including product owners and Scrum masters. We also need to build T-shaped, multi-functional teams. So, in advance of the transformation, HR needs to prepare new salary levels, job descriptions, job grades, associated performance and rewards arrangements and understand what skills and capabilities are required for these roles. For example, it took one international company three months to set up the Scrum master role in their HR system, by which time the business had already hired without the necessary administrative requirements in place. We've also seen adverts for roles that don't exist in Agile, like Scrum project manager or Scrum team leader, which reflect a lack of understanding of Agile on the part of the people recruiting (Wolpers, 2017).

---

**WHAT THEY SAY**

You need to get this right and get the correct people in the roles of PO and Scrum master to make this work, and they need to be doing the right things to create a self-organized system that accelerates. For example, there are too many Scrum masters who let teams do whatever they want, without challenging and stretching the team. If the Scrum masters are not improving the performance of the team, if they don't fix broken teams and collaboration, the role is not right for them.

Jeff Sutherland (Hellström, 2020)

HR TOP TIPS

- Start defining the descriptions for roles like Scrum master, product owner, chief product owner, programme manager, portfolio owner or manager, and Agile coach.

- Strengthen your understanding on what these roles do and the appropriate terminology to use. Prepare any necessary salary bands, grading scales, responsibilities, mandates and expectations for each role. The aim is to be ready to recruit at any time.

## Enable capability development

A big part of transformation is to support the development of Agile capabilities throughout the organization. While initial Agile training is appropriate, this type of development generally happens best through self-directed activities, such as building communities of practice, engaging early adopters, sharing knowledge, learning from other companies and developing a pool of active change agents who demonstrate the Agile values and vision in their actions. We also suggest designing recruitment practices to assess candidates against the Agile mindset, in order to attract and develop great talent to step into the roles of Agile coaches, Scrum masters and POs. Again, check out Chapter 17 for ideas on how to do this.

HR TOP TIPS

- Think about your recruitment process. How are you assessing whether new hires have an Agile mindset or are capable of handling uncertainty? Both of these are crucial when building an Agile culture. Indeed, some companies even recruit whole Agile development teams instead of individuals in order to accelerate this process.

- Define anchor roles such as PO or Agile coach that are vital to the success of the transformation and start identifying candidates for these roles as early as possible.

- Create an organization-wide Agile onboarding programme, ideally facilitated by Agile coaches. Even when we hire people based on an Agile mindset and experience using Agile methods, every business has their own Agile approach, and it's crucial to upskill new hires in the relevant practices, structures and language.

- Move beyond the traditional roles and career pathways when building skills. Learning should not and cannot be centrally mandated. Make it easy for individuals and teams to develop themselves. See Chapter 17 for suggestions.

## Design for workforce agility

Once a business has effective prioritization in place at the strategic level, the organizational network should be fluid enough to allow people and roles to move easily in response to end-customer needs. HR professionals should help create the practices necessary for this type of role adjustment and team transfer. In saying this, research demonstrates that a stable Agile team is more likely to achieve higher velocity and performance (ScrumPLOP, 2020). This implies the need for HR to constantly balance decisions within the business to move people and roles in response to end-customer needs against the benefits of keeping Agile teams as stable as possible. Team performance data can help in making these types of decision more evidence-based.

### HR TOP TIPS

- Ensure the HR systems and policies allow for this dynamic movement of people and teams across the organization when needed. However, keep in mind that moving people around the organization chart does not always add the intended value and can cause confusion.

- Involve people directly and co-create the new team compositions by discussing the strategic portfolio of work and how to organize to get it done. A great example is how Ericsson Finland assembled their first Agile teams through self-organization. The company invited people from different departments to discuss the logic and need for restructuring, as well as the ideal team composition, and then asked people to self-organize (within one big room) into cross-functional teams. The result was 15 cross-functional teams formed by the people themselves in the room (Haapio, nd).

- Fine-tune HR services to acquire and support a temporary workforce. For instance, build a pool of freelancers or, even better, form skilled freelancer teams that can serve as capacity buffers.

- Set up a pool of vetted Agile coaches who know your business and can step in on demand.

- Build effective onboarding processes for any outsourced or freelancer teams, so that they feel part of the value delivery instead of just a temporary workforce.

## Ensure extra support for virtual teams

Considering the often global nature of organizations, Agile team members or whole teams may not necessarily be working from the same physical location as other teams or team members. It's therefore crucial to support virtual teams and remote working. In order to build trust and continuously improve their way of working, they will need a Scrum master skilled in digital facilitation, as well as good digital tools. Associated workplace policies linked to flexible or out-of-hours working might also need to be updated.

---

HR TOP TIPS

- Ensure a great Scrum master or Agile coach has enough capacity for these teams.
- Leaders should also ensure extra resources for these teams, such as digital tools and equipment such as video meeting platforms and electronic Kanban or Scrum boards.
- Include a budget for the distributed teams to meet physically when possible, and at least to ensure a good kick-off and initial backlog refinement meeting with the PO and main stakeholders.
- Make sure Scrum masters help these teams agree on commitments and a way of working. For example, agree times when everyone is online and available for discussion and times when people will focus on their own tasks without distractions.

---

## Ensure a pull-based work system

At the heart of Agile are self-organizing teams prioritizing and improving work together. An unfortunate and common way to disturb this system is to start pushing work onto the teams instead of allowing them to pull their own work according to their true capacity. Ensure to watch out for this and coach leaders in how to support their teams effectively.

---

HR TOP TIPS

- Have people and teams flag conflicting priorities and create mechanisms to tackle these conflicts, for example inviting POs to sort it out together.
- When designing new organizational structures, try to minimize conflicting priorities for a team, for instance no longer allowing line managers to delegate work to team members who are now working 100 per cent in the new Agile team.

---

## Make it safe to discuss and solve impediments

Agile teams will need to raise any impediments they can't solve through stand-ups, retrospectives and continuous improvement. It's important to create forums with the right level of mandate where these impediments can be discussed and resolved. This process can be quite controversial for companies going through Agile transformation. Although impediments are often quite practical in nature, some can be highlighting shortcomings and flaws that have previously been swept under the carpet and are now made apparent. To promote transparent, we recommend the use of transparent impediment boards to prioritize and track the blockers raised and follow up their resolution.

---

### HR TOP TIPS

- Building psychological safety within the organization is crucial to enable these types of feedback conversation. For example, in one organization, two leaders who were not getting along recognized this was impeding their teams and creating a blocker. Realizing they needed to solve this impediment themselves, the two leaders talked about their personal differences openly through a cross-team forum. This kind of action requires a lot of courage and demonstrates a true belief in the Agile feedback loop.

- Getting people who don't believe in Agile practices contributing as devil's advocates, by helping to identify flaws and risks within the Agile operating model, is a huge benefit. Why wait for trouble to happen if these people can show us where the model will most likely break? In particular, invite people who specialize in quality, risk, compliance or process.

- Many people can feel threatened by impediment discussions if there is a legacy of a blame-game culture. HR professionals can help to make it safe to handle, prioritize and solve impediments together.

- Engage people in problem-solving events or hackathon days and make solving impediments fun and practical.

- HR can also prepare leaders by inviting them to participate in a facilitated and self-directed problem identification session with a coach skilled in conflict management. It's much better for the leaders to recognize the shortcomings of the organization and their own behaviours themselves from the start, rather than allowing them to fester and derail future impediment discussions.

---

## Support people and teams with performance issues

Agile practices help make our work more concrete and open and give HR the opportunity to work on performance issues early on. This means that Agile can be quite tough for people who aren't delivering or are experiencing personal problems that negatively impact their performance. One common mistake here is that the line management structure is kept alive for this purpose, rather than allowing the Agile feedback loop to directly support performance management within the organization. We recommend supporting these Agile performance mechanisms further with coaches, and employee health and well-being services, to help teams and individuals deal with conflicts and personal performance problems as they arise.

---

HR TOP TIPS

- Let teams deal with their own performance problems first through retrospectives, possibly with the help of an experienced coach.

- You will encounter performance issues both at the team and individual level, which often become visible within only a few sprints or cycles of work. Have support available to help the teams and people navigate through these issues.

- We can't always expect teams, Scrum masters or coaches to know how to handle these situations, and it's essential for support processes such as professional counsellors to be in place to care for people's well-being, as well as for legal reasons. It might be valuable for HR to handle deeper problems, behavioural misdemeanours or individual performance issues personally to ensure a professional and human approach.

---

## Evolve the role of leader

The theme of redesigning and rediscovering the role of the leader in Agile organizations is a huge topic in itself. As previously discussed, the role of the manager begins to shift, with prioritization of work happening through strategic portfolios or team backlogs, and the actual management of work is done by the team themselves. Within the Agile community, some people argue that managers aren't needed in Agile organizations, yet our experience shows that leaders and strong spokespersons are still very much required to guide successful Agile transformation. Depending on the level of Agile maturity, a leader's role can look very different from company to company. Some companies can abandon a middle manager layer altogether, because the tasks are distributed to new roles. Some companies want to keep the line management structure but redefine the role towards a leadership or administrative position. Research also suggests that a transformation might benefit from sourcing some leaders from the outside, who are lacking the baggage of the past (Dikert *et al*, 2016).

The traditional role of the line manager in Agile evolves into a servant leadership role, which helps align people around the vision and purpose while also enabling self-organization and continuous improvement at the team level. Leaders also solve organizational impediments and coordinate around dependencies with POs and Scrum masters. Actually, a lot of what we might traditionally view as leadership responsibilities resides in the Agile practices themselves, including planning, improvement, feedback and review of the deliverables.

---

### HR TOP TIPS

- Involve managers and the teams in conversations around what becomes of the line manager role. Explore what people need and expect from line managers. We recommend exploring the manager's role with a certain frequency, together with the leaders.

- Identify which decisions the team is ready to take on from line managers. It's useful to list these decisions and discuss where they sit. For example, some decisions will fully move to the team (such as deciding on holidays), while some will be achieved through joint consultation (such as the pricing of products or services), and some will remain with the manager (such as setting the salary). Some decisions will not be made at the team or manager level, so it's good to identify what sits outside the team's or manager's influence.

- Co-create the new manager roles with the managers themselves (see case study).

---

### CASE STUDY
*Co-creating the new role of the manager*

This is a great workshop to co-create the new role of a manager within Agile organizations, which we've run multiple times, often with up to 50 managers in the room. The main agenda is as follows:

1   Together with the managers, list all the decisions a manager currently makes on sticky notes.

2  Next, use green coloured dots to visualize which of these decisions can be undertaken by the Agile team instead. Then mark the decisions that the managers are reluctant to move to the teams with a red dot, and any items that are controversial, or 'it depends', with a yellow dot.

3  Visualize the roles within the Agile system roles on a wall, for example the development team, PO, Scrum master, Agile coach, portfolio manager, country leader and executive board.

4  Move the sticky notes that were marked with green dots under the team role on the wall, to demonstrate that everyone agrees that the Agile teams can make these decisions.

5  Discuss the items in the red or yellow categories. Explore whether any can be transferred to another role, by following the Agile principles and mindset. For example, prioritization can go to the PO.

6  Ideate on how other decisions can be made within the Agile system.

7  Discuss a way forward and ideate on what the new role of the leader should look like within the Agile system.

This exercise helps to explicitly visualize what kinds of decisions are handed over from the managers to other roles within the Agile system, and which decisions remain with them.

Instead of colour coding, you can also use estimation techniques and give a complexity number for each decision. The lower the number, the more confidence the group has that the teams are able to make the decision. It's been beautiful to watch how managers start to find different roles for themselves through this exercise.

An interesting outcome from one workshop was when a group of managers realized they were ready to let go of many of their decisions, but the teams themselves weren't ready to take on the accountabilities just yet. To help, we set up a team of managers who coached the teams in how to self-organize and called it 'leadership as a service'. The message was clear. Teams would have the accountability for most decisions and 'leadership as a service' would be available to help the teams make them.

---

## Invest in physical space

Aim to influence decisions about office space and workplace design to enable Agile ways of working. For example, provide multipurpose working areas with lots of wall space, whiteboards, charging sockets and movable furniture.

---

HR TOP TIPS

- Co-create with teams on what kind of working space they need.

- Don't plan an office 100 per cent or commit the whole budget before moving in, and save some of the budget to finance the co-creation mentioned. This also helps fine-tune the design and gives teams a sense of ownership of their own workplace.

- Specifically designing a space to accommodate multi-team planning or large events is recommended. Quite often this is solved by having a large room that can be separated into smaller working spaces with movable walls.

- Let Scrum masters and Agile coaches own the budget to run their own Agile learning events and buy supporting materials.

---

## Upskill HR in Agile

By now, the value of equipping HR with Agile knowledge and skills should be clear. Sometimes Agile coaches might bypass HR, not understanding how much preparatory organization design is needed for successful Agile transformation, and this can lead to HR practices becoming blockers later on.

---

HR TOP TIPS

- Participate in an Agile HR training delivered by HR professionals, not IT.

- Participate in the same Agile training delivered to other parts of the business.

- Invite Agile transformation leads from other companies to share learning through long lunch sessions, discussing the HR obstacles they have faced and how these were overcome or could have been prevented.

- HR is one of the best teams to role-model Agile at the start of transformation to guide wider organizational change.

---

WHAT THEY SAY

In the best Agile transformations I've seen, HR has had a central role and what they did was to start running their HR team as a Scrum team. When HR understood what Agile work is about, they realized that they need to start recruiting people who can work on teams, instead of individuals that aren't suitable for collaboration and teamwork.

Jeff Sutherland (Hellström, 2020)

# Partner with Agile coaches

Agile coaches help adopt Agile frameworks on scale or across several teams. They are highly experienced and often mentor and coach Scrum masters, as well as upskill stakeholders and partner with HR around structural and policy matters. Agile coaches are also great at understanding how the teams are doing, for example in handling impediments or making improvements. Agile coaches are important partners for the organizational development and design aspects of Agile transformation.

## HR TOP TIPS

- Agile coaches can begin to cover a lot of the areas traditionally seen as HR's accountabilities, and it's healthy to remain open to collaboration and letting go of things we previously controlled.

- To help Agile coaches who may lack HR experience build a more holistic view, we recommend sharing the HR strategy and service infrastructure.

- Agile coaches will most likely identify where there is Agile versus waterfall tension and HR can help access the right people within the organization to help resolve these issues.

- Agile coaches are constantly building their own collaboration, leadership and facilitation toolkits and HR can help them accelerate their learning by sharing our knowledge and resources.

- Explore the options of upskilling HR professionals to move into Agile coaching roles. Their skills in facilitation and organizational development make them great candidates.

- Choose your coaches wisely. There are several Agile certifying bodies that award certification for simply attending a training or passing a tick-the-box test rather than assessing coaching capability. Beginner coaches can sometimes find themselves overwhelmed with challenges they haven't experienced before. Additionally, Agile coaches that come from Agile-by-nature organizations can often lack the knowledge of how a traditional company operates and might therefore struggle with this type of transformation. It's crucial to thoroughly vet all Agile coaches, given their importance to the success of Agile transformation.

## Sync our own Agile HR operating model with the transformation

As we've explored in earlier chapters, it's important for the HR products and services as well as our operating model to evolve in line with the wider Agile transformation. Review the different Agile HR operating models in Chapter 10 and start evolving your own.

---

HR TOP TIPS

- To lead Agile transformation, we need to first change ourselves!
- Remember to consult HR stakeholders, such as employee representative groups, works councils and unions, to agree new ways of working and demonstrate how employee rights remain guaranteed within the new Agile structure. For example, Deutsche Telekom agreed on an Agile Manifesto with their works council, which stated that 'Agile does not override employee law' (Vey, 2019).

---

## Conclusion

HR plays a crucial role in Agile transformation and helps to accelerate the mindset change across the organization. However, by failing to upskill our teams in Agile and not fully appreciating the negative impact that traditional HR processes and systems can have on the success of Agile practices, we can also quickly become a blocker. We encourage you to see Agile transformation as a fantastic opportunity to take our experience in organizational design and development to the next level. It represents a unique learning experience that can support the development of our own capabilities and help HR become true partners in designing the future of work.

---

KEY POINTS FOR HR PROFESSIONALS

- Be Agile transformational leaders.
- While the role can be intimidating at first, the top tips provided in this chapter will help you understand where and how to start, as well as what to expect.

---

- Agile transformation needs to be done in an Agile way, and we encourage you to use Agile tools such as a transformation backlog, release planning and strategic reviews and retrospectives to shape their approach.

- Be ready to redesign HR processes and systems to enable Agile transformation and accelerate the change.

- This also means letting go of some of the things we did before and partner with roles such as Agile coaches and Scrum masters.

- Most of all, we need to upskill our own HR teams in Agile so that we can role-model and take a lead on the Agile practices being introduced as part of the transformation.

# References

Dikert, K, Paasivaara, M and Lassenius, C (2016) Challenges and success factors for large-scale agile transformations: a systematic literature review, *Journal of Systems and Software*, **119**, pp 87–108

Haapio, P (nd) Ericsson's M-MGw LeSS adoption, *LeSS* https://less.works/case-studies/ericson.html (archived at https://perma.cc/946G-8U7X)

Hellström, R (2020) Interview with Dr Jeff Sutherland, Co-creator of Scrum, 7 January

ScrumPLOP (2020) Stable teams, *ScrumPLOP* https://sites.google.com/a/scrumplop.org/published-patterns/product-organization-pattern-language/development-team/stable-teams (archived at https://perma.cc/4HES-JN6Y)

Standish Group (2019) CHAOS Report, *The Standish Group* www.standishgroup.com (archived at https://perma.cc/5MKD-QWQJ)

VersionOne (2019) 14th Annual State of Agile™ Report, *VersionOne* https://stateofagile.com/#ufh-c-473508-state-of-agile-report (archived at https://perma.cc/S6X2-W7MH)

Vey, A (2019) Guardrails Agreed for Agile Working, *Deutsche Telekom* www.telekom.com/en/media/media-information/archive/guardrails-agreed-for-agile-working-576692 (archived at https://perma.cc/E924-KGFD)

Wolpers, S (2017) 22 Scrum Master Anti-Patterns from Job Ads, *Age of Product* https://age-of-product.com/scrum-master-anti-patterns-job-ads (archived at https://perma.cc/JS9C-XRLX)

# 17

# Agile HR products and services

## Introduction

If you've jumped straight to this chapter looking for complete solutions, that's OK. This chapter will give you a great feeling for what can be achieved with Agile HR. However, there is a reason this chapter sits at the end of the book. As we've stressed, Agile HR is about designing fantastic products and services based on what our people need, instead of copying and pasting what has been done before. What's more, blueprinting can be dangerous because Agile HR is very contextual. This means that what works well for one organization may then not fit the culture, brand values and business strategy of another.

With this in mind, this chapter aims to, first, explore the design principles that HR teams, and indeed whole organizations, can use to develop human-centric people practices that enable business agility. We'll then dive into the important HR topics of performance, reward and talent, to investigate specific examples. These case studies provide a useful and highly practical starting point for all HR professionals to co-create awesome products and services with their people.

### Agile HR design principles

The values and principles that underpin the Agile mindset serve as a useful guide when it comes to designing HR people practices. For instance, two powerful design rules that stem directly from the Agile Manifesto are to always advocate people before process and to validate the value that any HR policy or system will deliver to its employees and business.

Transparency is a great illustration of how we can use the values of Agile to guide the design of HR products and services. In Agile, openly sharing information is a key enabler of quick decision making and self-organizing teams. It naturally follows that the same principle exists for HR, and that people tend to distrust the intentions and actions of others when information is kept secret. Reward is a good case in point; by simply sharing more detail on how people are paid, including the mechanisms used to determine salaries and the reasons behind any pay increase or bonus, employee perception of fair treatment can dramatically improve (Herner and Hanley, 2020).

Using the Agile mindset as our guiding light, we've compiled a checklist of design principles to help HR professionals develop the types of products and services that will both delight the internal customer and accelerate organizational performance. The list also serves as a recap of the tools and techniques outlined in this book. We recommend using these design principles in conjunction with a design thinking approach as outlined in Chapters 4 and 9, to ensure the solutions are co-created and tested from the perspective of our users:

1 **Customer-centric**. It's vital that our products and services not only reflect the actual needs of our internal customers, but their usefulness and value are validated through employee feedback and data.

2 **Value defined and prioritized**. As discussed in Chapter 8, HR teams need to clearly articulate the value that a specific product or service will deliver to the organization. This also includes any maintenance or improvement work required for existing products and services, which at times might be more important than designing something new.

3 **Innovate within constraints**. HR will always need to ensure the compliance and regulation requirements of a business are met when designing products and services. We'll also never have the ideal budget or timeframe, so it's important to plan our work based on true capacity and the resources at hand. Before we embark on any people initiatives, HR should map constraints and clearly define the parameters of a project. The goal is to innovate within these constraints rather than let the constraints dictate the design. For example, base the design on the user experience you want to create and then see how this delivers against the compliance needs, rather than leading with the compliance requirements, which inevitably produces unnecessary tick-boxes and over-engineered approval steps.

4 **Co-create.** To design customer-centric products and services we encourage HR to embrace design thinking and co-create the solution with their people as set out in Chapters 4 and 9.

5 **Incremental development.** The incremental delivery of value sits at the heart of Agile, and for HR this implies moving away from blueprinting whole end-to-end solutions upfront and implementing them onto the business through a big-bang change. Instead, for all our products and services, it's crucial to plan and prioritize how to release slices of value early and often.

6 **Fight process waste.** The best question to ask ourselves when designing HR products and services is: does this solution help our people succeed? Our aim is to build lean, streamlined processes and systems that enable organizational performance rather than hinder team collaboration or quick decision making. All process steps need to be evaluated, and if they block or slow the flow of work, such as an approval or control step, HR needs to assess and validate why they are necessary.

7 **Transparency.** As highlighted earlier, transparency not only fuels a culture of trust, it powers self-organizing teams and networks. From company restructures through to what people are paid, HR needs to seriously question and challenge why any piece of information is withheld from their employees.

8 **Evidence-based.** We're not sure we can say this enough, but it's crucial for HR teams to test an idea or hypothesis first, and only begin to work on a design once they've discovered what works and what doesn't.

9 **Trust.** Start with the design principle that our people are adults and able to make good business decisions, given the right information. It's time to move away from building HR systems and processes that either focus on how to weed out and manage the low performers or, alternatively, only single out and prioritize top talent.

10 **One-size-does-not-fit-all.** Given the dynamic nature of Agile organizations, it's unsurprising that different employee groups or parts of the business might require different types of people practices. Gone are the days that a one-size-fits-all approach should be assumed.

11 **Harness Agile ways of working.** When designing products and services for Agile teams, it's crucial to support the activities that already proactively drive feedback loops and improve performance, such as retrospectives and end-customer demos, rather than add processes on top of Agile ways of working and slow teams down.

Now, let's use these design principles to explore a range of HR topics, starting with performance management.

## Performance management and Agile

After years of eye-rolling and apathy at the mere mention of the word appraisal, it feels the times are finally changing within many organizations as Agile ways of working begin to influence the performance management process. For a long time, many suspected that the traditional approach was broken, and no matter how much HR developed managers to coach and trust their people, the old heavy force of hierarchy and top-down feedback would return every time a performance rating was discussed.

While the business value of improved productivity and the employee value of career development are worthy aims, there appears little evidence that an annual performance management process of cascaded goals and documented appraisal meetings delivers against these aims. However, rather than reassess the whole approach, up until now HR teams have tended to focus on activities like reengineering the performance rating scale or introducing a new IT system, hoping these actions alone would fix the problems. Often though, this felt like we were tweaking an already flawed system. With Mercer reporting that only 2 per cent of organizations feel their performance management practices deliver exceptional value (Mercer, 2019), let's consider some of the common problems:

- **Process waste.** Studies show that a huge amount of time is given to performance management activities within organizations, which often have little perceived value to managers and employees. For instance, Adobe calculated that 80,000 hours were invested by their 2,000 people managers every year, only for the process to be unappreciated by most employees (Morris, 2016). These examples of process waste are further supported by a worldwide Corporate Executive Board (CEB) survey of 13,000 employees that saw 60 per cent believe the performance management process hindered their productivity and 65 per cent thought it wasn't even relevant to their job (Meinert, 2015).

- **Fear state.** Neuroscience research suggests that many practices end up damaging the performance they are intended to improve, by creating a fight or flight response within people when feedback is associated with performance rankings or, even worse, bonus numbers (Rock, David and Jones, 2014).

- **Assumed links to reward.** Most performance management processes have assumed that a performance rating is required to decide on reward outcomes, such as the distribution of individual bonuses. As we'll come to explore in this chapter, these types of reward often fail to motivate people and can cause a direct conflict with the Agile principles of collaboration and self-organizing teams.

- **Backward looking.** The annual process of performance reviews and end-of-year rewards only serves to hold people accountable for past performance (Cappelli and Tavis, 2016), rather than how to improve in real time.

- **Ineffective goal setting.** Studies suggest that while specific goals suit roles involving clear and straightforward tasks, for more complex roles, which require the navigation of interrelated steps, adapting to unfamiliar cues or developing new skills, a 'do-your-best' type of objective that focuses on learning and behaviour may work better (Gifford, 2016).

Spurred on by tech companies, such as Adobe, Juniper Networks, IBM and Atlassian, and now joined by a range of businesses like Accenture, Deloitte, General Electric, Gap and Cargill, many organizations are finally rethinking the whole process. Most are moving away from annual performance management processes and fixed performance rating scales towards continuous feedback and more informal coaching check-ins. Furthermore, as a way of feeding into the social network and to harness collaboration, many are starting to incorporate real-time peer feedback and collective target setting (Bersin, 2017).

So, how can HR professionals start to redesign performance management, or as some commentators like to say, revolutionize it? First, we need to ask specific questions about the value that performance management brings to an organization and the type of culture we want the framework to support. To achieve this, we suggest exploring the following questions through discovery workshops and design thinking techniques:

- **What are the desired outcomes?** This is often quite tricky to answer. Common outcomes include an improved focus on strategic alignment, to support innovation or enable business agility. A healthy and modern human view, especially from senior leaders, is required when conducting these types of conversation. For example, these discussions will be limited if employees are perceived as replaceable resources.

- **What kind of culture should performance management support?** This can help to establish design principles such as: everyone is regarded as a talent, learning happens every day or feedback is our fuel.

- **What do we want to avoid?** Explicitly stating what outcomes or side effects an organization wishes to avoid is a powerful way to shape the design; for example, not wanting performance to be reduced to a number, or distrusting feedback because it's not transparently shared.

Next, through safe experiments, ideally with volunteering teams, explore methods that support a more continuous cycle of feedback and coaching, alongside adaptive and transparent goal setting. Once the process has been prototyped and validated by the teams involved, only then introduce and test a supportive IT or administrative system. This way, it's the people and organizational needs that drive the design rather than any pre-set tech system dictating workflow.

---

HR TOP TIP

Here is a great list of the common elements of modern and Agile performance management practices that HR professionals can start to prototype and test within their own organizational context:

**From**: Setting static annual goals that are difficult to update and change during the year.

**Towards**: Adaptive goal setting that aligns with business needs and the cadence of teams.

**From**: Functional goals cascaded down from the top.

**Towards**: Transparent goals set by employees and teams themselves, who sync and align inter-team dependencies as needed.

**From**: Individual targets.

**Towards**: Shared objectives.

**From**: Activity-based targets.

**Towards**: Outcome- or impact-based objectives.

**From**: Forced ranking.

**Towards**: Self-assessment, self-evaluations and transparent feedback or the use of calibration meetings where performance is assessed by a group of people (for example, managers) and drawing on data and other evidence to challenge individual bias.

**From**: Improvement based on a review of past performance.

**Towards**: Immediate improvement that is applied to the next iteration of work.

**From**: Individual assessment of performance based on number of actions or individual KPIs.

**Towards**: Holistic assessment of performance based on expectations in role, connections with others and organizational values or outcomes.

**From**: Feedback from the manager.

**Towards**: Different types of feedback (peer, product and end-customer) driving growth and improvement at both the individual and team level.

**From**: Feedback to improve the individual.

**Towards**: Feedback to improve collaboration and networked performance.

**From**: Low performers issued a low rating and managed through a performance improvement plan.

**Towards**: Real-time conversations to, first, explore why low performance is happening, and second, support immediate improvement. In many cases, professional help from coaches and HR is used if low performance continues.

**From**: Manager- and HR-led process.

**Towards**: Process owned by teams and supported by roles like coaches and mentors.

**From**: Performance, ratings, money and feedback discussed in one conversation.

**Towards**: Delinking the components and separating the discussion of each. For example, setting goals through the product vision or project kick-offs, holding separate and standalone reward conversations, and allowing ongoing feedback discussions within the teams, often supported by lightweight tech solutions.

**From**: Annual review.

**Towards**: Frequent and brief check-ins, alongside regular realignment discussions.

## Agile as the performance management system

What strikes us as surprising is that few people realize that Agile ways of working already act as an effective performance management system. As we've come to learn in this book, the Agile feedback loop of *plan, do, check, act* naturally drives a continuous cycle of target setting, followed by a review and assessment of *what* teams produce and *how* they go about it. This means that by directly supporting Agile, HR can proactively improve the performance of an organization. Within an Agile organization, performance management processes can feel like an add-on or unnecessary layers of bureaucracy. Instead, HR should step back and see what parts of the Agile system are already naturally supporting performance and feedback, and add in extra process steps only when something is lacking, or the business itself sees the need.

For instance, HR can have a huge impact on performance within an Agile organization by supporting and facilitating team retrospectives. Additionally, the people and team development tools commonly used by HR, such as self-assessments, team profiling and conflict resolution techniques, can offer immense value when used in conjunction with retrospectives. By helping teams develop psychological safety, where individuals feel supported and able to take moderate risks, speak their mind and be creative, HR can directly support innovation and help improve performance (Delizonna, 2017).

Objective key results (OKRs) are another great mechanism that can be used to support the Agile feedback loop acting as an effective performance management system. OKRs invite people and teams to set their own objectives, alongside 2–5 measurable key results to demonstrate achievements, while also being mindful of aligning to the wider company vision or business-level OKRs (re:Work by Google, 2020). The goals should be ambitious and hard to reach in order to encourage stretch and performance improvement. Generally, organizations that embrace these practices don't expect people to realize all their OKRs or consistently achieve high results.

All OKRs are transparent and openly shared throughout the organization, usually through a supporting tech system, to allow people to align and sync organically rather than by cascading down missions and KPIs. This can also be linked to a business or team cadence, such as monthly or quarterly goal-setting cycles, and backed by regular retrospectives and ongoing informal feedback discussions. Often, reward is decoupled from the OKR process, though the results sometimes serve as a data point in reward decisions. An OKR approach can also help to support individual development and achievement, which is important to single out within an Agile environment that is heavily focused on team goals and organizational purpose.

Excitingly, Agile can help HR professionals take a refreshing step back from traditional performance management practices and truly assess the value it delivers to the business and employees. As a minimum enabler for Agile ways of working, we recommend questioning the relevance of individual performance ratings and investigating ways to decouple direct links to individual bonuses and rewards.

CASE STUDY

*Evolving performance management at Sky Betting and Gaming*

Using an Agile approach, Amanda Bellwood, Head of People Experience, helped the online sports betting company challenge pre-held assumptions and iterate a new performance framework that harnessed their core values of 'do things better' and 'free to be me'.

The business challenge

Amanda started by questioning the business value of the existing one-size-fits-all process and whether a five-point performance scale could account for the diversity in talent within the organization. There was also evidence of process waste within the existing system, which linked a bell curve distribution of financial incentives with individual performance ratings. Managers and employees put a huge amount of time and effort into the process each year, only for it to be perceived as unfair, subjective and at times demotivating. The aim was to discover a new way to deliver a fair and predictable performance and reward framework, as well as to encourage creativity and collaboration.

Agile HR approach

- **Challenge leadership assumptions**. Senior leaders believed that a pay-for-performance culture should be driven through individual inspection, ratings and financial incentives. Indeed, some thought that people could hold something back if they didn't receive a financial incentive and that ratings were an essential component in understanding how a person performed. These views were challenged using the following evidence-based approach:
    - academic research on motivation and performance in the workplace;
    - internal customer feedback on existing processes and that people were primarily motivated by working on challenging tech and with amazing colleagues;
    - business and performance data;
    - information on Agile organizational design and the changing nature of creative and technical roles.
- **Start small and experiment**. A prototype was developed based on employee and business needs. A commitment was made to test the new approach for 12 months, with around 120 tech employees working within the 'Bet Tribe' of the business (out of approximately 1,400 employees in total). As Amanda points out,

'this was a massive step change for Sky Betting and Gaming, and the first people and culture change to be driven independent from HR!'

- **Test a holistic performance framework**. There were four components:

  - **Performance management**. Performance ratings were removed, and individual performance was decoupled from bonuses. Instead, the focus was on quality conversations and frequent check-ins between team members and their managers, with no requirement to record objectives. Assessment was based on managers answering four questions about what actions they would take, rather than what they *thought* about each individual. An example question was, 'if this person was to inform you that they were leaving for a new role, what would you do?' The responses were reviewed on a quarterly basis within manager peer groups, with the aim of building an open and trusting community of practice around people management skills.

  - **Reward**. A transparent and fixed 'thank you' bonus was introduced and paid twice a year to promote team collaboration. Everyone knew what was being paid and why, rather than it being linked to individual performance ratings. A 'now that' reward was also introduced, allowing managers to offer instant in-the-moment recognition, such as Amazon or Formula 1 Driving vouchers, without the need for prior approval. Additionally, peer rewards were introduced through an Oprah Bot on Slack, where anyone could instantly thank a colleague with an Amazon voucher.

  - **Learning**. Everyone received 10 per cent free learning time as well as a tech 'ninja fund' to spend on their own development. A learning toolkit was introduced to support individual coaching discussions between managers and team members, and action learning workshops helped people learn from real-life scenarios.

  - **Continuous feedback culture**. As well as encouraging ongoing one-to-one discussions, specific feedback activities were introduced. These included social evening events that explored people's job satisfaction and career growth in a safe and relaxed environment. At one stage this event highlighted that not everyone received valuable time with their manager, and Amanda was able to take this feedback to the people management community of practice and co-create solutions. Regular employee surveys were also used to constantly track data.

- **Results**. The 12-month test saw a strong level of engagement with the new framework, as evidenced by people using the allocated learning time and learning toolbox. Employee feedback was also positive, with 92 per cent saying they knew what was expected of them and 87 per cent receiving relevant feedback.

However, the big surprise was an increase in the net promoter score for that part of the business, which went from 36 in 2016 to 55 in 2017. This was a game changer for the senior leadership team and led to the new performance framework being introduced across the wider business the following year.

Dank (2020a)

Now, let's explore the HR topic of reward, so often intimately linked to performance in many organizations.

# Reward and Agile

Perhaps more than any other area of HR, reward is a topic riddled with personal preferences and strong opinions and can be greatly influenced by what already exists within an organization. For example, we've come across companies where Agile ways of working have started to influence their culture; however, their executive team remains wedded to a framework of individual bonuses and performance ratings despite the tension this creates with team-based collaboration. Given these dynamics, context is everything when it comes to designing reward-based products and services, and it's crucial that HR professionals co-create the solutions incrementally with their people through an Agile approach.

---

**WHAT THEY SAY**

Things need to radically change regarding bonuses, too. I've seen an executive go back from one of our training sessions to change the performance management practices within a couple of weeks, removing individual bonuses from interfering with Agile adoption. This was an executive who really *got* it.

Jeff Sutherland (Hellström, 2020a)

---

## Total reward strategy

We view reward holistically and follow what the CIPD defines as a 'total reward strategy', which includes all the areas of work that employees value, such as learning opportunities and the ability to work virtually from home, alongside any standard pay and benefits package (CIPD, 2020). This way of approaching reward is also intimately linked with employer branding and can go a long way in helping organizations attract talent through workplace design and employee perks, like the provision of onsite yoga classes, free restaurants and market-leading healthcare. A good illustration is the brewery company BrewDog, which has connected their dog-themed brand with employee benefits that encourage people to bring their dog to work, as well as take a week of 'pawternity' when caring for a new puppy or rescue dog (BrewDog, 2017).

These trends show the importance of moving beyond just money as the mechanism to reward employees. While much debate exists on how to best recognize and incentivize people within the workplace, there is little evidence that the traditional approach of paying individual bonuses based on an annual performance review encourages people to work harder (Adams, 2017). Instead, there is a growing body of research that demonstrates positive links between intrinsic motivators and rewarding people based on the value they contribute, and increased performance and employee engagement (Chamorro-Premuzic, 2013). This becomes even more relevant within an Agile organization where individual incentives can destabilize or block team collaboration and lead to sub-optimizing behaviour. All of this has led to some organizations fundamentally reshaping how they approach reward, with companies like Netflix (McCord, 2014) and Atlassian (Luijke, 2011) leading the way and essentially taking money off the table. Instead, the focus within these companies is on how to pay people well and at competitive market rates, rather than attempting to motivate through individual bonuses.

---

WHAT THEY SAY

The way we pay people has to change. More companies are moving towards more Agile incentives and pay practices, where they review compensation much more regularly than once a year. They reflect contributions in different projects, and team-based rewards. Team-based rewards are outperforming individual rewards.

Josh Bersin, Global Industry Analyst (Hellström, 2020b)

---

## Reward transparency

The Agile value of transparency perhaps constitutes the most influential factor when designing reward frameworks, as it can dramatically shift employee perceptions around fairness and trust. For example, a CIPD report (CIPD, 2019) on UK-based organizations showed that only half openly communicate how pay decisions are made and what a person needs to do to receive a pay rise. Interestingly, the report also found that while 75 per cent of HR professionals thought their organization paid fairly, only 33 per cent of employees agreed. These findings suggest that when organizations are not transparent about their pay practices, employees are less likely to trust reward decisions or be able to judge whether they are being treated fairly. This type of research also indicates an opportunity to use design thinking to better empathize with employee pain points when it comes to rewards.

It's good to clarify at this point that paying people fairly does not assume everyone is paid the same. Rather it's about rewarding people for their contribution in a clear and easily understood way. The push for greater reward transparency is also gaining traction with an increased focus on pay equity for gender or race within society. For example, countries like the UK, France and Switzerland now require companies of a certain size to publicly report on their gender pay gap, and research suggests that pay transparency can help reduce gender and racial inequalities within the workplace (Jacobs, 2019). Further fuelling these transparency trends are websites like Glassdoor and PayScale that share salary levels for different roles and organizations based on anonymized and crowdsourced data.

These developments have led some organizations to completely transform the reward landscape by embracing full pay transparency. For instance, companies like Whole Foods (Loudenback, 2017) and SumAll (Weller, 2017) openly share salary data with employees, while other organizations go even further, such as Buffer (Terry, 2019), which publicly shares the information via their website, and GrantTree (Kellner, 2018), which invites their employees to research and set their own salaries. Such levels of transparency might seem radical for more traditional organizations, but helping to shift the mindset of senior executives, and at least explaining the frameworks and formulas used within a business to make reward decisions, can go a long way towards building a culture of trust with employees.

---

HR TOP TIP

To help HR professionals prototype and test new reward offerings that fit their own organizational culture, let's explore the main trends influencing Agile organizations:

- **Delink reward from individual performance ratings**. Owing to the subjective nature of individual performance ratings and the temptation for people to game a bonus system, many organizations are instead linking rewards to a collection of outcomes, such as team and organizational results, expectations in a role, company values and peer feedback.

- **Pay people well**. To remove the contentious aspect of individual bonuses altogether, as well as challenge previous practices where companies topped up low salaries with the promise of bonuses, some organizations now use their budget to pay competitive market rates instead, which are regularly reviewed against benchmarks or even an employee's own research.

- **Transparent salary formulas**. Like Buffer, companies are building mathematical salary formulas, based on multipliers like location and cost of living, work experience, role level and business impact, as well as behaviours linked to cultural values, and openly sharing these with employees to ensure clarity and fairness.

- **Pay transparency**. Inspired by Semco and by Ricardo Semler's (2004) book, *The Seven Day Weekend: Changing the way work works*, some organizations are opting for full pay transparency, alongside frameworks that enable employees to set their own salaries, with the view of limiting office gossip and building a culture of trust (Putter, 2018).

- **Review and adjust regularly**. To better reflect Agile ways of working and a faster pace of change within the marketplace, companies are beginning to review and update rewards more frequently, for instance quarterly assessments of salaries against benchmarks and applying cost of living adjustments once a year (Bersin, 2019).

- **Team-based reward practices**. Quite a few organizations are testing out ways for people and teams to reward their peers in the moment and without the need for prior approval.

- **Creative benefits and perks**. Often attracting a lot of social media attention, and supported by a growth in tech solutions that distribute the rewards, such as Perkbox and Kudos, there are some great innovations happening in this space and it can be an effective way to harness peer recognition and offer experience-based rewards. However, when it comes to perks, it's good to remember that it's not just about ping-pong tables and free meals but nurturing the whole person and building a culture that attracts talent.

- **Workplace design**. Companies like Google, Sky and Red Bull are great examples of how to build a strong employer brand through inspiring office design and working environments that boost a happy work life, collaboration and creativity. On the flipside, some commentators argue that this can lead to people spending too much time in the office, and a crucial component to all designs is how to support a healthy work–life balance as well as flexible working outside the office (Jacobs, 2018).

- **Employee ownership**. Spurred on by the tech start-up scene, many organizations have begun to offer all employees, not just top executives, the opportunity to own shares and often link the distribution to individual and team-based achievements as well as company results.

- **Reward learning from failure**. To harness innovation and experimentation, some organizations harness a culture that celebrates learning from failure. An inspiring example is the gaming company Supercell, which toasts failure, such as a failed game, with a glass of champagne and hosts an open discussion where the team involved share details on what went right and what went wrong so that everyone can learn from the experience (Mickos, 2015).

- **Build a rewarding culture**. Building a purpose-led, social enterprise, where people feel deeply connected to the company brand and each other, is a powerful way to motivate employees and drive loyalty.

Just as the business needs to iterate their product offering in response to end-customer demands and a fast-moving market, HR professionals should be evolving their total reward strategy to continually attract the best talent and keep pace with changes within the organization. Indeed, research shows that high-performing companies follow an evidence-based and data-driven approach, and iteratively evolve their reward offerings through small-scale experimentation and testing (DeBellis, 2019). The fact that the topic of reward is highly contentious within an organization is then even more reason to apply an Agile approach.

---

CASE STUDY

*Building a rewarding culture at Beyond*

Led by Kate Rand, Group Employee Experience and Inclusion Director, the people team at Beyond live and breathe a truly Agile approach. By viewing the culture of the design and technology agency as their product, the team have co-created an award-winning environment that attracts great talent from across the industry. What Beyond has managed to do through Agile HR is build a company that competes on the basis of culture and a sense of belonging, rather than just salary and bonuses.

## The business challenge

A market-leading and innovative workforce is an absolute must in order to win in the agency world. To achieve this goal, Beyond needed to attract and harness diverse talent through an inclusive workplace. However, given the poor reputation traditionally associated with design agencies and an industry generally known for not being inclusive, the people team recognized a need to redefine their whole approach to HR and organizational development.

## Agile HR approach

Feeding off the way the business works with their end-customer, the people team set about building a culture that was essentially the people experience product that internal customers wanted. The team apply five core elements to their Agile HR work:

- human-centric design;
- principles that trust people as adults instead of prescribed policies telling them what to do;
- adaptable processes;
- full transparency;
- data-driven and evidence-based.

As Kate explains, 'By mirroring the way we interact with our clients, we have become a client-first team with a human-centred, agile approach to #GSD (getting stuff done).'

## Example products and services

- **Belong frameworks**: a series of great workplace practices to support people well-being as well as diversity, equity and inclusion. These frameworks are publicly shared for others to learn from and are currently used by companies across 29 countries (Beyond, 2020).
- **Grow beyond**: a suite of learning and development solutions based on what people need to learn and grow their skills. These solutions can take the form of

anything from digital learning content through to a coaching conversation within the business.

- **Feedback culture**: what the people team are most proud of. Mirroring the Agile feedback loop, this ensures that the people within the organization directly shape the culture and what HR focuses on.

- **Fluid career development**: recognizing that the average tenure within the agency industry is under two years, Beyond focuses on helping their people develop the skills they need for their next big career move, rather than trying to get them to stay longer. Many people at Beyond go on to run their own business or work at places like Google, and before they leave their skills are hugely impactful on Beyond's business results.

Results

In recognition of their inclusive and open culture, Beyond has won a range of awards in diversity and inclusion and is a top 100 company in the UK. Their eNPS (employee net promoter score) always remains over 20 and the London office has a Glassdoor rating of 4 out of 5.

Dank (2020b)

Now, let's look at the topic of talent within Agile organizations.

## Talent and Agile

Talent is all about attracting, developing, engaging and retaining great people within our organizations. This area of HR is also littered with frameworks and processes that have tended to control and limit the approach up until now, such as 9-box grids, competency frameworks and high-potential programmes. However, like the other topics reviewed in this chapter, the talent landscape is rapidly evolving. These changes are driven by a more holistic view of what constitutes talent, alongside the need to build an end-to-end employee experience that many organizations now see as beginning at the candidate stage and continuing through to how a business can stay connected with great talent even once they have exited the organization.

> **WHAT THEY SAY**
>
> The talent practices in Agile are very different: HiPo (high potential), succession planning, annual reviews... all of this has to become a bit different. Individuals will be rewarded for their projects, their experience, their reputation and their skills. Not anymore according to how far up the hierarchy they have gone or according to what their bosses think. Bosses are actually not bosses anymore but tend to be more like career managers or project managers.
>
> Josh Bersin, Global Industry Analyst (Hellström, 2020b)

## Widening the talent profile

The concepts of growth mindset and creating an environment where everyone has the potential to learn are having a profound impact on how organizations attract and develop talent. David Clutterbuck (2012) likens this to setting talent free, and argues that many of HR's past practices have not only failed in promoting the right people but tended to view the relationship with talent as too simple and linear. Instead of relying on simplistic models that put people in boxes or attempt to predict talent in a static way, HR should tap into the dynamic nature of an organization's talent needs and build an approach that is more adaptive and networked-based. For example, rather than sending people to a leadership development programme, encourage them to take the initiative and access new experiences within their existing role to strengthen leadership capabilities. Another good illustration is offering people or teams their own learning budget, which often leads to innovative investment choices and encouraging more on-the-job learning such as mentoring or project work.

Agile organizational design and the flattening of hierarchy are also influencing the approach to identifying and developing talent. Within many successful Agile brands, roles that were perhaps considered lower than a management position in the past, such as a coder or technical engineer, might now be one of the most important contributors to business success. We also need to consider the rapidly changing nature of our organizations, and that many of the key roles required within a business might not even be needed within five years. These developments dramatically alter how we develop talent and bring into question the expensive high-potential programmes that were commonly used in the past, which mainly focused on developing people for specific leadership roles. This view also aligns with a report showing that 73 per cent of high-potential programmes fail to deliver any return on investment (Gartner, 2018) and with research suggesting that these types of programmes only served to divide our workforce rather than bring them together (Riddle, 2012).

Within Agile organizations, instead of climbing a predetermined career ladder, the concept of T-shaped teams implies a need to create situations where people can access new experiences and move from role to role to master different skills. This approach becomes even more powerful when linked to rewards based on achievements and outcomes, rather than just seniority and role.

---

### HR TOP TIP

Agile can help innovate our talent practices. Common themes influencing the design of products and services in this area include:

- **On-demand learning**. Linking into a view that learning should reflect what people need at specific times in their job as well as help them fix on-the-job problems, some organizations are building learning suites or platforms from which people can access different learning experiences as and when they need them. Additionally, this taps into the trend of social learning, where employees share knowledge through these tools. The products available within these platforms are diverse and wide ranging, and include solutions like short, targeted digital content, having a coaching conversation or attending a formal training programme. To design these products, many HR teams are embracing Agile methods and design thinking to truly capture the employee need, as well as track impact through the data on touchpoints like when the learning is accessed, by whom and subsequent business results. Another interesting aspect is the need to use a language that employees recognize when designing the different learning solutions, rather than using HR-based language that stems from competency frameworks or job descriptions.

- **Learning organizations**. Intimately linked with the Agile feedback loop driving an environment of continuous improvement, this looks at how learning can become a core value that is ingrained within the organizational culture. Within these companies, learning is seen as a core component of the work itself, rather than something that happens separately. This means that time is scheduled for people to learn during their working day or it's directly incorporated into team activities and workplace events. For example, this might be time allocated for people and teams to innovate and test out new ideas on anything they want, as well as participate in a hackathon or host a meeting where people discuss failure and what they've learnt.

- **Team-based learning budgets**. Teams or even individuals make their own development decisions and choose how a set budget will be invested. As mentioned earlier, this often leads to a more innovative use of the learning budget and people tapping into the social network around them to learn from others or access development opportunities.

- **Social learning**. Many Agile organizations encourage an organic creation of learning events by allowing scheduled time and money to be invested in activities like meetups, competence hubs, speaking at external events and inter-company learning visits. Often these activities are further supported through the provision of creative office space that is dedicated to company events and allows for external people to easily attend as well as internal employees.

- **Fluid career development**. Role profiles are becoming more fluid within Agile organizations, which allows people to move between different roles more easily. By bringing the T-shape concept to life, Agile organizations are encouraging people to broaden their skills base and access new experiences through horizontal career moves, secondments and project-based work. This can even lead to people holding several different roles simultaneously or to roles being occupied by several different people. For example, as discussed in earlier chapters, it's common to see domain experts taking on roles as capability leads, previous line managers moving into PO roles and HR professionals becoming Scrum masters or Agile coaches. This more fluid approach to career development also allows for changes in people's aspirations and motivations over time, such as when people need to take a career break or when they're ready to take on more responsibility or business travel.

- **Career coaching**. As teams become more self-organizing and less dependent on a line manager, there is often a need to create a role for career coaches or capability leads to support individual development. For illustration, a capability lead might oversee the development needs of people who hold a particular skill set within the business, such as coding or graphic design, or a career coaching expert might be allocated to a certain part of the business so that people access their services whenever they want to discuss their learning needs.

- **Transparent and flexible talent pools**. Open tech systems allow teams and project leads to link up with people who have the skills they need in real time. A good example was a company that developed a 'talent visualizer', which provided a search mechanism that sourced talent from across 600 tech consultant profiles. Some other companies are creating in-house talent markets, where anyone can offer their skills as a service that can then be utilized by teams who require those capabilities.

- **Digital coaching and support**. Linked to many of the trends explored above, there are numerous apps and tech-based solutions coming into the learning market that offer organizations a digital method of providing targeted coaching or support individual development. For example, coach bots that use AI and chatbot technology to host development discussions with individuals or teams are increasingly common within workplaces (Saberr, 2020). Another good example is a digital career development framework co-created by the People Operations team at Infinity Works, in Leeds, UK, that allows individuals to self-assess their skill levels across different areas of expertise, and then use the interactive tool to map out a development roadmap and seek new experiences and project-based work to develop their career (Dank, 2019).

Agile is helping HR redefine the meaning of talent within the workplace and embrace a more holistic approach to how we attract, develop, engage and retain great people. By applying design thinking techniques, HR professionals can co-create innovative talent solutions that support people's lifelong learning.

## Conclusion

Great Agile HR products and services are the foundations for building a fantastic organizational culture and support people to be awesome in their job. From redesigning administrative and compliance-driven processes to be more user friendly, through to creating a new and innovative performance management framework, HR professionals can use the Agile mindset to design the types of products and services that our people need and want to use. The more we see Agile HR in action and learn about the inspiring case studies that show what some HR teams are achieving, the more certain we have become that Agile HR is revolutionizing our profession and helping to prepare us for the future of work.

> KEY POINTS FOR HR PROFESSIONALS
>
> - Designing great Agile HR products and services is about putting into action everything you've learnt throughout this book!
> - When building products and services, we recommend applying the 11 Agile HR design principles outlined at the start of this chapter, to ensure that the values that underpin the Agile mindset guide your work.
> - Don't forget that Agile is a natural performance management system and our role should be to support this feedback loop rather than add processes and systems.
> - It's important to view the employee experience holistically and understand how our Agile HR products and services support the whole person at work, not just the 9-to-5 bit.
> - Great Agile HR products and services deliver value to the whole organization and support the individual to succeed in their job.

# References

Adams, L (2017) *HR. Disrupted: It's time for something different*, Practical Inspiration Publishing, Basingstoke

Bersin, J (2017) HR Technology in 2018: Ten Disruptions Ahead, *Josh Bersin*, 3 November https://joshbersin.com/2017/11/hr-technology-in-2018-ten-disruptions-ahead (archived at https://perma.cc/MQ3S-F3ZQ)

Bersin, J (2019) Performance and Rewards in the Future of Work, *Josh Bersin*, 18 December https://joshbersin.com/2019/12/performance-and-rewards-in-the-future-of-work (archived at https://perma.cc/3CUP-FB7H)

Beyond (2020) The Belong Frameworks, *Beyond* https://frameworks.bynd.com (archived at https://perma.cc/A9LY-MN5E)

BrewDog (2017) HQ News: Puppy Parental Leave, *BrewDog*, 13 February www.brewdog.com/blog/dog-days (archived at https://perma.cc/NVF6-NACJ)

Cappelli, P and Tavis, A (2016) The Performance Management Revolution, *Harvard Business Review*, October https://hbr.org/2016/10/the-performance-management-revolution (archived at https://perma.cc/377E-LRJM)

Chamorro-Premuzic, T (2013) Does Money Really Affect Motivation? A Review of the Research, *Harvard Business Review*, 10 April https://hbr.org/2013/04/does-money-really-affect-motiv (archived at https://perma.cc/D3TW-T8NH)

CIPD (2020) Strategic Reward and Total Reward, *CIPD*, 14 May www.cipd.co.uk/knowledge/strategy/reward/strategic-total-factsheet (archived at https://perma.cc/JKM4-B93Y)

CIPD (2019) Reward Management Survey, *CIPD*, 3 December www.cipd.co.uk/ knowledge/strategy/reward/surveys (archived at https://perma.cc/C2N2-TKWU)

Clutterbuck, D (2012) *The Talent Wave*, Kogan Page, London

Dank, N (2019) Interview with Charlotte Goulding, People Operations Manager at Infinity Works, 15 November

Dank, N (2020a) Interview with Amanda Bellwood, Head of People Experience at Sky Betting and Gaming, 20 February

Dank, N (2020b) Interview with Kate Rand, Group Employee Experience and Inclusion Director at Beyond, 19 February

DeBellis, P (2019) 3 Approaches to Enhancing Rewards Agility, *Bersin, Deloitte Consulting LLP* www2.deloitte.com/content/dam/Deloitte/us/Documents/ human-capital/us-human-capital-bersin-lt-3-approaches-to-enhancing-rewards-agility.pdf (archived at https://perma.cc/B9Z8-4DJ8)

Delizonna, L (2017) High-Performing Teams Need Psychological Safety. Here's How to Create It, *Harvard Business Review*, 24 August https://hbr.org/2017/08/ high-performing-teams-need-psychological-safety-heres-how-to-create-it (archived at https://perma.cc/7UU5-2477)

Gartner (2018) Create Agile HIPO Strategies: Ensure Future Leadership Success With Agile HIPO strategies, *Gartner* www.gartner.com/en/human-resources/ insights/leadership-management/high-potentials (archived at https://perma.cc/ 3NEU-49PB)

Gifford, J (2016) Could Do Better? Assessing What Works in Performance Management [Research Report], *CIPD*, December www.cipd.co.uk/Images/ could-do-better_2016-assessing-what-works-in-performance-management_tcm18-16874.pdf (archived at https://perma.cc/B7QF-AC7W)

Hellström, R (2020a) Interview with Dr Jeff Sutherland, Co-creator of Scrum, 7 January

Hellström, R (2020b) Interview with Josh Bersin, Global Industry Analyst, 20 January

Herner, M and Hanley, P (2020) The Pay Transparency Challenge: Deciding Where to Fall on the Salary Transparency Spectrum [PayScale webinar], *PayScale* https:// resources.payscale.com/hr-thanks-webinar-recording-the-pay-transparency-challenge. html (archived at https://perma.cc/PCY2-HGGZ)

Jacobs, E (2019) Why Radical Transparency About Salaries Can Pay Off, *Financial Times*, 6 May www.ft.com/content/11403170-6cc9-11e9-a9a5-351eeaef6d84 (archived at https://perma.cc/YL74-VCYL)

Jacobs, K (2018) Has the Silicon Valley Revolution Changed HR Forever?, *People Management*, 12 July www.peoplemanagement.co.uk/long-reads/articles/ dark-side-silicon-valley-workplace-revolution (archived at https://perma.cc/ 97JR-WMBB)

Kellner, R (2018) I Set My Own Salary. It Blows People's Minds [Blog], *GrantTree*, 16 October https://granttree.co.uk/i-set-my-own-salary-it-blows-peoples-minds/ (archived at https://perma.cc/TS8A-3NX4)

Loudenback, T (2017) More Tech Companies Have Stopped Keeping Employee Salaries Secret – and They're Seeing Results, *Business Insider*, 3 May www.businessinsider.com/why-companies-have-open-salaries-and-pay-transparency-2017-4?r=US&IR=T (archived at https://perma.cc/K6GZ-6XTX)

Luijke, J (2011) Atlassian's Big Experiment With Performance Reviews, *Management Innovation eXchange*, 16 January www.managementexchange.com/story/atlassians-big-experiment-performance-reviews (archived at https://perma.cc/7468-6G8H)

McCord, P (2014) How Netflix Reinvented HR, *Harvard Business Review*, January–February https://hbr.org/2014/01/how-netflix-reinvented-hr (archived at https://perma.cc/X2J5-UAUE)

Meinert, D (2015) Is It Time to Put the Performance Review on a PIP?, *SHRM HR Magazine*, 1 April www.shrm.org/hr-today/news/hr-magazine/Pages/0415-qualitative-performance-reviews.aspx (archived at https://perma.cc/BKZ3-YCQV)

Mercer (2019) Performance Transformation in the Future of Work: Insights from Mercer's 2019 Global Performance Management Study, *Mercer LLC*, 2 July www.mercer.com/our-thinking/career/performance-transformation-in-the-future-of-work.html (archived at https://perma.cc/ZW8K-SWWW)

Mickos, M (2015) Ilkka Paananen of Supercell: Celebrate Learnings From Failures [Blog], *School of Herring*, 19 July https://schoolofherring.com/2015/07/19/ilkka-paananen-of-supercell-celebrate-learnings-from-failures (archived at https://perma.cc/7LR7-AJX6)

Morris, D (2016) Death to the Performance Review: How Adobe Reinvented Performance Management and Transformed Its Business, *World at Work Journal*, Second Quarter www.adobe.com/content/dam/acom/en/aboutadobe/pdfs/death-to-the-performance-review.pdf (archived at https://perma.cc/8VKG-MPNZ)

Putter, B (2018) Why Let Your Employees Choose Their Own Salaries?, *Medium*, 4 June https://medium.com/swlh/why-let-your-employees-choose-their-own-salaries-35588fe53014 (archived at https://perma.cc/MKG8-C2RC)

re:Work by Google (2020) Guide: Set Goals With OKRs https://rework.withgoogle.com/guides/set-goals-with-okrs/steps/introduction/ (archived at https://perma.cc/JQ9V-M8YV)

Riddle, D (2012) Your High-Potential Program Could Ruin Your Business, *Harvard Business Review*, 17 July https://hbr.org/2012/07/your-high-potential-program (archived at https://perma.cc/WH4U-7G8S)

Rock, D, Davis, J and Jones, B (2014) Kill Your Performance Ratings, *Strategy+Business*, Issue 76, 8 August www.strategy-business.com/article/00275?gko=586a5 (archived at https://perma.cc/Q7LE-L57F)

Saberr (2020) CoachBot, *Saberr* www.saberr.com/coachbot (archived at https://perma.cc/ND9S-DKVM)

Semler, R (2004) *The Seven Day Weekend: Changing the way work works,* Portfolio, New York

Terry, J (2019) Continuing to Improve on Pay: Our Latest Changes to the Salary Formula and How Much It Costs, *Buffer* [Open Blog], 25 February https://open.buffer.com/salary-formula-changes-2019/ (archived at https://perma.cc/Y9M4-QA65)

Weller, C (2017) A CEO Who Makes Everyone's Salary Transparent Says People Are More Productive Than Ever, *Business Insider*, 8 May www.businessinsider.com/sumall-ceo-says-salary-transparency-makes-people-more-productive-2017-5?r=US&IR=T (archived at https://perma.cc/5T9M-SBSM)

PART FIVE

# Conclusion

# 18

# Conclusion: Let's get going

Excited? We hope so! However, many HR professionals will get to this point and ponder two things:

1  How to get started and begin to apply the mindset within our HR teams and projects.

2  What will happen to the HR profession from here?

## How to start

After reading this book, you will be keen to get cracking and put lots of new ideas into action. Some people may feel overwhelmed, and struggle to absorb everything in one go. It might also be unclear where and how to start. The key thing to remember is that just like Agile, we need to start small and use an experimental approach to build learning and capability over time.

As we've explored in this book, HR professionals need to understand the power of Agile for HR, and applying these ways of working within our own teams and projects, to fully appreciate how to lead HR for Agile, and begin to redesign existing people practices to enrich the employee experience and enable business agility throughout the organization.

---

WHAT THEY SAY

Agile has shown us that the focus (or project) can be absolutely anything. But you do need to stick to some basic rules, and initially go-slow to go-fast (in part, because you are also managing your team through a change journey). You'll then get this back ten-fold.

Tracey Waters, Director of People Experience, large media and telecommunications company (Waters, 2018; Dank, 2019)

Use our Agile for HR checklist to help get started:

- **Start small.** While the Agile operating models that we've reviewed in this book offer some great next evolutionary steps for the HR function, we don't recommend jumping straight into a full team restructure. Instead, start small. Either form a cross-functional Agile team to run a project or select an HR team within the wider HR function, for example Learning and Development (L&D) or Recruitment, to test Agile first. Remember, Agile is all about learning through doing, and the aim is to build a working model that can be scaled up across the wider function or organization.

- **Solve a complex problem.** While we can apply Agile to any topic to get us started, it needs to be a complex problem which, if solved, will deliver very apparent and beneficial results to the whole business, not just HR. For example, a project that previous attempts using traditional HR methods, or a waterfall approach, have failed to solve.

- **Determine the value.** As we've explored in this book, it's crucial to assess and clearly define the value of the project or initiative selected, and what will result if the problem is solved. Remember that this can be multifaceted and will most likely include business value as well as employee value.

- **Help your team prepare.** Sow the seeds for a successful change by helping everyone get familiar with the terminology and concepts that make up the Agile mindset. Share videos, blogs, not to mention this book, and help others get comfortable with the concepts that sit within Agile.

- **Commit to a timeboxed experiment.** Treat the adventure like an Agile experiment. It's OK not to have all the answers and it's OK to get some things wrong. By engaging in regular retrospectives and review sessions, the Agile feedback loop will actively support continuous improvement. This approach also helps reassure people who are initially uncertain about the change. Some of this pressure can be relieved by inviting people to experiment for a timeboxed period, for example three months, on the agreement that if it doesn't work the experiment will end there.

- **Build a backlog.** Take plenty of time to build the backlog together. It also helps everyone feel better once they can visualize all the potential work and identify the most important tasks to start with.

- **Set up a support ecosystem.** Finding office space to set up a Scrum or Kanban board might sound obvious, but it often becomes a hurdle for new Agile teams to overcome, and it's vital to aid collaboration and self-organization. Additionally, we suggest a few good digital tools, especially if working virtually, such as Trello, Slack or Microsoft Teams. Aim also to give the team the best chance of success by ensuring that there is enough capacity and that people have allocated time in their diary. Agile doesn't work if it's an add-on to the day job, and at best the team should reserve days to work together using Agile, separate from BAU days. Also, set up clearly defined roles, such as PO and Scrum master, and an Agile coach can be invaluable at the start to help facilitate learning.

- **Test a prototype, don't just pilot.** Fully embrace design thinking and see how it feels to explore the problem and quickly test a prototype with internal customers. Challenge the team to do this within a short period of time, like a week, so it really is an experiment. Get used to sharing something that is not yet perfect, but from which people can learn.

- **Step outside the HR silo.** An Agile team or project should be cross-functional and multi-skilled. Even if you start within a team like L&D or Recruitment first, draw on multiple skills and ideally get people from the wider business involved.

- **Self-organize as a team.** Again, there is no use trying to work Agile if the team members continue to operate as single-point topic owners or individual project managers. Let go of the traditional HR roles and truly self-organize around the product or project vision.

- **Create a safe space to learn.** For the Agile mindset to thrive, people need to feel safe enough to try. Teams new to Agile can begin to deliver results very quickly but only if they don't fear repercussions or penalties if things go wrong. Instead, create a safe space where people try things out, talk about how it felt, explore what worked and what failed, and most of all, decide what to do next.

---

CASE STUDY
*How to get started with Agile*

Tracey Waters, Director of People Experience, and her team offer an inspirational case study on how to get started with Agile. Faced with the need to respond to a rapidly changing business landscape and the demands of digital transformation, not to mention tight budgets, the team set out to evolve their ways of working by letting go of the existing rules.

The business challenges

Tracey and the team faced four key challenges that seemed ripe for an Agile experiment:

- **Pace**. The previous luxury of taking 3 or even 12 months to deliver something of value to the business, like an L&D programme, was now simply too slow in comparison to the needs of the business.

- **Waste**. Up until now, the team would aim to make solutions perfect or complete before releasing them into the business, only to find they didn't always deliver the intended value or that work had to be redesigned.

- **Opinion overload**. A lot of projects were being influenced by the loudest voice or the highest paid person's opinion (HiPPO) because the team often lacked the data to make an evidence-base counterargument.

- **Silos**. Like many HR teams, each person was responsible for their own specific topic and skill set, leading to multiple projects being worked on but slow delivery of results and being consistently limited by the capability or capacity of a single person.

Agile HR approach

Guided by the Agile mindset, Tracey and the team embraced a test-and-learn approach. As Tracey points out, 'none of us knew what we were doing! So, we had to take a test-and-learn approach'. Their adventures included:

- **Ninety-day experiment**. Before starting, the team took a couple of months to informally research and get comfortable with Agile concepts together. This meant everyone was a leaner, not an expert. They then made a deal to experiment for 90 days, and if at the end it didn't solve their problems, they would revert to previous ways of working. This invitation to experiment provided the freedom and underlying psychological safety for the team to learn rapidly.

- **Embrace a framework**. The team embarked on a cadence of two-week sprints using the Scrum framework (see Chapter 6 for more detail). While the approach was a great starting point, the team began to struggle with managing strategic projects at the same time as getting BAU done, and the sprint work often took priority over maintenance and improvement work.

- **Inspect and adapt**. Modifications were introduced to evolve the operating model and the team decided to use a Kanban method to track all work on a continuous basis, including BAU and strategic, and to interweave short targeted five-day sprints on specific business challenges. The team also swarm for on or two days to solve ad hoc problems or clear blockers as they arise.

- **Break the rules**. The team has fundamentally reshaped their approach by letting go of assumed HR design principles such as competency frameworks. Instead, the team co-create solutions by empathizing with the user experience and rapidly prototyping, testing solutions that solve organizational and people development problems at the source and in real time.

- **Become data hungry**. Tracey and the team found that the quickest and easiest way to have a sensible conversation with stakeholders was with real data. Instead of programmes or projects, they treated their outputs as products. Just like a Tech or Marketing team, the team learned to show metrics such as user (ie employee) activations, repeat visits, consumption, differences between user segments and so on. Rapid trials and experiments now provide rapid sources of data.

Results

The team has grown from a small team of multi-skilled professionals working individually into People Experience squads, each aligned to specific employee groups (people, manager, leader) and covering a larger HR remit. Instead of sourcing Scrum Masters from alternate squads and Tracey representing the PO, the squads now have a permanent Scrum Master and PO. Overall, the business impact has been strong. One of the most significant changes has been to manager development which was previously a three-month linear, cohort-based programme capped at 15 participants. Today it includes digital resources via an app, on-demand 90-minute workshops on points of need, a social peer-to-peer group, and seven-week guided programmes for more than 100 managers at a time. During the coronavirus lockdown, the team pivoted rapidly and within 10 days were providing weekly support for 12 continuous weeks to more than 2,000 managers. The level of employee engagement at Sky is market leading and it's all been achieved on less budget and faster than before the team started using Agile. The team even shared all their early adventures through a public bog (Agile in Learning, 2020).

---

# An Agile HR future

The second key question that is likely comes to mind after reading this book is what will happen to our profession from here.

## Letting go of the HR shackles

Over the past few years, we've been privileged to share in the delight of people reenergizing and reengineering how they work after learning to apply Agile HR. Many talk of the joy in rediscovering their passion for HR, after losing their way within the profession. For a long time, HR professionals have felt frustrated by a perception from other parts of the business that we're a type of workplace police, implementing top-down, compliance-driven processes and policies. It's time to fundamentally reshape how HR delivers value within an organization and no longer to manage people as resources but trust them to succeed. Agile HR provides the crucial skills to achieve this vision and help to transform our profession into a human-centric, evidence-based and value-driven business partner.

---

**WHAT THEY SAY**

My recommendations to HR people about Agile:

- You need to be cross-trained in other areas of HR, build your T-shape [skills].

- Look for people that have done Agile HR and listen and follow them; this is a very fast-changing space. Look at it as a part of your professional development, and it will really change your career.

- Go find a company that will let you work on some new, different Agile-focused projects. If you are stuck in a siloed job, you are not going to learn this. You've got to be in this to learn this.

Josh Bersin, Global Industry Analyst, 2020

---

Agile is also the future of business, not just HR. This book reflects numerous conversations with HR leaders who are feeling ill-equipped and unprepared to help their brand respond to wide-scale market disruption and mind-boggling technological change. Some have shared how their business might not even exist within a few years if they don't embrace a huge organizational redesign to facilitate innovation and speed to market. This challenge is why so many organizations across all types of industries are seeking ways to improve business agility and reskill their people. HR, as the professional experts in organizational design and development, can help lead this transformation if we too embrace an Agile mindset.

Also, Agile HR just works! As we've explored through out this book, HR professionals have begun to co-create solutions with the business in products and services such as performance, reward and talent using Agile HR techniques. More importantly, an Agile HR practitioner becomes a type of coach guiding organization-wide change and facilitating the Agile feedback loop to lift performance and harness career development. While Agile does not provide a predefined blueprint to follow, by embracing the mindset and methods of working outlined in this book and joining the growing network of Agile HR enthusiasts we'll become a better profession together.

Let's do this!

# References

Agile in Learning (2020) Agile in Learning, *Agile in Learning, Medium*
     https://medium.com/agile-in-learning (archived at https://perma.cc/GY8Z-H3KR)

Dank, N (2019) Interview with Tracey Waters, Director of People Experience at
     Sky, and Agile HR Pioneer [Blog], *The Agile HR Community*, 29 July
     www.agilehrcommunity.com/agilehr-community-blog/interview-with-tracey-
     waters-from-sky (archived at https://perma.cc/CVK5-4HWF)

Waters, T (2018) The Psychology of Agile, *Agile in Learning, Medium*, 27 April
     https://medium.com/agile-in-learning/the-psychology-of-agile-87f92521a5ed
     (archived at https://perma.cc/4MNX-GA6U)

# APPENDIX

## *From traditional HR to Agile HR*

| Traditional HR | Agile HR |
|---|---|
| HR as a support function | People operations creating people and business value |
| Siloed HR operations, process owners and service centres | End-to-end and T-shaped people operations teams connecting into business value streams |
| Big-bang roll-outs and implementations | Products and services co-created incrementally with internal customers |
| One-size-fits-all HR processes and policies | Personalization, choice, segmentation and customization |
| Benchmarking and best practice | Contextualizing |
| HR processes (HR focused) | Employee and manager services (employee experience focused) |
| People are resources that should be managed and controlled | Values employees as human beings that have emotions, needs, passions and ideas |
| Change management | True employee involvement in creating and validating change |
| Assumed knowledge | Hypothesis, experimentation and validation |
| HR push implementation | HR release planning |
| Policy generally designed to minimize the risk of misdemeanour or poor performance | Values-based policies that trust people as adults |
| Extrinsically reward, retain and control | Intrinsically inspire |
| Secrecy first | Transparency first |
| Assessment and development | Fluid learning organization |
| Employee engagement | Employee experience |
| Metrics, benchmarks and reporting | Continuous listening and people analytics |
| Job roles relatively stable and defined | Job roles continuously evolving |
| Workforce are employees on payroll and within a perceived organizational boundary | Workforce is part of a wider ecosystem, beyond a perceived organizational boundary |

*(continued)*

(Continued)

| | |
|---|---|
| Invest and develop high potentials | Create conditions for high potentials to build own career networks and pathways |
| Measure and identify talent | Create conditions where talent can emerge |
| Talent management and succession | Talent portfolios and opportunities |
| Potential fixed and measurable | Potential contextual and hard to measure |
| Individual focus | Individual within a network and team |
| Pay for performance | Collective and Agile reward |
| HR services primarily developed from a risk management and compliance perspective | Agile HR services designed to support people succeeding in their jobs |
| Policies that account for everything and all exceptions | Principles and values that enable real-time decisions |
| Everything needs to be perfect | Prototyping and testing to discover what works and what doesn't |
| The endless HR wish-list | Strategic portfolio of work and the motto of 'stop starting and start finishing' |

# INDEX

Bold page numbers indicate figures, *italic* numbers indicate tables.